Democracy o

Manchester University Press

Democracy on demand

Holding power to account

Matt Qvortrup

Manchester University Press

Published by Manchester University Press
Oxford Road, Manchester M13 9PL
www.manchesteruniversitypress.co.uk

British Library Cataloguing-in-Publication Data
A catalogue record for this book is available from the British Library

ISBN 978 1 5261 6421 6 hardback
ISBN 978 1 5261 5895 6 paperback

First published 2021

Typeset by Newgen Publishing UK
Printed in Great Britain by TJ Books Limited, Padstow

The most potent, and possibly the only remaining weapon to involve [wo]men in the destiny of their country is to make them share government.

Alexis de Tocqueville, *Democracy in America*

Meiner Muse gewidmet!

Contents

Figures

Tables

Foreword: on demand democracy?

Voters are sophisticated. California is a case in point. In November 2020, a large majority of the voters in the Golden State opted for Democratic Presidential Candidate Joe Biden, however they were not uniformly voting for liberal issues. For in California – like in roughly half of the US states – voters can vote on ballot propositions (also called initiatives). When they did, they were not siding with the left. Indeed, the voters in California passed Proposition 22, opting to let companies like Uber and Lyft exempt their drivers from state labour laws, and 24 years after banning it, voters again rejected affirmative action, which allows diversity to be considered in public-sector hiring and college admissions. At other times the process is reversed. In 2018, the voters in Florida approved Amendment 4, which restored the right to vote for most people with prior felony convictions upon completion of their sentences. The initiative was opposed by Ron DeSantis, a Republican running for Governor. The voters rather liked their former Congressman and voted him into the Governor's mansion in Tallahassee, the state capital, but they disagreed with him on former felons' right to vote. Like in California two years later, they were able to distinguish between measures and men. In both cases, the voters showed that – democratically speaking – they can have their cake and eat it; that we can have a system of bespoke democracy. This is what *Democracy on demand* is about.

Foreword

Are referendums and ballot propositions (as they tend to be called in America) a kind of "democracy on demand", the democratic equivalent of Netflix or other streaming services, where voters decide when they want to get involved? Are referendums and initiatives a recipe for populism? Will they lead to unwise decisions? Based on a survey of the past 227 years – and occasionally further back still – the book looks at why referendums have been held, why they have been won, and what implications they have had for public policy.

Generally, the book finds that referendums provide the voters with a veto. It is a mechanism for keeping politicians in check. The book also shows that countries with many referendums tend to be richer and more equal. Referendums can however degenerate into populism, with the device having been abused by demagogues and power-hungry politicians in democratic countries and by a large number of dictators. Referendums tend not to have positive effects for the economy and political culture if it is up to the politicians to decide when to hold them. Ultimately, the referendum needs to be a people's shield – not the politician's sword.

In this day and age, democracy is susceptible to sinister influences from darker forces which abuse the process via the internet using a digital toolkit which includes the implementation of bots and algorithms. This arguably helped those who fought to take the United Kingdom out of the EU. As this book shows, other countries have successfully banned the abuse of online advertising, especially the Baltic countries but also, in part, France.

Referendums can sometimes lead to harsh debates and even violence. This is, of course, unacceptable, however there are ways in which the debate can become more grown up. In Ireland, so-called citizens' juries, where a representative sample of citizens discuss the issue before coming up with a question, have taken the heat out of controversial and divisive questions.

Finally, there is evidence to suggest that citizens use their powers wisely, when they have the right to propose legislation, or repeal laws, if they can gather a specified number of signatures. Democracy does not always yield the results we like but that is the way the system works; sometimes conservatives win, at other times liberals are triumphant. Regardless of party preference, as this book will argue, provided they are regulated, referendums can create a more responsible and representative system of government.

London, 11 November 2020

Acknowledgements

The author is grateful to colleagues who submitted questionnaires and answered questions. These include, in no particular order, Eleanor Craven, Paul Preston, Christina Fasone, Rachel Hammersley, Paul Jacob, Arjen Nijboer, Markku Suksi, Ilker Gökhan Sen, Daniela Vancic, Uffe Elbæk MF, Zoltán Tibor Pállinger, Petia Gueorguieva, David Altman, Dorota Maj, Ron Levy, Stefan Vospernik, Steen Sauerberg, Markku Suksi, Ana Alonso, Hildur Margrét Jóhannsdóttir, Tor Bjørklund, Henrik Qvortrup, Henrik Ekengren Oscarsson, Louis Massicotte, Theresa Reidy, Laurence Morel, Saskia Hollander, Benjaman Baker, Tiago Tiburcio, Ruichuan Yu, Guy Lachapelle, Søren Søndergaard, Miroslav Nemčok, Alex Ahrendtsen MF, Mitsuhiko Okamoto, Uwe Serdühlt, Andrew Blick, Caroline Wakesho, Veronica Anghel, Pedro Tavares de Almeida, Octavio Amorim Neto, Ugo Medrado Corrêa, Peter Spáč and Vicky Triga. The author also wishes to acknowledge his gratitude to Dane Waters, Greta Ríos, Caroline Vernaillen, Bruno Kaufmann, Andrea Adamopoulos and colleagues at *Democracy International*. Thank you! I could not have written this book without you! The author is grateful to the National Research Institute, Port Moresby and the Westminster Foundation for Democracy for financial support. The results and findings are those of the author and do not necessarily represent the views of supporting organisations. I am grateful to Ms Renate Lodge and Mr Mason Waters for research assistance. The usual caveat applies.

Introduction: the spectre of direct democracy

A spectre is haunting Europe – the spectre of direct democracy. It is tempting to paraphrase Karl Marx and Friedrich Engels' famous opening bars to the *Communist Manifesto* and even to go on, that the "powers of the old establishment have entered into an unholy alliance to exorcise this spectre". Though, confusingly, sometimes, these self-same "powers" have – paradoxically – done this by using democracy against itself. As far back as 1800, Napoleon Bonaparte rhetorically asked the people to consent to him becoming consul – and two years later asked them to approve that he became consul for life[1]. Needless to say, he was supported by a majority but even such votes can be lost; politicians as different as Augusto Pinochet in Chile, Robert Mugabe in Zimbabwe and David Cameron in Britain have all lost plebiscites.

Verily, "history repeats itself, first time as tragedy and second time as farce"[2]. As already noticed, these plebiscites – to use a French term – are not popular referendums. The "history of all hitherto existing society is the history of struggles between elites and the people", to once more paraphrase the aforementioned revolutionaries[3]. The same is true for democracy today, however, in this day and age, the people have more mechanisms at their disposal for holding the rulers to account.

Once, the state was perhaps but "the executive agency for managing the common affairs" of the ruling classes.[4] That was until the emergence of direct democracy! The referendum (especially, but not exclusively, in the form initiated by the people) is the mechanism for holding the ruling classes to account. It is for this reason that many politicians in powerful positions have entered into an alliance to "exorcise its ghost".

On the few occasions when the people have been allowed to make decisions in plebiscites or in constitutional referendums, they have occasionally said no. The Australian voters, to take but one example, have tended to vote "no" to schemes developed in the capital Canberra, which were deemed excessive in the states. Of course, a narrow majority of the British voters did the same in 2016 when they voted to leave the European Union. Generally speaking, however, referendums initiated by governments are unlikely to serve their purpose as checks on the elected representatives.

Mandatory constitutional referendums – as opposed to plebiscites (top-down votes) – can be a good safety valve against excessive elite control. As this author has written elsewhere, such votes can be the citizens' shield and not the rulers' swords[5].

It is possible to go one step further and let the people (or rather a percentage of them) decide whether they want to have a say. Imagine, for example, if that were the case in Scotland. Then the voters would decide, and they would not be a pawn in a party-political game between the First Minister Nicola Sturgeon and the UK Prime Minister Boris Johnson, who, at the time of writing, are locking horns over whether there should be a second referendum on independence for Scotland. This is how the mechanism works in several US states, Uruguay and in the German *Länder*. (We shall look at these examples throughout this book.)

Referendums (popular votes on decisions by representatives) and initiatives (votes on policy initiated by the people) are not meant to be an alternative to representative democracy. They never were. As far back as Roman times, the historian Tacitus wrote approvingly of the system of the northern tribes: "on small matters the chiefs decide; on larger the community". But he also added the caveat that "matters were first handled by the chiefs"[6].

It is a common misconception that more referendums would lead to direct democracy gone amok; to a system where everything is decided by everyone. That was never the intention. Even Jean-Jacques Rousseau (1712–1778), the prophet of popular government, was adamant "that a direct democracy would be impracticable"[7] – especially as one can "hardly imagine that all the people would sit permanently in an assembly to deal with public affairs"[8]. Rather, he argued, the people should have the right to veto laws proposed by the magistrates. Rousseau was from Geneva, and that Swiss city state had a system much like the one that exists in Switzerland today. The voters in the latter country can demand a referendum on any law passed in the legislature, provided that they can muster the signatures of 50,000 citizens.

It is this type of referendum – not some idea of grass-roots participation – that can ensure legitimacy and popular consent. The referendum would only be called if there are enough voters who demand a referendum. Such a mechanism would leave it to the voters to decide when they want to exercise their power of veto.

Some have reservations about referendums. Lord Norton, a Conservative member of the House of Lords (and a political scientist), is one. "With a referendum", he writes, "there is no accountability. Electors cannot hold themselves to account for the outcome of a referendum"[9]. This is a reasonable objection, but if democracy is "the will of the people", there needs to be a mechanism which ensures that the representatives do not go beyond their mandate. For, as John Macintosh, a Labour MP in the 1970s, said in a Commons debate, when the device was first discussed, "the fundamental assumption behind the referendum is that this House does not adequately represent the feelings of the country"[10]. This is even more true today!

This is a book about direct democracy – about how it works now, and about how it can be, and should be, improved. The book was intended to be an updated version of my book *Direct Democracy*, which was published by Manchester University Press in 2013. However, momentous events in the United Kingdom, such as the referendums on Scottish independence in 2014 and the Brexit vote in 2016, forced me into a radical rethink.

The negative and sometimes even intolerant atmosphere surrounding especially the latter referendum led many to question the use of mechanisms of direct democracy. Some felt – rightly or wrongly – that the debate had been overly simplified and that the voters were deceived. Moreover, the suspicion – and probably more than that – of outside interference, as well as the use of money, and the role of the media, necessitated much more than a mere revision or updating. Hence, I wrote a completely new book based on completely new data and based on more empirical evidence and a thorough review of legislation and regulation all over the world.

My conclusion is that referendums and direct democracy are forces for good but *only* if they are structured and properly organised. This conclusion was strengthened by the successful use of citizens' forums in Ireland in that country's two referendums on, respectively, marriage equality (2015) and on abortion (2018), but also by examples of regulation in countries such as Estonia, of which I had not previously been aware.

The book is divided into four parts.

- Part I is an overall introduction to the ideas of direct democracy;
- Part II deals with the referendum in the form of a detailed historical overview of the direct democracy provisions and their history in Europe (Chapter 2), followed by a study of referendum on national self-determination in a comparative perspective (Chapter 3);
- Part III deals with the regulation of the referendum and initiatives in democratic countries and is based on an original survey;
- Part IV deals with proposals for reform, such as citizens' assemblies (Chapter 5), the recall (Chapter 6), and citizen-initiated referendums (Chapter 7).

This book is written with a purpose. It is, largely, a defence of direct democracy against its critics. To paraphrase Marx and Engels, "democrats disdain to conceal their views and aims". They openly declare that their ends can be attained only by a democratisation of all existing social conditions. Let the ruling elites tremble at a democratic revolution!

Notes

1 Robert Alexander, *Napoleon* (London: Arnold, 2017), p. 22.
2 Karl Marx, *The Eighteenth Brumaire of Louis Bonaparte* (London: Charles H. Kerr & Company, 1914), p. 9.
3 Karl Marx and Friedrich Engels, *The Communist Manifesto* (London: Penguin, 2015), p. 6.
4 Ibid.
5 See Matt Qvortrup, *Government by Referendum* (Manchester: Manchester University Press, 2018).
6 Tacitus, *Agricola, Germania, Dialogus* (Cambridge, MA: Harvard University Press, 1970), p. 147.
7 Jean-Jacques Rousseau, "Sur l'economie politique", in *Oeuvres Complètes III* (Paris: Gallimard, 1964), p. 251.
8 Jean-Jacques Rousseau, "Du Contrat Social", in *Oeuvres Complètes III* (Paris: Gallimard, 1964), p. 404.
9 Philip Norton, *Governing Britain: Parliament, Ministers and Our Ambiguous Constitution* (Manchester: Manchester University Press, 2020), p. 76. See A. Breuer, "The use of government-initiated referendums in Latin America: Towards a theory of referendum causes", *Revista de ciencia política (Santiago)* 29(1) (2009), pp. 23–55.
10 House of Commons Debates, 11 March 1975, col. 336.

Part I

Philosophy

Chapter 1
The ideal of on demand direct democracy

> Government has no rights; it is a delegation from several individuals for the purpose of securing their own. It is therefore just, only so far as it exists by their consent, useful only so far as it operates to their well-being.
>
> Percy B. Shelley, "Declaration of Rights", 1812[1]

At the time of writing, Jason Kenney, the Conservative Premier of Alberta, Canada, won support in the local legislature for a Bill that will allow referendums to be held on issues that the government deems should be decided by the voters. Mr Kenney said that the people wanted more referendums, "Albertans", he said, "continue to tell us that they want a greater say in the politics in this province – and that is what we're doing"[2]. The opposition cried foul[3].

Why? Why was this not democratic? Because the premier did not allow the people themselves to decide when an issue is of great importance. In Britain, Bolivia and Burundi – to name but three different examples – referendums are usually held when it is convenient for the government. These polls are often referred to as *plebiscitarian referendums*. In dictatorships *plebiscites* have been (ab)used by authoritarian regimes – often after extensive rigging and cheating – the culprits include Hitler, Napoleon and Papa Doc Duvalier, to take some of the most notorious ones.

To be truly democratic the people must be given the right to demand a vote (an initiative or a citizens' referendum) – or the vote must be stipulated by the constitution. Referendum must limit the power of the government; it is not meant to strengthen the executive, but rather to hold it to account.

However, Kenney was right that people want to vote in referendums. Empirical research is pretty unequivocal on this point, "a median of 70 percent of European adults believes that public referenda would be a good way to govern their country. This includes nearly eight-in-ten Greeks and roughly three-quarters of the Spanish, Germans, and French", according to a 2017 study of ten European countries conducted by the Pew Research Centre[4].

People want choices. Once we were content with package deals. We used to buy music albums and boxsets; nowadays, we download selected tracks and bespoke playlists on Spotify. Once, we were happy to watch whatever was scheduled on TV; now, we enjoy bespoke selections and we go on Netflix. As consumers we want individualised choices. Politics is catching up with this trend through what we call "democracy on demand".

Thus, it is in this context of the ubiquitous individualised shopping lists, that we should see the demand for more referendums and the like. For political parties – and the system of representative government – is in many ways characteristic of the old system of one-size-fits-all; the system under which we were content with package deals, under which a basket of goods had been selected for us by the benevolent shopkeeper. Sure, we are able to choose between different packages, but the shopping baskets on offer in the political supermarket were – and to some extent still are – essentially the same.

This current system will no longer do; as individuals and as consumers we are no longer content with a system that leaves us to choose between different packages. This idea of the political package deals was suited for the twentieth century when information was limited, sparse and tightly controlled by a political oligopoly but it is not suited for an age characterised by the internet, Twitter, and bloggers and "bespoke" consumers.

Furthermore, the system is especially not suited for a time when people are more and more interested in single issues, causes and individual campaigns.

This tendency has been going on for over a decade. A good example is the Downing Street e-petition website launched in November 2006. In the spirit of a more technological age, the government asked visitors to its website to create online petitions on any subject. And, others could then add their support at the click of a mouse. Within two months of launching the initiative there were 2,860 active petitions. One petition in particular stood out. 1,274,362 "signatures" were "signed" against road pricing. The government dropped the proposal unceremoniously![5]

Thus, for better or for worse, we live in a consultative democracy. Since 1997 there have – according to Cabinet Office figures – been more than 500 consultations per year. This means that there are 1.5 new consultations every day.

The fact of the matter is that we now vote online and support causes – not political parties. As of July 2019, according to the House of Commons Library, "Labour had 485,000 members, compared to the Conservatives, who had 180,000 members. The SNP had around 125,500 members, the Liberal Democrats 115,000 (August 2019), Green Party 48,500 (July 2019), UKIP 29,000 (April 2019) and Plaid Cymru 10,000 (October 2018)"[6]. That is a total of 992,500. Yet, the combined membership of political parties is below the total membership of The Royal Society for the Protection of Birds.

So, while we are, in fact, more (not less!) political than ever before, we are no longer happy with the system of representative democracy as it has existed hitherto. While turnout in elections has gone up in the past decade, we trust the system less and less. At the time of writing just 14 per cent of the British voters, according to

IPSOS/MORI, say they trust politicians. That is down by 5 per cent on the year before[7].

Is that the reason why direct democracy is experiencing a renaissance? In part, certainly, but also, because referendums and initiatives conform to our norms and expectations as individualised consumers. Politics is infinitely more important than the films we watch on Netflix, yet our system of government remains stuck in the consumer model of the 1950s – if not earlier. This is in part why many request an upgrade.

No political system can be, will be, or ought to be seen as legitimate if it does not conform to the norms and expectations of the citizens. Moreover, the voters of today are increasingly individuals, who make individual choices. We see this, for example, in the concept of the so-called "ethical consumer", i.e. those people who buy fair-trade coffee and the like.

This individual consumer is not merely an economic agent, but also a political actor. This, indeed, is already recognised among political geographers. "Ethical consumption campaigns aim to provide information to people already disposed to support or sympathise with certain causes; information that enables them to extend their concerns and commitments into everyday consumption practices"[8]. That is, consumers become empowered to act ethically and politically in and through their actions as shoppers[9]. But why just rely on the market? Why not extend politics to its natural sphere, the forum, and to the world of voting and collective decision-making?

By allowing people to vote for individual issues in referendums, and indeed by allowing people to initiate votes on single issues (so-called citizens' initiatives), mechanisms of direct democracy provide a mechanism for upgrading democracy. The question, of course, is if this is sustainable, if these mechanisms have any value, if they increase trust and choice, or if they – paradoxically – do the opposite, as some have suggested[10].

It is in this context we should see the debate about direct democracy. What the debate is about is not just traditional models of engagement and deliberation, though it is about that too. What is at stake is an urgent upgrade of the political system's hardware (its constitutional arrangements) as well as its software (the way we do politics).

Karl Marx once argued that revolutions occur when there is a discrepancy between the fundamental underlying structures of society and the political superstructure. When the economic system changes, when the way we consume, produce and interact in the marketplace changes, then begins "an era of social revolution. The changes in the economic foundation lead sooner or later to the transformation of the whole immense superstructure". That is, "at a certain stage of development, the material productive forces of society come into conflict with the existing relations of production"[11], he wrote.

Without carrying the analogy too far, we may be at a critical junction in history. The underlying structure of society, the way we think, the way we consume and so on, is out of sync with the way we govern our societies. We live in a world of the individualised consumer, of mass information and choice, yet the political structures are still those of the collectivised society of the post-Second World War era.

But, of course, we cannot simply transplant the consumer model from its natural setting into the world of politics. The task here is to inquire *if* a system of direct democracy would work. Many think that these mechanisms provide the "political consumer" or "customer" with the opportunity of selecting their personal choices, but this does not mean that the old system is entirely obsolete. The system of representative government is not doomed because we introduce mechanisms of direct democracy. Just as we still watch general news bulletins, buy package holidays, etc., there is still a market for one-size-fits-all products in politics. It is just that this is not the only option. Politically – so the argument runs – we want to have our cake and eat it. Whether this is possible – or ultimately – desirable, is the question that this book seeks to answer.

Direct democracy (i.e. allowing people to recall their MPs, proposing new legislation, etc.) is not a substitute for representative democracy. It is not a system that should be used on a daily basis, but – as we shall see – a last resort; a democratic safety valve. It provides a means of rebooting the political hard disk. If all else fails, we turn off the computer and restart it. The same is true for politics.

Opting for a referendum is a more modest approach. It is based on the premise that voters are given a second say over a policy that has typically been approved by the legislature. For example, in Ireland, voters have on several occasions voted against policies supported by the two major parties, and yet continued to support these parties at general elections. This might be seen as the very justification of the referendum.

Although it is consistent with the ethos of the individual consumer generation, it is not a novel view. Indeed, A.V. Dicey, the famous British constitutionalist, was one of the first to make a case for the referendum[12]. According to Dicey, the referendum was the "only check on the predominance of party which is at the same time democratic and conservative"[13]. The referendum is – as a matter of logic – a conservative device. It allows the voters to say no.

India is one of the countries that has never held a nationwide referendum. However, the case for having this type of popular vote was discussed in the Constituent Assembly, when Brajeshwar Prasad, a representative for the Congress Party, made this case for its introduction:

> I am in favour of a referendum, because [the] referendum has many advantages. [The] Referendum is democratic as it is only an appeal to the people, and no democratic government can have any objection to resorting to referendum in order to resolve a deadlock, when there is a conflict between Parliament and provincial governments. Secondly, I am in favour of referendum because it cures patent defects in party governments. People think that it is too radical a weapon and that a conservative people like ourselves ought not to

> use it without proper consideration and thought. It is conservative since it ensures the maintenance of any law or institution which the majority of the electors effectively wish to preserve. Therefore, it cannot be a radical weapon. Thirdly, Sir, [the] referendum is a clear recognition of the sovereignty of the people. Fourthly, it would be a strong weapon for curbing the absolutism of a party possessed of a parliamentary majority[14].

The rationale for this use of the referendum is, of course, small "c" conservative. It had long been a popular view among British theorists that change was dangerous and uncontrollable. David Hume – the Scottish philosopher – represented this view. He wrote:

> It is not with government as with other artificial contrivances; where an old engine may be rejected, if we can discover another more accurate and commodious, or where trials may safely be made, even though success may be doubtful. An established government has an infinite advantage by that very circumstance of being established … To tamper, therefore, in this affair, or try experiments merely upon the credit of supposed argument and philosophy, can never be part of a wise magistrate[15].

Hume did not write about the democratic checks on power, but he was inspired by the often-overlooked English republican James Harrington, who had proposed an early form of democracy on demand in the wake of the English Civil War (1642–1651). The latter believed that laws "derived" their powers and legitimacy "from the authority received and confirmed by the vote or command of the people"[16]. Harrington himself was not explicitly in favour of referendums but his ideas had impact. A century later they were picked up and applied by figures who did believe in the referendum. Where Harrington insisted that the Senate should propose legislation and the lower house vote on the proposal to decide whether it should become law, some French revolutionaries adapted this to suggest that the legislative assembly propose potential laws. The figures proposing this were all members of the

Cordeliers Club. In a key essay, *Republicanism adapté à la France*, the now largely forgotten writer François Robert proposed the use of referendums[17]. As we shall see in the next chapter, one of the writers who toyed with the idea of making the referendum a reality was the mathematician Condorcet though he could not quite bring himself to wholeheartedly endorse national referendums[18].

A hundred years later A.V. Dicey, the conservative constitutionalist, adopted the idea of the referendum[19]. Through his theory of the referendum, Dicey developed a mechanism that ensured that "experiments" based on "supposed argument and philosophy" were tested in the court of public opinion; through a referendum.

In some countries – most notably Uruguay, Switzerland and Italy – referendums are held at the citizens' behest. For example, in Switzerland, according to the official website, "When citizens disagree with the decision of Parliament and they gather 50,000 valid signatures within 100 days of the official publication of the act, or eight cantons submit a request, the act is submitted to a vote of the People (an optional referendum). The act only comes into force if it is accepted by the majority of the People". In Italy and Uruguay, the voters can demand a referendum on an already existing law if they can gather a specified number of signatures. The latter type is known as the *abrogative referendum*. Some have been sceptical as regards the benefits of this type of complementary democracy. Others have been more optimistic, and found that these abrogative referendums have generally been "hospitable for social movement activity", as Donatella della Porta and colleagues write[20].

The initiative is a bit more radical. Unlike the referendum, the citizens' initiative is a progressive instrument that allows citizens to propose and vote on legislation or the constitution – and bypass the legislature. For example, in Switzerland the voters can trigger a vote on a proposed change to the constitution if they can gather signatures from 100,000 citizens. In Uruguay, they can propose an ordinary law if they can get signatures from 25 per cent of the voters.

Hence, the initiative is more drastic than the referendum. It addresses the legislature's "sins of omission" rather than merely their "sins of commission". Some people believe that such a mechanism is likely to lead to populism. The evidence – as we shall see – does not really support this, at least not unequivocally, but we shall return to this later.

But we can do more than merely vote on propositions and policy issues. We can also change the guard. This is the recall. It is a mechanism that "allow voters to limit an official's term and remove him or her from office" and to hold a special election to recall their representative[21]. This is a comparatively uncommon institution (it is mainly used in some American states, some German *Länder* and a handful of very different countries ranging from Taiwan and Romania to Ethiopia, the Philippines and Venezuela), but it can – in certain circumstances – be useful.

Democracy on demand in Uruguay

Uruguay stands out as one of the Latin American countries that has employed direct democracy most intensively[22]. While there were several attempts to use various provisions for citizen involvement in Costa Rica, Mexico, Ecuador and Peru (to veto laws, not to promote them), none of these have resulted in legislation. In the words of two regional experts, "Despite this legal expansion, with the notable exception of Uruguay, the use of Citizens' Referendum Initiatives has demonstrated to be poor"[23].

Since 1990, Uruguayans have voted in six popular initiatives. Of these, only two were approved, a vote that banned privatisation of the water supply (2004) and one to prevent the reduction of pension payments (1994). However, an initiative on lowering the age of criminal responsibility (*Baja edad de imputabilidad*) was defeated in 2014, as was one on stiffer sentences (*Endurecimiento del derecho penal*) in 2019. These results seem to indicate that the Uruguayan voters opted for more liberal causes. Yet, they were not consistent in this. Thus, in 1994, they rejected a left-leaning initiative that would have ringfenced 27 per cent of the national budget for public education. Maybe the voters were able to make up their own minds and disregard the views of the political parties? In fact, they tended not to do so. According to one scholar, it was rather the other way around, "Uruguayans are extremely consistent in following their political parties' advice … when [they] go to the polls to vote on a popular initiative, their vote choice is primarily the result of their party loyalty"[24].

In the United Kingdom, we historically had very little experience with referendums. This changed in 2014 with the Scottish referendum on independence and still more in 2016 with the vote on Brexit. After a long and bitter campaign, the "leave side" won. Many felt that this proved that referendums were ill-suited for solving controversial and complex issues. Certainly, the Brexit referendum was not ideal, however, the option of not having referendums in the future seems unlikely. Referendums are here to stay but their conduct can be and should be improved. We shall return to this in the second part of this book, but first, let's consider how the referendum has actually worked worldwide since it was first used over 200 years ago.

Notes

1 Percy Bysshe Shelley, "Declaration of rights", in *The Prose Works of Percy Bysshe Shelley* (London: Chatto & Windus, 1906), p. 284.

2 www.cbc.ca/news/canada/edmonton/opinion-kenney-referendums-political-illusion-1.5627689 (accessed 28 September 2020).

3 www.cbc.ca/news/canada/edmonton/alberta-opposition-ndp-label-referendum-bill-a-covert-jason-kenney-power-grab-1.5624698 (accessed 30 July 2020).

4 www.realclearworld.com/articles/2018/01/31/europeans_want_direct_democracy_112694.html (accessed 30 July 2020).

5 http://news.bbc.co.uk/1/hi/magazine/6354735.stm (accessed 11 November 2020).

6 https://researchbriefings.parliament.uk/ResearchBriefing/Summary/SN05125 (accessed 26 January 2020).

7 www.ipsos.com/ipsos-mori/en-uk/trust-politicians-falls-sending-them-spiralling-back-bottom-ipsos-mori-veracity-index (accessed 28 September 2020).

8 Nick Clarke, Clive Barnett, Paul Cloke and Alice Malpass, *Political Geography* 26(3) (2007), p. 231.

9 On this see Russell J. Dalton and Mark Gray, "Expanding the electoral marketplace" in B.E. Cain, R.J. Dalton, B. Cain and S.E. Scarrow (eds), *Democracy Transformed? Expanding Political Opportunities in Advanced Industrial Democracies* (Oxford: Oxford University Press, 2003), pp. 23–43.

10 Liz Gerber, *The Populist Paradox* (Princeton: Princeton University Press, 1999).

11 Karl Marx, *A Contribution to the Critique of Political Economy* (Moscow: Progress Publishers, 1977), p. 6.

12 A.V. Dicey to J. St Loe Strachey, 6 May 1895, quoted from Richard A. Cosgrove, *Albert Venn Dicey: Victorian Jurist* (Basingstoke: Macmillan, 1981), p. 108.

13 Ibid.

14 India Constituent Assembly, Vol. 9, No. 143, Para. 479.

15 David Hume, "The idea of a perfect commonwealth" (1754), in David Hume, *Essays* (Indianapolis: Liberty Fund, 1982), p. 24.

16 James Harrington quoted in Rachel Hammersley, *James Harrington: An Intellectual Biography* (Oxford: Oxford University Press, 2020), p. 71.

17 On this see R. Hammersley, *French Revolutionaries and English Republicans: The Cordeliers Club, 1790–1794* (Woodbridge: Boydell & Brewer Ltd, 2005). See also R. Hammersley, "English republicanism in revolutionary France: The case of the Cordelier Club", *Journal of British Studies* 43 (2004), pp. 464–481.

18 See Jean-Antoine-Nicolas de Caritat marquis de Condorcet, *Sur la nécessité de faire ratifier la constitution par les citoyens, et sur la formation des communautés de campagne* (Paris: De l'imprimerie de Ph. D. Pierres, premier imprimeur ordinaire du Roi, 1789).

19 The first formal proposal for introducing the referendum into the UK was made by the Liberal MP Robert Wallace in 1896. He moved that both the referendum and the initiative were introduced. On this, see Philip Norton, *Governing Britain: Parliament, Ministers and Our Ambiguous Constitution* (Manchester: Manchester University Press, 2020), p. 68.

20 D. Della Porta, F. Portos O'Connor and Anna Subirats, *Social Movements and Referendums from Below: Direct Democracy in the Neoliberal Crisis* (Bristol: Policy Press, 2017), p. 5.

21 Shauna Reilly, *Direct Democracy: A Double-Edged Sword* (London: Rienner, 2018), p. 37.

22 See A. Breuer, "The use of government-initiated referendums in Latin America: Towards a theory of referendum causes", *Revista de ciencia política (Santiago)* 29(1) (2009), pp. 23–55.

23 S. Linares and Y. Welp, "Las iniciativas ciudadanas de referéndum en su laberinto", *Latin American Review of Comparative Politics / Revista Latinoamericana de Politica Comparada* 15 (2019), pp. 55–77 (p. 55).

24 D. Altman, "Popular initiatives in Uruguay: Confidence votes on government or political loyalties?" *Electoral Studies* 21(4) (2002), pp. 617–630.

Part II

Practice

Chapter 2

A brief history of the practice and consequences of referendums

> So, two Cheers for Democracy: one because it admits variety and; two because it permits criticism.
>
> E.M. Forster[1]

Referendums have always attracted negative comments: "The Referendum is tried and found to be a failure", wrote the Russian revolutionary Pyotr Kropotkin, in *Conquest for Bread*[2]. The anarchist theoretician rejected the view of socialist and populist progressives of his day. In his succinct summary, "As to the political system, it would be the parliamentary system, modified by positive instructions given to those elected, and by the referendum – a vote, taken by noes or ayes by the nation. Let us own that this system appears to us simply unrealizable"[3]. This sentiment is not limited to the beginning of the twentieth century. In the twenty-first century the American political scientist Andrew Moravcsik opined that referendums produce a "politics in which individuals have no incentive to reconcile their concrete interests with their political choices". Writing specifically about a failed Irish referendum on further EU integration, in which the voters had the audacity to vote "no", the Harvard professor went on that the voters' "ignorance was so great that the slogan 'if you don't know, vote "no"' carried the day"[4]. That this statement was *not* based on survey data or similar is perhaps telling. Yet the statement is not unique, another political scientist similarly wrote, "one only needs to look at … the Brexit referendum in Britain to see that the impact of [this decision] can reach far beyond the understanding of typical voters (and maybe even politicians)"[5]. These views, probably, reflected gut-feelings (and undoubtedly a fair share of sour grapes), but the same can be said of those who eulogise direct democracy.

President George W. Bush, for example, believed that "the initiative and [the] referendum make government more responsive to its citizens, neutralize the power of the special interests and stimulate public involvement in state issues"[6]. Despite this, Mr Bush did nothing to promote these instruments during his years in power. He was not the first supposed enthusiast to abandon the referendum once he was in office. Margaret Thatcher, before she became prime minister, suggested that industrial relations issues, such as the relations with the trade unions, should be put to a referendum[7]. Once in office, she forgot about this and enacted a divisive policy that would have been more legitimate if it had been given the seal of popular approval.

Was Kropotkin correct, and was it a wise decision to abandon the referendum once in office? Representative government is the norm. It is – at the present time, at any rate – impossible to conceive of a system which is not based on indirect democracy. But that does not mean that this is the only show in town. What we need is to complement representative institutions to better enable people to voice criticisms and concerns. We might define these institutions and practices as examples of "complementary democracy", that is, all the different forms of democracy that complement the election of representatives. To this category belong mechanisms such as deliberative democracy and mini-publics (see Chapter 5) and the recall (Chapter 6). But the most important institution of complementary democracy is undoubtedly the referendum. Any discussion of the nature of complementary democracy must start with this institution.

First, we need to understand the logic of this democratic device. One can look at "democracy on demand" using a metaphor from economic theory. Thus, the demand curve for direct democracy in a polity with pure representative institutions is a case of what economists call *cross price elasticity*. The concept usually refers to a situation where two so-called *substitution goods* compete. If the price of one goes up the demand for the other will increase. For example, if the price of a coffee from Costa Coffee increases, the demand for Starbucks will rise. The same is, conceptually speaking, true for the relationship between the substitution goods representative government and complementary democracy.

When the "price" of representative democracy goes up – when citizens feel that their voices are not heard – because the cost of elections, lobbying of representatives, etc. go up, other mechanisms must be found to voice their grievances. Historically, measures of what we might call complementary democracy in the form of referendums and initiatives were perceived as providing genuine outlets for the citizens' grievances. In the populist era (1890–1910) and in the Progressive era (1915–1925) in America these mechanisms were introduced when monopolised capitalism was driving up the

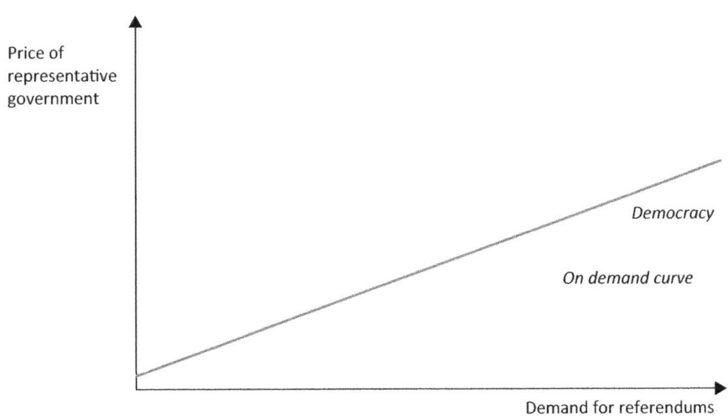

Figure 2.1 Demand for representative government and referendums.

price of representative government[8]. But did it work? To answer this question, we need to survey the history of the referendum in practical politics since it was introduced shortly after the French Revolution.

The use of the referendum around the world, 1793–2020

Over the past 200-plus years, the use of the referendum has varied. The original idea was to provide a veto by the people. The first nationwide referendum was held in France in 1793. The voters were asked to endorse the so-called *Montagnard Constitution*, drawn up by the radical Maximilien Robespierre. The constitution was not only endorsed by the people, it also contained provisions for citizens' initiatives[9].

This new constitution replaced the so-called *Projet de constitution girondine* of 1791 – which had been drawn up by the notable mathematician and political theorist Nicolas de Condorcet. The Projet was a based on constitutional monarchy, and it made no mention of the referendum. However, after the proclamation of the republic in late 1792, and the execution of the king in early 1793, a new constitution was drawn up, which – on the face of it – was more democratic and afforded the citizens direct rights[10].

It is, perhaps, a bit surprising that the first constitution had not been ratified by the people. Its author had been the first major political theorist to make a case for referendums. Interestingly, Condorcet had made a case for popular ratification. In an early treatise from 1789 with the title "On the Need to have the Constitution Ratified by the Citizens, and on the Formation of Rural Communities," he posed the question of whether "a nation can give an assembly the power to give it a constitution … or does the people have the right to reserve this prerogative to themselves?"[11]. He answered that, "to form a constitution is separate from the right to ratify it"[12].

While he was in principle in favour of letting the people decide, the aristocrat sounded a note of caution, noting that, "when a nation reserves the power to ratify the constitution it is not actually exercising it. We can in fact assure, without fear of being mistaken, that given the state of education [the people are] not sufficiently enlightened to judge a plan of constitution"[13]. This probably explains why he was reluctant to allow the people a vote – at that time at least.

Notwithstanding these reservations, he went on to develop an argument for democracy, and purported to show mathematically that democracy is the best form of government. He thus developed the so-called Condorcet Jury Theorem to show that more opportunities for participation lead to optimal outcomes. In simplified form without too much mathematics, the probability of a correct majority decision, when the individual probability p is close to $1/2$, grows linearly in terms of $p - 1/2$. Basically, for every voter added, the closer the chance of them reaching a correct decision. Well, at least in theory!

The constitution was not in effect for long. In 1795 it was replaced by another constitution, which established Le Directoire, the five-person collective executive. This document was also ratified by referendum.

In 1799, when the Directorate was overthrown by Napoleon Bonaparte, one would, perhaps, have expected that it was curtains for direct democracy. That was not the case. Indeed, Bonaparte held several referendums to add legitimacy to his autocratic regime. Thus, there were referendums in 1800 to approve Napoleon as Consul, two years later to make him ruler for life, and in 1804 on hereditary rule for Napoleon's descendants. After Napoleon's return from Elba (he had been forced to abdicate in 1814), he asked the liberal constitutionalist Benjamin Constant to write a more liberal constitution. This, so-called *la Benjamine*, was also ratified by referendum. However, Napoleon's defeat at Waterloo meant that it didn't come into effect.

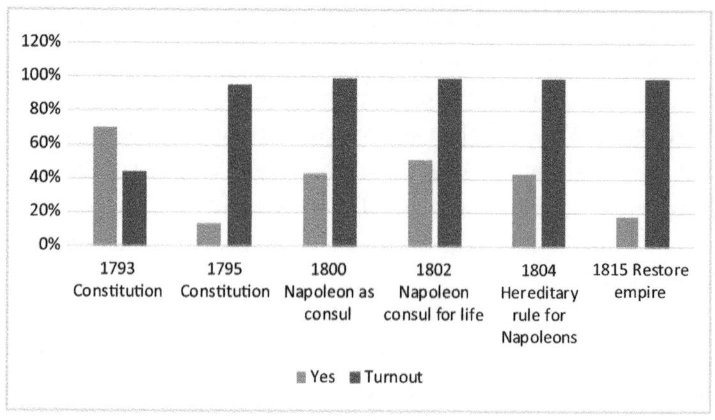

Figure 2.2 Referendums after the Revolution and under Napoleon Bonaparte.

After the fall of Napoleon, the use of referendums fell into abeyance. There were few other referendums in other countries at this time. Only two stand out. In 1802, Switzerland voted on a new constitution. The country had been occupied by the French who came on a promise to establish democracy. The constitution intended to form a centralised regime on the French model. The vote was in keeping with Napoleon's professed (but skin-deep) belief in popular sovereignty. However, a majority voted against the constitution: 92,000 voted no and 72,000 voted yes. Initially, the French decided to treat the abstainers (in total 167,000) as yes-voters[14], hence, the constitution was approved. However, Napoleon withdrew it, as he appreciated that its enactment would cause resentment which he could ill-afford at the time. Even referendums held under autocracy and semi-democracy can have effects that were not foreseen by their initiators, and may have unintended consequences that lead to more democracy, although this requires miscalculations on the part of the autocrat, which is relatively rare. In any case, the no-vote solidified Swiss national sentiment. In a way, the episode (the first nationwide vote in the country's history) created Switzerland; rather appropriately, the Helvetic Confederation was born in a referendum.

Another early pioneer was Chile. This country had voted in a referendum on whether to become an independent country in 1812 (the vote was precipitated by Joseph Bonaparte's usurpation of the Spanish throne – he was Napoleon Bonaparte's brother). It was an interesting example of countries using the French rhetoric of popular sovereignty against the revolutionaries in France. Thus, the Chileans, at the instigation of their leader Bernardo O'Higgins Riquelme, took this as an opportunity to shake off the colonial fetters, and – in keeping with the revolutionary ideas of Rousseau – sought popular approval for this[15].

Despite the rhetoric, O'Higgins was far from democratic. The referendums he organised in, respectively, 1817 and 1818, were plebiscites very similar to the ones held by Bonaparte in France at the turn of the century. Chile did not become a democracy when it became independent.

It was only after 1848 that we saw the re-emergence of the view that momentous decisions had to be ratified by the people; that the citizens were the ultimate masters. But apart from the Risorgimento referendums that led to the unification of Italy (see next chapter), the few that were conducted were farcical. For example, the Mexican referendum of 1863 to institute Maximilian (a handpicked French candidate) to become emperor of Mexico (he was later deposed and executed) was anything but free, and even less fair. The same was true for the vote in 1867, when Mexico instituted a new constitution after another blatantly rigged plebiscite[16]. These examples were similar to the votes held elsewhere, such as Liberia, Peru and Honduras, among other places.

As Table 2.1 shows, there were only a total of 16 nationwide referendums (outside Switzerland) during the nineteenth century.

The referendum continued to be a mainly French institution. After the overthrow of the constitutional monarchy and King Louis Philippe I in 1948, who governed under a semi-democratic constitution, the French soon turned to the referendum – in its plebiscitary form.

Table 2.1 Nationwide referendums, 1817–1900

Country	Year	Issue	Turnout	Yes-vote
Chile	1812	Constitution		Majority
Chile	1817	Independence	N.A.	Majority
Chile	1818	Constitution	N.A.	Majority
Liberia	1846	Independence	N.A.	52
Liberia	1847	Executive and legislative functions	N.A.	78
France	1851	Constitutional powers for Napoleon III	79	92
France	1852	Napoleon III as emperor	79	96
Mexico	1863	Maximillian as emperor	N.A.	100
Peru	1865	Colonel Prado as interim president	N.A.	100
Mexico	1867	Constitutional reform	N.A.	100
Ecuador	1869	Constitution	N.A.	96
Costa Rica	1870	Colonel Guardia for president	N.A.	100
Dominican Republic	1870	Annexation to the USA	N.A.	100
France	1870	Constitution	83	82
Honduras	1870	Extend president's term	N.A.	99
Dominican Republic	1873	Lease of Samara Peninsula	N.A.	100
Canada	1898	Prohibition	44	51

The first elected president was Charles Louis Napoleon Bonaparte. A playboy and a revolutionary in his youth, he fled France after an unsuccessful coup in 1836. His contemporaries did not have much regard for the new president. The novelist Victor Hugo despairingly called him *Napoléon le Petit* in a book with that title[17]. Yet, the new president was a wily political operator, he was popular among the people and used this popularity to stage an autogolpe – a self-coup.

Instead of a straight *coup d'état* Charles took a leaf out of his uncle's playbook and appealed to the people – in a way that was later used by other dictators including Adolf Hitler in the 1930s, Haiti's Papa Doc Duvalier in the 1960s and Peruvian strongman Alberto Fujimori in the 1990s. The French referendums in, respectively, 1851 and 1852, were successful, even if they were anything but fair. The writer George Sand described Napoleon III's referendums "as an attack on liberty itself"[18]. This view is supported by recent scholarship on the French plebiscites[19].

Yet, they were able to convey the impression that Napoleon III had the support of the people. The votes were held when the president (soon to become emperor) clashed with the elected representatives.

In his essay "The Eighteenth Brumaire of Louis Napoleon", Karl Marx observed that the president, through the use of the plebiscite, "possesses a sort of divine right; he is president by the grace of the people"[20]. While Napoleon III was undoubtedly popular, his regime left nothing to chance. The voting was tightly controlled, and voters were not given a meaningful opportunity to express dissent. While it is a myth that voters were only given the option "oui", campaigning for a "non" was non-existent and the emperor's control over the bureaucracy meant that he could not lose.

It is tempting to conclude, therefore, that all the plebiscites in the nineteenth century were rigged, unfair and undemocratic. This would be inaccurate. Even in France.

Occasionally, especially in the French literature, a distinction is made between referendums and plebiscites[21]. The former, as we have seen, are votes in democracies and can be lost by the proposer. The latter are votes held in more or less autocratic states, votes that tend to be rigged and are almost always won by the incumbent. However, this intrinsically undemocratic nature of the plebiscite does not necessarily mean that the ruler is unpopular. Thus, the vote in 1870 (held shortly before Napoleon was forced from power after the Franco-German War) was regarded by some observers as his desperate attempt to hold on to power. Marx wrote to Engels, "[that] the referendum is held, is the last blow to the empire"[22].

This assessment seems reasonable in hindsight and after the war. However, at the time it was held, the referendum was actually seen as a stroke of political craftmanship which strengthened the beleaguered emperor. Louis Napoleon won 82 per cent of the votes. Léon Gambetta, the leader of the opposition, noted in despair, "we were crushed. The Emperor is more popular than ever"[23]. Emperor Napoleon III did not lose power because he lost the trust of the people but because his army was defeated by Prussia.

The first properly democratic referendum outside Switzerland (see next section) took place in Canada in 1898. The first French-speaking prime minister, the Liberal Wilfrid Laurier, had promised the Canadians a say on the issue of prohibition. By offering a referendum, he was able to neutralise the matter and appeal to voters in both the more conservative English-speaking provinces as well as the voters in his native – and more liberal – Quebec.

But the turnout was a mere 44 per cent. And when 81 per cent of the Quebecois rejected the proposal, Laurier (rather bravely) decided to abandon the temperance measure. He recognised that in a multi-ethnic state one part (even if it is a majority) cannot ride roughshod over the minority. It is unlikely that Laurier would have pushed ahead with Brexit – which was rejected by the Scots and the Northern Irish in 2016. Maybe it is this bravery, this willingness to make a bold decision, even on unpopular issues, that makes Laurier one of Canada's greatest prime ministers. The ones who decided to push ahead with Brexit in Britain 118 years later are perhaps less likely to be remembered in the same way in Britain's history books.

Switzerland

Overall Switzerland has held more than 550 nationwide referendums. The total number of referendums held in other countries at the time of writing was 1,101. This makes Switzerland *sui generis*. This is nothing new. Throughout the nineteenth century, Switzerland followed its own pattern. More than any other country, the Alpine republic is a special case, a *Sonderfall*, in the local vernacular. It was not inevitable that this would be the case.

The *Sonderbund War*, in which seven conservative Catholic cantons' attempted secessions were halted by the liberals, led to the introduction of a new constitution, which was endorsed by the voters. The Liberal Party was dominant in the *Bundesrat* but did not have a majority in the Second Chamber (*Der Ständerat*). This prevented them from introducing liberal and secular reforms to the education system.

However, the dominance had political costs for the Liberals. The Swiss politician and writer Andi Gross has noted that the introduction of the citizen-initiated referendum – at least indirectly – was precipitated by the Liberals' mishandling of the cholera epidemic in Zürich. The local government was forced to change the cantonal constitution and introduce more direct democracy. This change put the popular referendum – democracy on demand – on the agenda[24].

But the party was still in a strong position at the national level, and they were desperate to keep it that way. For this they needed an institutional device that could strengthen the Lower House at the expense of the more conservative Upper House. To this end, a new constitution made it possible for the people to challenge ordinary legislation through optional referendums. The objective was to pass legislation that made education a federal matter and thus to check the power of the Catholics.

The Liberals expected the Protestants would prevent the Catholics from using the referendum mechanism. This was not a case of turkeys voting for Christmas for the Liberals, rather they believed another sacrificial animal would lead to the metaphorical slaughter.

It was this miscalculation that was responsible for the introduction of the referendum as a centrepiece of the Swiss political system. Unexpectedly, Catholics and Protestants, despite their theological disagreements, started to challenge legislation passed by the government through the new referendum provision for democracy on demand. This eroded the Liberals' virtual monopoly on legislative power in the period before the First World War. The result of this collaboration was the rejection of a law on the establishment of the federal ministry of education in 1884, the introduction of the constitutional initiative in 1891 and the rejection of a more liberal temperance law in 1903 – all examples of how non-liberal groups prevented radical legislation.

Through the referendum, parties in opposition were able to shape public policy. In the view of one observer, "strong political minorities were able to threaten and mobilize for an activation of the optional referendum, until they were eventually co-opted into the government"[25]. This tendency became stronger when Switzerland became a multi-party system after the introduction of proportional representation in 1918[26]. At this time, the dominance of the Liberals was over. The rise of the Social Democrats meant that no party was able to dictate policy, and, in any case, any elite compromise could potentially be vetoed by the people.

Generally, the system was not – and is not – one of unrestrained direct democracy. The voters can propose constitutional amendments, but these rarely succeed – fewer than 20 per cent have resulted in a yes-vote. In many ways, the system of direct democracy as practised in Switzerland today is close to the ideal envisaged by that country's most famous philosophical son, Jean-Jacques Rousseau, who wrote that "the people … [should] only give their consent to these laws … if they had time to be convinced"[27].

The referendum before the Second World War

There were 19 referendums between the turn of the century and the end of the First World War, of which 13 were constitutional amendments in Australia.

In the nineteenth century, all referendums were ratified. This changed after the turn of the century. Seven out of 19 were rejected, thus proving that the referendum could perform the

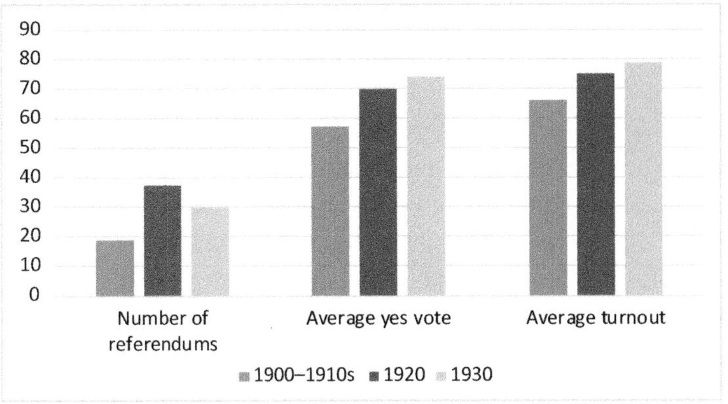

Figure 2.3 Referendums, 1900–1940.

function of what the English constitutionalist A.V. Dicey had called a "People's veto"[28].

The average number of referendums increased the 1920s, and then fell back in the 1930s, and only very few referendums were held during the Second World War – a notable exception being the vote on conscription in Canada. In this, the Liberal prime minister – who had campaigned against conscription – sought, and was given, a mandate to change his manifesto commitment[29].

During the period the average yes-vote increased, as did the turnout rate. In the first decades of the century the average yes-vote was 57 per cent. This increased to 70 per cent in the 1920s and to 74 per cent in the 1930s. It is tempting to suggest that this increase was due to a relatively large number of referendums being held in dictatorships – authoritarian as well as totalitarian ones. Countries like Haiti, Nazi Germany, Greece and Spain held referendums in which the official results were suspiciously high approval rates.

Certainly, one should not discount these plebiscites in authoritarian regimes. Yet, there were also referendums in democratic polities. In fact, the vast majority were held in countries that were nominally polyarchies. Many of these were on institutional issues, for example the attempted abolition of the Landstinget (Senate) in Denmark (1939), and the votes on the role of the monarchy (in Luxembourg in 1919 and in Greece in 1935). However, the second most salient issue (after constitutional referendums) was prohibition. Norway voted twice on the issue (1919 and 1926), and the issue was submitted to the voters in Sweden (1922) and Finland (1931)[30]. There were also votes in Iceland in 1933 (this country was formally under the Danish Crown until the independence referendum in 1944) and the Faroe Islands (1907), which is still a devolved territory under the Danish Crown.

Why were these referendums held? It seems there was a pattern of sorts. All the votes were a result of split political parties or disagreements between coalition partners. In Sweden prohibition was an issue that divided the bourgeois parties and had to be defused[31]. In Finland, the issue "cut across parties"[32]. And, in Norway, the parties in the centre-right bloc had divergent views on the subject, which made governing difficult. Three governments fell as a result of the disagreement over the prohibition issue. There were also similarities in the outcome of the referendums. While Norway voted to introduce prohibition in 1919, this was reversed in 1926. The votes in the Faroe Islands (1907), Sweden (1922), Finland (1931) and Iceland (1933) all resulted in yes-votes for those opposed to prohibition.

The referendum during the Cold War

The number of referendums continued to rise after the Second World War. As we can see in Figure 2.4 there was a steady rise in the number of referendums, though with a slight fall to 73 in the 1980s from the peak of 95 in the 1970s.

However, there were uneven numbers of referendums in the different continents, but on the face of it the differences in number were minimal, as we can see from Figure 2.4. Indeed, the democratic countries in Oceania (predominately Australia and New

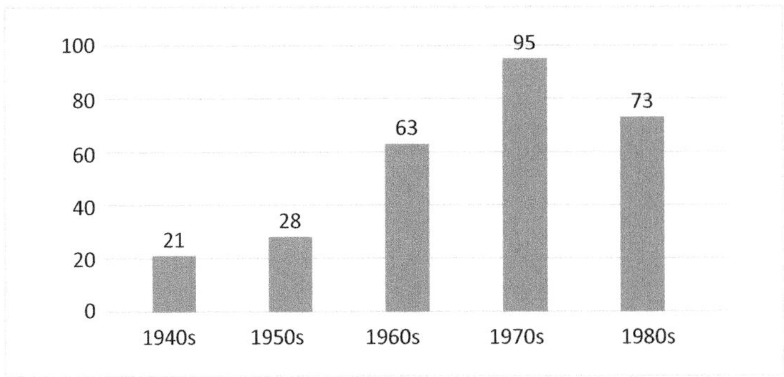

Figure 2.4 Number of referendums per decade.

Zealand) held fewer referendums than the largely undemocratic countries in Africa.

Overall, it is fair to say that the tendencies were far from uniform. In Europe and Oceania – overall, the two most democratic continents – the number of referendums increased throughout the period. In the Americas (covering the Caribbean, Latin America and North America) the development defied any pattern, and in Asia and Africa there was a sharp drop in the 1980s (see Figure 2.5).

It might be useful to look at the data to see if we can detect a similar trend? Or, if the different continents, and indeed the different countries, simply follow different trajectories?

But it is necessary to begin with the fundamental political difference. Europe was divided between Eastern communist countries, Southern European dictatorships and Western democracies. There were very few referendums in the former two. Only Bulgaria, East Germany and Romania in the communist bloc held referendums, and the number was similarly low in Spain, Greece and Turkey. The vast majority of the votes during the period were held in Western countries.

Apart from Switzerland, where there were hundreds of votes, the countries that asked the people most frequently were Italy (with

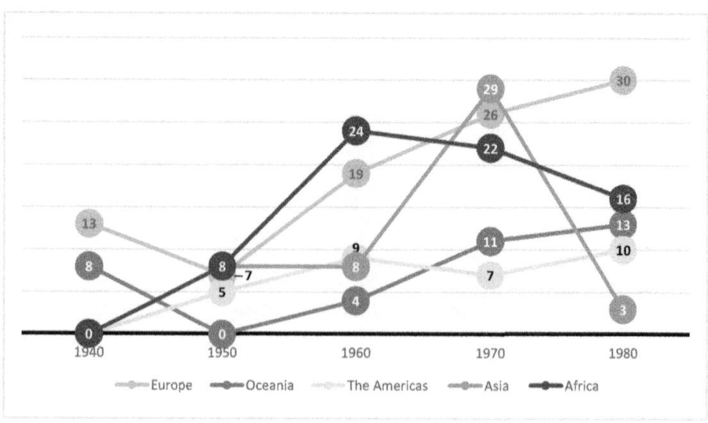

Figure 2.5 Number of referendums per continent, 1944–1989.

13 votes, all but two of which were so-called abrogative referendums initiated by the people), Ireland (with 12 – all constitutional referendums), Denmark (10) and France (11).

What is interesting about these referendums in Western Europe is that they were held on miscellaneous issues like driving on the right in Sweden, wage-indexation in Italy, and other issues that did not fit into the traditional left–right divide that characterised the era of what Stein Rokkan called the "frozen party system"[33].

The referendum is constitutionally speaking a "people's safeguard", a barrier against the encroachment by the elected representatives. And this is also (pretty much) the story of the use of the device after the Second World War. The category containing by far the largest number of cases is that of constitutional referendums (such as the total revision of the Danish and French constitutions in, respectively, 1953 and 1958, or the numerous amendments to the Irish constitution).

These referendums were "uncontrolled", to use the terminology of Gordon Smith's classic paper[34]. The other referendums were – in many cases – characterised by crossing across ideological divides. Matters such as nuclear energy, membership of the EEC

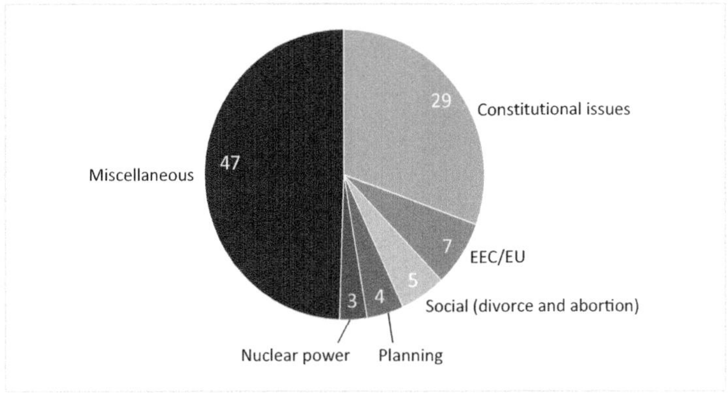

Figure 2.6 Referendums by type in Europe, 1944–1989.

(the forerunner of the European Union) and planning. These did not quite fit into the cleavages that had shaped the party system. Hence, like in the case of temperance (prohibition), political parties kicked issues into the long political grass by submitting them to referendums. This is true, for example, of the Danish and Norwegian referendums on EEC membership, the Austrian and Swedish votes on nuclear power, and even to the vexed issue of abortion in Italy – over which the Christian Democrats and the Communists "agreed to disagree".

The pattern is very much the same in Oceania. Indeed, even more so. All but four of the 36 referendums held in Australia, New Zealand and the smaller Pacific islands were votes on constitutional changes or reform. In general, democratic countries used the referendum as a constitutional safeguard. Not a radical device, not one used often, but one used when the government wanted to expand the legal framework of governing, in other words the constitution.

This is very different from the use of the referendum in Asia and in African countries. Only 14 out of the 90 referendums held in Africa during the period were constitutional – but in many cases they were held in countries with single-party systems.

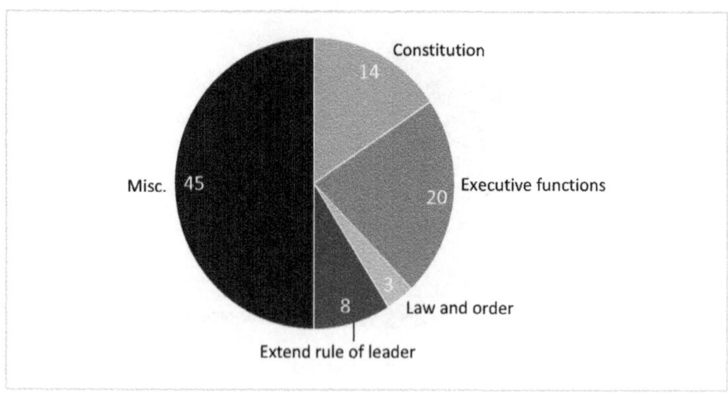

Figure 2.7 The most common issues put to referendums in Africa, 1944–1989.

Another category of referendums was on executive-legislative functions. That is votes that gave the president increased powers. These votes, which in other countries would have been of constitutional importance, were held as plebiscites without any real alternative. For example, in 1970 in Burkina Faso (then Upper Volta), the military leader Sangoulé Lamizana organised a vote that enabled the president (himself) to dissolve congress. This vote effectively granted him an extension of his day-to-day powers and was a way of circumventing term-limits. In other countries, above all Egypt, they did not bother with the pretence; in eight cases there were referendums on the extension of the terms of leaders, and a large number of referendums on martial law and security measures.

In Africa too, of course, there was a large number of miscellaneous issues that were put to a vote. A handful of these were genuine referendums (on a new electoral system in Botswana in 1987, for example) but most of these were plebiscites held to provide a façade of legitimacy for restrictions of freedoms. For example, the 99 per cent support for "Measures for the protection of the nation and social peace" in Egypt in 1981 was an example of this. It is perhaps instructive to note that this vote was held only a month before the assassination of Anwar Sadat.

The pattern we find in Asia is almost identical. Indeed, in the largest continent an even larger number of referendums were on the extension of the rule of authoritarian leaders, such as Al-Asad in Syria and Ferdinand Marcos in the Philippines. Constitutional referendums were largely ceremonial and, in any, case rigged. One example will suffice. When, in 1955 Jean Baptiste Ngô Đình Diệm hailed the result of the referendum on the abolition of the monarchy, he proclaimed that the people took "an enthusiastic part" and concluded that it was "an approval of the policies pursued"[35]. This "approval" was reiterated in Washington, where the Department of State was "gratified that according to reports the referendum was conducted in such an orderly and efficient manner and that the people of Viet-Nam have made their choice unmistakably clear"[36]. The outcome of the vote was inarguably "unmistakably clear". Indeed, official figures initially showed that 600,000 voters supported Diệm. Though, somewhat puzzlingly, the number of electors who turned out to vote was a stunning 450,000, that is a "yes" vote of 133 per cent[37].

Apart from the 1980s, there were few genuinely democratic referendums like the one in South Korea in 1987 that formally ended the dictatorship.

The same pattern could be observed in Latin America. There too – but perhaps to a lesser extent – referendums were held by authoritarian leaders such as General Pinochet in the 1970s and 1980s, and a couple of decades earlier the votes to instate and perpetuate the (mis)rule of Papa Doc Duvalier in Haiti. With the exception of Uruguay (with a total number of 11 constitutional referendums), it was only in the 1980s that referendums in the Americas became democratic, and it was only in this decade that there were constitutional referendums worthy of the name.

But much as referendums were billed as "democracy on demand" and the voice of the people only one of the 29 votes in the Americas were initiated by the people, namely the 1989 Uruguayan referendum on the repeal of *Ley de Caducidad de la*

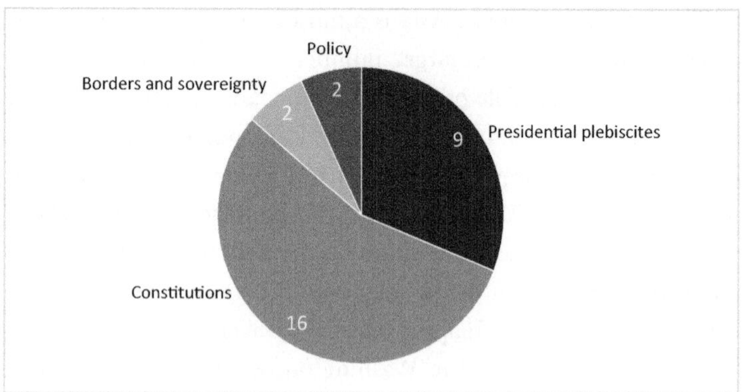

Figure 2.8 The most common issues put to a vote in the Americas, 1944–1989.

Pretensión Punitiva del Estado, which granted immunity for crimes during the years of dictatorship. Interestingly, and perhaps as an indication of the maturity of Uruguayan democracy, the voters voted to uphold the law.

The referendum after the fall of communism

There were 665 referendums in the three decades after the fall of the Berlin Wall in 1989. The number of referendums worldwide reached an all-time high in the 1990s and while it plateaued somewhat in the decade after, the total number was significantly higher than in the decades before the end of the Cold War.

Some countries that had previously held no referendums at the national level joined the list of nations with direct democratic experience (e.g. Granada, Bahamas, the Netherlands and Taiwan). Interestingly, in the latter two cases the majority of votes were initiated by the citizens.

In general, there were many more cases of genuine "democracy on demand" – for example the majority of the votes in Italy,

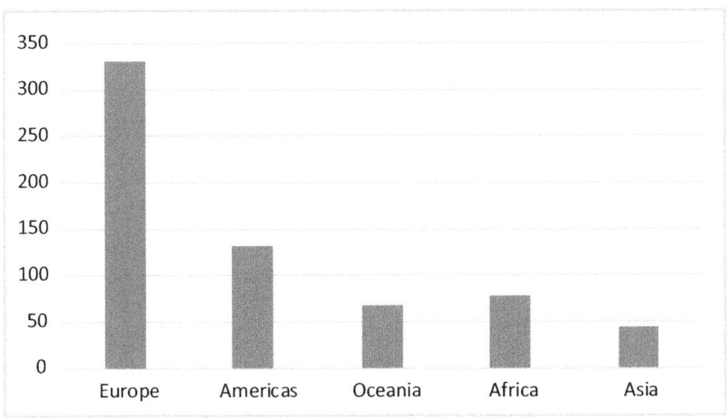

Figure 2.9 Total number of referendums per region.

Slovenia, Slovakia and Liechtenstein fell into this category. There were also initiatives in Uruguay and Colombia – though many of these votes were invalid due to a low turnout.

The number of referendums in Asia was lower, mainly because there were fewer dictators who held plebiscites on their continued powers – though such vote did take place in Syria (during the war!) and in Kyrgyzstan, Turkmenistan and Uzbekistan, with respectively, seven, three and four votes.

The referendums held in Africa continued to be strongly top-down – though there were exceptions such as the 2005 constitutional referendum in Kenya (which was a rare example of a rejected African referendum). But in the main, the abysmal record of rigged plebiscites continued to be the order of the day. Though, even autocrats can lose if they don't do their homework – and their due diligence. This is what happened to Robert Mugabe, when a proposed new constitution was rejected by 54 to 46 per cent in a referendum in 2000.

Without there being a perfect correlation, it seems that the decline in the number of referendums has corresponded to the

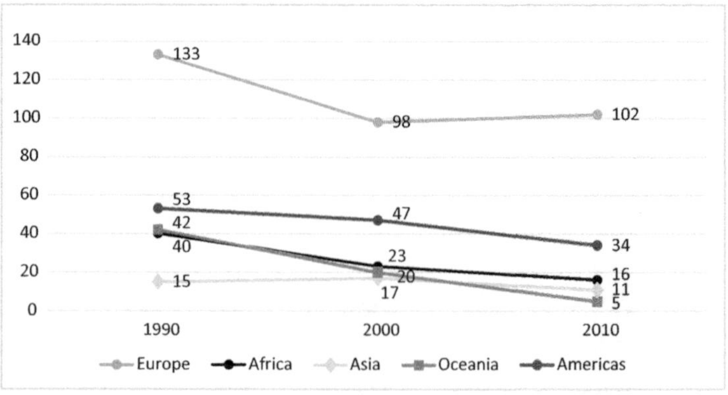

Figure 2.10 Number of referendums per continent, 1990–2019.

decline in the number of democracies that accelerated in the second decade of the 2000s[38]. However, there are still more referendums per decade than at any point before 1990. In the 1970s, there were, on average, 9.5 nationwide referendums per year, and 7.3 per year in the 1980s. In the first two decades of the twenty-first century, by contrast, there were 20.5 referendums per year between 2000 and 2009, and 16.8 referendums between 2010 and 2019.

The independence referendum in South Sudan: referendums in Africa

I was in an amusement park just outside London with my children when the phone rang. It was the Foreign Office. "Our colleagues in Washington have asked us to find an expert for President Obama's Africa Envoy Team", said the lady at the other end of the phone. "Yes, but I am a referendum expert", I tried. "Exactly. It is for the referendum on independence in

South Sudan". She explained that the Americans were mediating between the Khartoum government and the would-be separatists in Juba. Within 48 hours I was on a plane to Africa. Two hours after landing, I was part of a negotiation between hardened rebels and the national government over the practicalities of holding a vote on independence, as they had agreed in 2005. My boss, Major General Scott Gration, had not spent much time studying referendums and asked me for a briefing. "But a short one, god damn it". So, this is what I wrote for him: "While there were early votes for freed slaves in Liberia in 1846 and 1847, the referendums in Africa that can properly be called thus were held in 1950, where six votes were held in newly established states. This figure rose to 17 in the 1960s, and further to 27 in the 1970s before the figure fell back to 20 in the 1980s. In line with other parts of the world there was a massive increase in the 1990s. And, like elsewhere the number has fallen subsequently. Egypt is by a distance the most frequent user of referendums with a total of 30. Morocco with nine is a distant second. There have been relatively few referendums in Sub-Saharan Africa. The average yes-vote was a high 88 per cent." He took a brief look at the note. "It's short alright. That's good. What I need to know. Right, so, these guys – the South Sudanese – won't lose, right? So, we can safely allow some of the turnout requirements that the Khartoum are asking for", he said. I nodded, but added that this was a "political decision", and not one that I had a say in. The South Sudanese accepted the conditions. In January 2011, 98 per cent, on a 97 per cent turnout, voted for secession.

So far, we have only looked at the numbers, but political science is not just about recounting facts. It is also about finding patterns. So, were there any? This is the question we now turn to.

The policy effects of referendums

The big question is if referendums actually have any effects on public policy? Given the relative paucity of them, this is difficult to test empirically. The annual number per year is simply too small. However, often referendums – even when they are rare – have profound effects.

The Brexit referendum in the United Kingdom was a momentous political event that fundamentally shook the political debate – and did so in a way that no general election had done since 1945. Similarly, the Swedish referendum on nuclear power (1980), the Danish referendum on the Maastricht Treaty – and further afield the referendum on amnesty for the crimes committed under the years of dictatorship in Uruguay (1989) created political fault lines that impacted on subsequent political developments.

Hence, referendums can shape politics and can have a profound effect on subsequent politics. This is, admittedly, difficult to capture, but one way of gauging the effect of referendums is to look at the total number of referendums held in a decade and then contrast and correlate that figure with social and economic indicators.

In line with research by John Matsusaka[39], there is a positive correlation between the number of referendums and GDP per capita (R=0.433**, statistically significant at the 0.01 level, 2-tailed, N=172).

Yet, as Figure 2.11 shows, Switzerland is an outlier, and without this country the correlation falls to just below R=0.20, statistically significant at the 0.05 level. But referendums certainly are not bad for the economy. Similarly, there is a small, but statistically significant, negative association between high levels of CO_2 emissions and the total number of referendums (R=-0.174, statistically significant

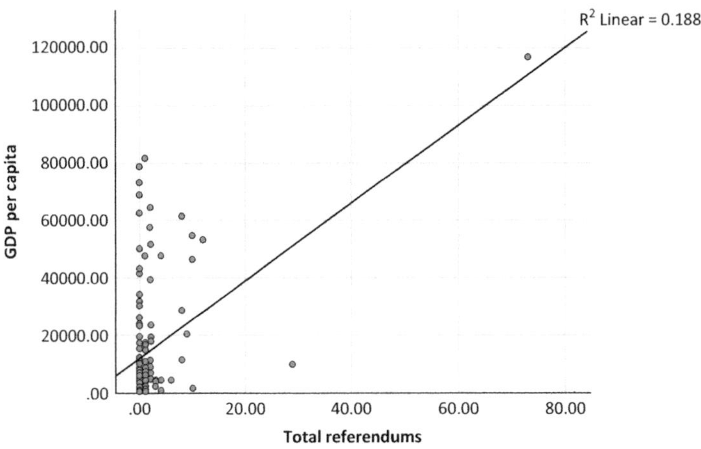

Figure 2.11 Total number of referendums and GDP per capita.

at the 0.05 level, 2-tailed, N=173). Put simply, more referendums equal lower emissions of carbon dioxide. Not a massive correlation, but certainly not a falsification of the claim that direct democracy provisions in Switzerland led to better environmental protection[40].

Of course, there are other institutional factors that might conceivably play a role. For example, second chambers, presidentialism, semi-presidentialism and federalism might be conducive for better economic performance. Or, conversely, it is possible that one-party states (like China or Vietnam), or even traditional monarchies (like Saudi Arabia and Brunei) do better. Indeed, it is possible that having a democracy is not good for economic well-being. This is an empirical question.

In research for this book, we tested this, using dummy variables for one-party states, presidentialism, parliamentarism, semi-presidentialism and monarchies. We have also added the Freedom House score for the country in question, and finally the number of referendums held in the past ten years. The findings corroborate the earlier pattern that referendums are positively associated with a high average GDP per capita. We find a number of interesting factors.

Overall, we find that the most statistically significant factor is having a democracy. This is by a considerable distance the best predictor of wealth. The confident claims regarding the supposed benefits of authoritarianism – as espoused by the likes of the Chinese Communist Party, are simply not supported by statistical evidence. For every notch up the 100-point Freedom House scale, the average citizen gains nearly US$300. Other variables do not fare quite so well. Federalism, according to political theorists such as Montesquieu, was an ideal form of government, one that, in the view of the French sage, had "all the internal advantages of republican government and the external force of monarchy"[41]. Alas, this factor (while positive) is not statistically significant.

Table 2.2 Institutional factors and GDP per capita (standard errors in brackets)

Variable	B
Presidential	−7570.8*
	(4536.6)
Parliamentarism	815.391
	(4988.4)
Semi-presidentialism	−10348.2**
	5230.329
Federalism	6837.9)
	(4574.1)
Senate dummy	523.664
	(2651.8)
Total number of referendums, 2010–2018	884.1**
	(427)
Democracy	284.041***
	(.000)
Constant	−1124.601
	(5058.3)

Dependent variable: GDP per capita. R-Squared: 0.33; N=173; *** significant at p<0.001, ** significant at p<0.05, * significant at p<0.1.

The same is true for the dummy variable for senates or second chambers. The proposition that upper houses are good for the economy is not supported statistically. Further, having a presidential system (like in the United States and Brazil) where the president is independent of congress has, statistically speaking, a negative effect on the economy. The same is true for a semi-presidential system (like the French model with *both* a prime minister *and* a president), which, statistically, is also directly harmful for the economy. In contrast to these absent or negative effects, the number of referendums seems to have positive effects. Statistically speaking, there is a significant relationship between the number of votes and the average wealth. In purely numerical terms, for every referendum held citizens become US$884 richer. Admittedly, there are outliers – and Switzerland is certainly one. However, this statistic is consistent with earlier research that suggested that "allowing the general public to participate in law-making often seems to improve the performance of government"[42].

In the same vein, though perhaps some readers will find this frivolous, statistically speaking, for every referendum held you live a few months longer. Conversely, living in a presidential system shortens your life by nearly five years. That presidential and semi-presidential systems are directly harmful to your life expectancy, might have many explanations, above all gridlock and the inability to get things done in these systems.

Not everything can be measured by statistics, but figures are a good start. Overall, there are many positive effects of having referendums. The doomsayers who hold that people are too stupid to vote rationally are not vindicated. The opposite if anything is true. Indeed, there are far better arguments against presidential systems than against systems that allow a modicum of direct democracy. Though, as we shall see in the next chapter, not all issues can be resolved through referendums.

Table 2.3 Institutional factors and life expectancy (standard errors in brackets)

Variable	B-coefficients
Presidential**	−4.740**
	(1.672)
Parliamentarism	−2.148
	(1.838)
Semi-presidentialism**	−5.886
	(1.928)
Federalism	0.586
	(1.686)
Senate dummy	0.183
	(0.977)
Total number of referendums, 2010–2018	0.367**
	(0.158)
Democracy	0.130***
	(0.021)
Constant	67.368***
	(1.864)

Dependent variable: life expectancy, R-Squared: 0.33; N=173; *** significant at $p<0.001$, ** significant at $p<0.05$, * significant at $p<0.1$.

When are referendums actually held: towards a statistical pattern?

"Referendums are held infrequently, usually only when the governments think that they provide a useful ad hoc solution to a particular constitutional or political problem or to set the seal of legitimacy on a change of regime"[43]. That is one of the more positive utterances. But not everybody has been this optimistic. Arend Lijphart struck a pessimistic note, writing that "the question of why referendums occur much more frequently in some countries than in others cannot be answered satisfactorily"[44]. And more recently, an even less pessimistic observer, Dag Anckar, conceded that "patterns are not well developed"[45]. At some level, there is reason to concede the

Table 2.4 Institutional factors and referendums (standard errors in brackets)

Variable	B variables
Ideology (right)	0.323**
	(0.106)
Federalism dummy	−6.356*
	(3.347)
Provisions for referendums	−1.640
	(2.016)
Proportional representation	−3.121*
	(1.527)
Parliamentary system dummy	−0.131
	(2.552)
Presidential	−1.348
	(2.259)
Senate index	1.389
	(1.467)
Constant	−8.200
	(5.538)

Dependent variable: total number of referendums, 2010–2018, N=257; R-Squared: 0.82. *** $p>0.001$, ** $p>0.05$, and * $p>0.1$

point. For example, there is no suggestion that the actual number of referendums follow sociological patterns. There is no correlation between inequality and the number of referendums, nor between the effective number of parties and the frequency with which referendums are held. (Respectively, these indicators are statistically significant at $p>0.50$, and in both cases the R is below 0.15.)

However, when we include other factors a different pattern emerges. Yes, it is true that there is no statistical relationship between the number of referendums and, respectively, presidential or parliamentary systems. But there is a clear, and statistically significant, negative relationship between, respectively, federalism and proportional representation.

Using Lijphart's terminology, federalism and proportional representation are both "consensus institutions"[46]. In a federal system, it is necessary to keep a delicate balance between states, this means that politicians at the central level have to do their utmost not to appear to override the concerns of the states. This might explain why Switzerland, the perennial exception to the rule, is the only federal state to use referendums. Referendums are absent from the politics of federations like Germany, Mexico, the United States at the national level, and while they used to be held frequently in Australia, this country has not held a single referendum in the twenty-first century. (The 2017 Australian Marriage Law Postal Survey was not a referendum but formally a large-scale consultation[47].)

Referendums – as the Brexit vote showed – can be divisive. And division is not what political leaders in federations cherish. Hence, they don't hold referendums, whereas the same is not the case in more centralised states, such as France and Malta.

Similarly, political systems based on proportional representation are based on a sense of compromise. John Stuart Mill valued proportional representation precisely because it would "enable any assemblage of voters, amounting to a certain number, to place in the legislature a representative of its own choice, [and] minorities will not be suppressed"[48]. For this reason, there is little incentive to hold divisive referendums in countries where cooperation and compromise is the norm, such as Belgium and Norway. In a majoritarian system, by contrast, such concerns are less important. The aim is not consensus, but efficiency[49]. For this reason, a political party can call a referendum to marginalise the opposition – or simply to overrule it, as has been the case on a number of occasions in the United Kingdom, such as when Tony Blair (1997–2007) held several referendums to wrong-foot the Conservative Party.

Another interesting factor is that referendums tend to be held in countries that are ideologically more right-wing.

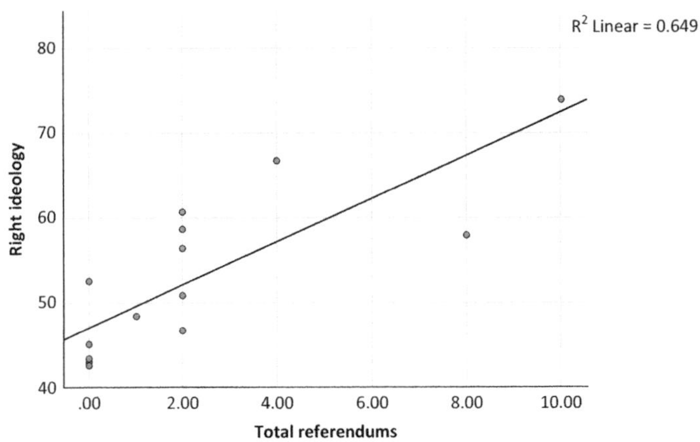

Figure 2.12 Referendums and right-wing political ideology.

If we use the data for the Manifesto Project[50], which used content analysis to code political parties' manifestos on a scale from 0 to 100, with a higher score meaning that the country's political parties are to the right, we find a statistically significant tendency that countries where the *bourgeois* parties are strong are more likely to hold referendums. In fact, this correlation is very strong (R=0.80, statistically significant at the 0.01 level (2-tailed), N=174).

Maybe this is not surprising. Political parties on the left have always had an uneasy relationship with referendums. In Germany leading theoreticians like Karl Kautsky and Eduard Bernstein were opposed to referendums[51]; in Italy, Arturo Labriola, the foremost theoretician of the left, published a short book with the telling title *Contro il referendum*[52]; and in the United Kingdom the Fabian Society early on published a tract entitled *The Case Against the Referendum* – almost literally the same title as Labriola's tract[53].

It was not surprising therefore that the first Labour prime minister, Ramsay MacDonald, railed against referendums. In his book *Socialism*, he declared himself, "perfectly content as a democrat to regard the responsibility of electors under a democracy as the responsibility for electing a government"[54]. He stayed true to this belief. When the Conservative MP Frederick Penny, in 1924, asked Prime Minister MacDonald, "whether he will introduce legislation to establish a system of referendum to form a part of our constitution, in order to save the country from the inconvenience and disturbance of frequent elections?", the latter responded curtly and monosyllabically, "No"[55].

As alluded to, the other side of politics was fonder of the idea of referendums. In Britain, this institution was "mooted repeatedly throughout the [twentieth] Century … by Conservatives who saw it as a break on change", wrote David Butler in a pioneering study[56]. Thus Arthur Balfour, called attention to the "admirable use" that had been made of it in Australia, where it was "a living and effective part" of "the constitution of the new Commonwealth". Balfour also noted that the referendum has "its proved value as used by local authorities and trade unions in England"[57].

From a more theoretical perspective (though with opportunistic undertones) the aforementioned A.V. Dicey, true to his conservative instincts, championed the referendum, which he believed would "prevent the passing of any important Act, which does not command the sanction of electors"[58].

In light of this, it is not surprising that most referendums have taken place in countries where the centre-right has been in control of government, and where socialist parties have been less electorally successful, such as Ireland, Italy and Switzerland.

One of the interesting factors is that provisions for citizen-initiated votes are *not* correlated with the use of referendums. This is largely a result of many provisions for mechanisms of direct democracy in places that are patently *not* democratic, such as Belarus, and in recent years Hungary, where the provisions for citizen-initiated referendums have fallen into disuse under the rule of Viktor Orbán. Provisions for holding referendums on demand require more than simply enabling constitutional rules. That such votes are not held might also have something to do with supermajority requirements which render results void if the turnout is low, which, in turn make the exercise of gathering signatures and campaigning a bit of a waste of time.

The world of direct democracy is far from perfect, and there is plenty of room for improvement. Yet, in its own little way, the referendum – and still more the initiative – provides mechanisms through which the people can have a say. Perhaps the novelist E.M. Forster had a point when he wrote, "We may still contrive to raise three cheers for democracy, although at present she deserves only two"[59]. The same would also be accurate for the use of referendums.

Notes

1 E.M. Forster, *What I Believe* (London: Hogarth Press, 1939), p. 229.
2 Pyotr Kropotkin, *The Conquest for Bread* (Paris: Adansonia, 2018 [1906]), p. 83.
3 Ibid., p. 84.
4 Andrew Moravcsik, "The European constitutional settlement", *World Economy* 31(1) (2008), pp. 158–183 (p. 178).
5 Shauna Reilly, *Direct Democracy: A Double-Edged Sword* (London: Rienner, 2018), p. 3.
6 George Bush quoted in Mike Ford, "Letting the people take the initiative", *Veritaseritas – A Quarterly Journal of Public Policy in Texas* (October, 1999), pp. 26–41 (p. 30).
7 Vernon Bogdanor, *The People and the Party System: The Referendum and Electoral Reform in British Politics* (Cambridge: Cambridge University Press, 1981), p. 92.
8 T. Donovan, "Referendums and initiatives in North America", in Matt Qvortrup (ed.), *Referendums around the World* (London: Palgrave Macmillan, 2014), pp. 122–161.
9 See Laurence Morel, "The referendum experience in France", in Julia Smith (ed.), *The Palgrave Handbook of European Referendums* (Basingstoke: Palgrave, 2021), pp. 179–202.
10 Jean-Antoine-Nicolas Condorcet, *Sur la nécessité de faire ratifier la constitution par les citoyens, et sur la formation des communautés de campagne* (Paris: De l'imprimerie de Ph. D. Pierres, 1789).
11 Ibid., p. 1.
12 Ibid., p. 2.
13 Ibid., p. 11.

14 Jean François Aubert, "Switzerland", in David Butler and Austin Ranney (eds), *Referendums: A Comparative Study of Practice and Theory* (Washington, DC: The American Enterprise Institute, 1978), p. 40.
15 J.E. Rodríguez and J.E.R. Guez, *The Independence of Spanish America* (Cambridge: Cambridge University Press, 1998).
16 J.J. Cortés, "Endogenous direct democracy: The case of Mexico", *Journal of Politics in Latin America* 12(2) (2020), pp. 200–218 (p. 216).
17 V. Hugo, *Napoléon le petit* (London: W. Jeffs, 1862).
18 Georges Sand, *Journal d'un Voyageur pendant la guerre* (Paris: Michel Lévy, 1871), p. 306.
19 Malcolm Crook, "Protest voting: The revolutionary origins of annotated ballot papers cast in French plebiscites, 1851–1870", *French History* 29(3) (2015), pp. 349–369.
20 Karl Marx, *Der achtzehnte Brumaire des Louis Bonaparte* (Berlin: Piper, 2016 [1852]), p. 16.
21 H. Duval , J. George and P.Y. Leblanc-Dechoisay, *Referendum et plébiscite* (Paris: FeniXX, 1970).
22 K. Marx, "Marx an Engels. 18 Mai 1870", in *Marx-Engels Werke* (Berlin: Dietz Verlag, 1974), Vol. 32, pp. 516–517 (p. 516).
23 Gambetta quoted in P. Séguin, *Louis Napoléon le Grand* (Paris: Bernard Grasset, 1990), p. 370.
24 Andi Gross, *Die unvollendete Direkte Demokratie* (Thun: Weber, 2016), p. 25.
25 Uwe Serdült, "Referendums in Switzerland", in M. Qvortrup (ed.), *Referendums around the World* (London: Palgrave Macmillan, 2014), pp. 65–121 (p. 85).
26 Ibid.
27 J.J. Rousseau, "Discours sur l'origine et les fondements de l'inégalité parmi les hommes", in *Oeuvres III* (Paris: Galimard, 1955 [1755]), p. 321.
28 M. Qvortrup, "AV Dicey: The referendum as the people's veto", *History of Political Thought* 20(3) (1999), pp. 531–546.
29 J.P. Boyer, *Direct Democracy in Canada: The History and Future of Referendums* (Louisville, Quebec: Dundurn, 1996), p. 37.
30 In the year of this referendum Finland was not a full democracy. Due to the far-right Lapua Movement, which used kidnappings and violent attacks to forward its anti-communist ideology, the country slipped to 4 on Polity IV in 1931 (see T. Raunio, "The changing Finnish democracy: Stronger parliamentary accountability, coalescing political parties and weaker external constraints", *Scandinavian Political Studies* 27(2) (2004), pp. 133–152).
31 Olaf Ruin, "Sweden: The referendum as an instrument for defusing political issues", in M. Gallagher and P.-V. Uleri (eds), *The Referendum Experience in Europe* (London: Palgrave Macmillan, 1996), pp. 171–184.

32 M. Suksi, "Finland: The referendum as a dormant issue", in M. Gallagher and P.-V. Uleri (eds), *The Referendum Experience in Europe* (London: Palgrave Macmillan, 1996), pp. 52–65 (p. 52).
33 S. Rokkan, *Citizens, Elections, Parties: Approaches to the Comparative Study of the Processes of Development* (Colchester: ECPR Press, 2009).
34 G. Smith, "The functional properties of the referendum", *European Journal of Political Research* 4(1) (1976), pp. 1–23.
35 Jessica M. Chapman, "Staging democracy: South Vietnam's 1955 referendum to depose Bao Dai", *Diplomatic History* 30(4) (2006), pp. 671–703 (p. 380).
36 William Brownell, *The American Mandarin: A Study of the Life of Diem and of the Origins of the American Involvements* (Ithaca, NY: Cornell University Press, 1963), p. 158.
37 Stanley Karnow, *Vietnam: A History* (New York: Penguin, 1997), p. 239.
38 See Larry Diamond, *Ill Winds: Saving Democracy from Russian Rage, Chinese Ambition, and American Complacency* (London: Penguin Books, 2000).
39 J.G. Matsusaka, "Direct democracy works", *Journal of Economic Perspectives* 19(2) (2005), pp. 185–206.
40 Philippe Thalmann, "The public acceptance of green taxes: 2 million voters express their opinion", *Public Choice* 119(1–2) (2004), pp. 179–217.
41 Charles Montesquieu, *The Spirit of the Laws* (Cambridge: Cambridge University Press, 1989), p. 131.
42 Matsusaka, "Direct democracy works", p. 185.
43 D. Butler and A. Ranney, "Summing up", in David Butler and Austin Ranney (eds), *Referendums: A Comparative Study in Practice and Theory* (Washington, DC: American Enterprise Institute, 1978), p. 221.
44 Arend Lijphart, *Democracies: Patterns of Majoritarian and Consensus Government in Twenty One Countries* (New Haven: Yale University Press, 1984), p. 197.
45 Dag Anckar, "Why referendums: On appearances and absences", in Laurence Morel and Matt Qvortrup (eds), *The Routledge Handbook to Referendums and Direct Democracy* (London: Routledge, 2018), pp. 107–122 (p. 118).
46 Lijphart, *Democracies*, p. 1.
47 See B. Hegarty, D. Marshall, M.L. Rasmussen, P. Aggleton and R. Cover, "Heterosexuality and race in the Australian same-sex marriage postal survey", *Australian Feminist Studies* 33(97) (2018), pp. 400–416.
48 John Stuart Mill, *Autobiography* (Oxford: Oxford University Press, 2018), p. 145.
49 P. Norton, "The case for first-past-the-post", *Representation* 34(2) (1997), pp. 84–88.
50 For a general introduction to the Manifesto Project see: https://manifesto-project.wzb.eu/down/data/2019b/codebooks/release_notes_MPDS2019b.pdf

51 Robert Michels, *Zur Soziologie des Parteiwesens in der modernen Demokratie. Untersuchungen über die oligargischen Tendenzen des Gruppenlebens* (Leipzig: Alfred Kröner Verlag, 1925), p. 430.
52 A. Labriola, *Contro il referendum* (Milan: Uffici della critica sociale, 1897).
53 Clifford Sharp, "The case against the referendum", Fabian Tract, No. 155 (London: The Fabian Society, 1911).
54 Ramsay J. MacDonald, *Socialism: Critical and Constructive* (London: Cassell, 1925), p. 223.
55 House of Commons Debates, 18 February 1924, Vol. 169, Col. 1304.
56 David Butler, "United Kingdom", in David Butler and Austin Ranney (eds), *Referendums: A Comparative Study of Practice and Theory* (Washington, DC: The American Enterprise Institute, 1978), pp. 211–219 (p. 211).
57 Balfour in Herbert W. Horwill, "The referendum in Great Britain", *Political Science Quarterly* 26(3) (1911), pp. 415–431 (p. 426).
58 A.V. Dicey, *An Introduction to the Study of the Law of the Constitution* (Indianapolis: Liberty Fund, 1983), p. cix.
59 E.M. Forster, *Two Cheers for Democracy* (London: Penguin, 1965), p. 12.

Chapter 3

Referendums, nationalism and separatism

"It is in general a necessary condition of free institutions, that the boundaries of governments should coincide in the main with those of nationalities", wrote John Stuart Mill in *Considerations on representative government*[1]. It was this sentiment that prompted groups in multinational countries to seek referendums in recent years; to create new boundaries that coincide with those of "nations". For example, in Scotland in 2014, Catalonia in 2017 and Bougainville (a part of Papua New Guinea) in 2019[2].

These referendums were but some of the recent cases of votes on independence, which have been described as a new wave of separatism. From one perspective, these votes can be seen as democratically legitimate because there ought to be a rule that stipulates that "a state's territorial integrity can be challenged from inside by a self-defined community"[3]. From another perspective, however, such referendums – and more generally such acts of secession – can be dangerous. When a constitution "is silent on secession, it is not clear that the central government sanctions such movements, and if it turns out that it does not, secessionist disputes can burst out in violence"[4]. In this chapter, this development towards more secessionism will be put into context by providing an overview of the votes on independence and nationalism in the past two hundred years, and even further back in history.

The brief history of independence referendums

Speaking in Sevastopol in Crimea on 12 May 2012, President Vladimir Putin called on all countries "to respect the right of Russians to self-determination"[5]. This came a few weeks after he had backed and probably helped organise the plebiscite in Crimea[6]. After the collapse of the Soviet Union, Russia has on several occasions encouraged referendums on self-determination in areas with a large number of Russian speakers, such as in Abkhazia in 1999, in Transnistria in 1995, 2003 and 2006 and in South Ossetia in 2001, 2006 and 2011 – and arguably in Eastern Ukraine in the spring of 2014[7]. Yet at other times, this principled commitment to "the self-determination of the people" has been less forthcoming. Russia – to name but one example – was less than enthusiastic about the independence referendum in Tatarstan in 1992[8].

While history is not a perfect guide for the future, it is instructive to consider how the concept of self-determination through plebiscites has evolved throughout history. This chapter is intended to provide a prolegomenon to future study of the subject.

"Discussion of the doctrine of national self-determination falls naturally into three periods", wrote Sarah Wambaugh[9]. She identified the votes held by the French after the 1789 revolution, the referendums at the time of the Italian Risorgimento (1848–1870), the votes held in the aftermath of the First World War. And, we might add, the more recent referendums, above all the one held in Catalonia in 2017[10].

A Foucault-inspired analysis of concepts

In analysing a concept or a historical phenomenon, we are often tempted to go back to the origins as if the first instance is in some way its true representation. However, there is another approach; one that stresses the changes concepts undergo as a part of their *Wirkungsgeschichte*. Without being too constrained by the epistemological constraints that go with borrowing theoretical frameworks from different disciplines, Foucault's notion of *genealogy* may be useful for studying the phenomenon of self-determination referendums.

Inspired by Friedrich Nietzsche, Michel Foucault made a distinction between a concept's *Ursprung* (origin) and its *Herkunft* (descent). Whereas the "origin" of a phenomenon is the pursuit of the "immobile form" and the "primordial truth"[11], the *Herkunft* is the study of the "myriad of events through which – thanks to which, against which – they [the concepts] are formed"[12].

A genealogical approach to studying the discourses of self-determination referendums is not just about the "origin" – i.e. the first referendums held – but more about the changes the discourse has undergone over a period of centuries, in short its *Herkunft*. For the historian of political ideas, the aim is to understand the different and sometimes interwoven ways in which thinking about a concept proceeded through history. That said, this does not purport to be a genealogical study in the true sense espoused by Foucault. But the chapter is based on the *a priori* assumption that it is more important to understand the *Herkunft* of a concept than its *Ursprung*.

Earliest referendums on self-determination

Historically, the first instances of self-determination referendums in anything like the present-day form date back to 1527 when the French King Francis I (1494–1547) held a plebiscite in Burgundy on whether to transfer the area to the Spanish king in 1527 as he had agreed to in the Treaty of Madrid[13]. The people rejected the transfer and stayed with France. Sarah Wambaugh speculates – though without concrete evidence[14] – that Francis was inspired by Erasmus of Rotterdam (1466–1536) who – in 1517 – had made a case for the view that "what power and sovereignty soever you have, you have it by the consent of the people"[15].

Of course, "the people" in those days was a rather small number of people. In these votes those so entitled were merely property-owning males. Whether a practical man like King Francis devoured texts of renaissance theologians – as suggested by Wambaugh[16] – can perhaps be questioned. A few years later, Francis' son, Henry II (1519–1559), "organised a plebiscite in 1552 in Verdun, Toul and Metz before their annexation [to France]"[17].

Before the vote, Bishop de Lénoncourt is reported to have said to the inhabitants of Verdun, "that the King of France had come as a liberator who will treat the citizens as good Frenchmen … He appealed to the vote of the people"[18].

It is remarkable – and possibly a result of Solière's enthusiastic recounting of the vote – that Bishop Lénoncourt used words such as "citizens" and "people" at a time when Jean Bodin (1530–1596) expounded his theory of divinely sanctioned absolutism by the grace of God in *Six livres de la République* (1576), and famously stated that "[only] the prince is responsible before God"[19].

However, we have few contemporary accounts of what motivated the use of referendums at the time and it took almost one hundred years before these practices of proto-self-determination were placed on anything like a theoretical footing. Hugo Grotius (1583–1645) observed in *De Jure Belli ac Pacis* that "in the alienation of a part of sovereignty, it is required that the part which is alienated consent to the act"[20].

Samuel Pufendorf (1632–1694) was even more explicit when he wrote in *De jura naturae et gentium* (1672) that "in the alienation of a part of the kingdom, there is required not only the consent of the people which continues to be with the old king, but the consent of that part too, especially, whose alienation is at stake" (and for those who want it in the original Latin: *sed maxime consensus illius partis, da qua alienda agitur*)[21].

Grotius and Pufendorf were not the only ones expressing this view. Emer de Vattel (1714–1767), roughly one hundred years later, cited the example of a vote held in Burgundy in 1527 in which the citizens had objected to a plan to transfer them to the Spanish king. Though Vattel added realistically that "Subjects are seldom able to make resistance on such occasions; and, in general, their wisest plan will be to submit to their new master, and endeavour to obtain the best terms they can"[22].

As diplomat and scholar Wolfgang Danspeckgruber has noted, the concept of self-determination had its roots in the enlightenment and the ideals of the idealistic philosophers like Kant and Fichte who championed the notion of freedom[23].

Not surprisingly, therefore, the concept of self-determination as a recognised doctrine of practical politics first appeared in the wake of the French Revolution when the Constituent Assembly in Paris passed a degree renouncing conquest and decreeing that henceforth "*la nation française renounce à entreprendre aucune guerre dans la vue de faire de conquétes*" ["the French nation renounces to undertake any war with a view to making conquests"][24].

As a consequence, the annexation of Avignon in 1791 only took effect after a referendum had been held in the area. True to the letter of the aforementioned law, Robespierre (1758–1794) stated in debate about the referendum that "if we have no right over this country, we cannot send an army there without being oppressors"[25]. The vote was an endorsement of French rule. As a contemporary report concluded:

> Considering that the majority of the communes and citizens have expressed freely and solemnly their wish for a union with Avignon and France ... the National Assembly declares that in conformity with the freely expressed wish of the majority ... of these two countries to be incorporated into France[26].

It would be almost trite to point out that the Congress of Vienna dealt a blow to the doctrine of self-determination. As Griffiths points out, "The Congress of Vienna in 1815 did not accept self-determination as a basis for reshaping the map of Europe"[27].

The perception was that the excesses of revolutionary fervour and the horrors of the Napoleonic wars gave self-determination a bad name. However, this changed after the revolutionary year of 1848 when referendums once again became fashionable. As Eric Weitz has pointed out, self-determination of the people was accepted again, and the ideals espoused by the Vienna Congress faded – though not in a uniform fashion[28].

Two areas are of particular interest: Italy (where several referendums were held in the name of self-determination as a part of the process to unify the country); and Schleswig-Holstein (between present-day Denmark and Germany) where a referendum was proposed – but not held – over the fate of the province. It was a conflict that received a fair bit of coverage, and which mystified pundits and politicians alike. The Russian novelist, Fyodor Dostoevsky, described it as "that ridiculous Schleswig-Holstein" in *Notes from the Underground*[29].

More cheekily Lord Palmerston famously said that only three people knew the solution to the problem, Prince Albert, a German law professor, and himself. Alas, Prince Albert was dead, the professor had gone mad, and Palmerston himself had forgotten. One solution that was not taken seriously at the time was to let the people in different parts of the region decide – as they did in the end[30].

In 1920 two referendums in, respectively, North and South Schleswig resolved the matter. The North voted to re-join with Denmark, and the South overwhelmingly opted to stay as part of Germany.

Independence referendums in the Confederate states

It is a paradox of democracy that those who deny other people equal rights often justify their actions with reference to democratic principles. The Confederate states in the United States – the ones that opposed the abolition of slavery – are a case in point.

In the early 1860s, the US states of Arkansas, Tennessee, Texas and Virginia held referendums on independence following the election of Abraham Lincoln to the US presidency. All the referendums were won but no country recognised the results[31].

The outcome of the referendum in Virginia is particularly noteworthy. Before the vote, representatives from counties in Western Virginia declared that they, in the event of a "yes" vote for independence, would establish a new state and that the constitution of this new state would be subject to the approval of the voters in a referendum.

Virginia as a whole voted for secession: 21,896 were in favour and 16,646 were against. However, in the western counties 8,375 out of the 9,758 votes cast were against secession[32]. The western counties sent delegates to a specially convened convention, which declared that the referendum in Virginia was "illegal, inoperative, null, void and without force and effect"[33]. They then "passed an ordinance providing for the formation of a new state out of the portion of the territory of this state [Virginia]. This ordinance was to be and was submitted to a plebiscite"[34]. Some 18,000 voted for a new state and 781 voted against it[35].

After the American Civil War, the US Supreme Court established in *Texas* v. *White* that unilateral declarations of independence are unconstitutional[36]. This principle was sustained most recently when the Alaskan Supreme Court in 2006 in *Kohlhaas* v. *Alaska* ruled a constitutional initiative for independence for this state to be *ultra vires*. In the words of the court, "secession from the United States is clearly unconstitutional and therefore an improper subject for the initiative"[37].

Risorgimento referendums

The Risorgimento referendums were held to put pressure on the great powers that were reluctant to change the status quo. In a series of votes held between 1848 and 1870 different parts of

Italy voted to join the new unified state under the constitutional monarch Victor Emmanuel of Sardinia. Camillo Benso di Cavour (1810–1861) expressed the consensus among those advocating the use of referendums at the time in a letter before the votes in Tuscany and Emilia in 1860, in which he wrote:

> I await with anxiety the result of the count, which is taking place in Central Italy. If, as I hope, this last proof is decisive (*questa ultima prova*), we have written a marvellous page in the history of Italy. Even should Prussia and Russia contest the legal value of universal suffrage, they cannot place in doubt the immense importance of the event today brought to pass. Dukes, archdukes and grand-dukes will be buried forever beneath the heap of votes deposited in urns of voting places of Tuscany and Emilia[38].

Cavour was perhaps correct in expressing doubt about the sincerity of the commitment on the part of more autocratic powers such as Prussia and Russia. Yet even these countries were surprisingly positive towards referendums on independence in 1850 and 1860 – at least as long as the aspiration of self-determination supported their own foreign policy goals. As Sarah Wambaugh observed, "There was not one of the great powers, not even Austria or Russia, which did not participate in those years [1848–1870] in some form of appeal to national self-determination to settle Europe's numerous territorial questions"[39].

As noted, Britain's mediation between Denmark and Prussia following the first part of the First Schleswig War in 1848–1851 is a case in point. Lord Palmerston (British Foreign Secretary 1846–1851) suggested to Christian von Bunsen, the Prussian ambassador in London, that the dispute should be decided "with reference to the ascertainable facts", and that these could only be found through a referendum[40]. The Prussian diplomat responded:

> Germany [technically this country was not established before 1871] cannot give up the principle declared on all occasions that no

> separation of any part of Schleswig can ever be thought of, unless the population in the northern districts themselves declare, by an open and unbiased manifestation of their intention to that effect[41].

The proposal was, however, rejected by the Danes who militarily had the upper hand. But this was not to last. In 1864 the Prussians (with help from Austria) once again attacked the Danes. Though the hostilities were caused by the new Danish king who annexed the Duchy of Schleswig, which had hitherto not been part of the Danish realm. The king himself was hardly responsible for this. Born in Schleswig, Christian IX, paradoxically a German speaker, was politically naive. His actions were a result of a long-standing policy of the ruling Danish National Liberal Party. It used the Schleswig Question as part of its agitation and demanded that the duchy be incorporated into the Danish kingdom under the slogan "Denmark to the Eider" (the river that separated Holstein from Saxony in the Middle Ages). This proved fatal for the Danes.

This time, the Prussians were more successful. During an armistice following Prussian victories in the first part of the Second Schleswig War, the Prussian Foreign Minister Peter Graff von Bernsdorff maintained at the London Conference that he was guided by the conviction that the conference should be "aware of the wish of the people whose future they were debating" and that "the inhabitants of Schleswig should be consulted on the subject"[42].

The Danes rejected the proposal believing – wrongly it turned out – that the British would oppose Prussian annexation. After the Prussian defeat of Denmark, the Treaty of Prague made annexation conditional upon the consent of the people. However, in January 1867, Prussia (having realised opposition against its rule) annexed Schleswig-Holstein in toto without a referendum[43]. Once again, pragmatism had triumphed over idealism. The referendum on self-determination played a very minor role in the years following the Franco-German War. Interestingly, given that the referendum often is used in an opportunistic way, leading German lawyers now rejected the use of referendums whereas French international lawyers and intellectuals rediscovered the attractions of letting the people decide.

Referendums on self-determination after the First World War

In the wake of the First World War – at the behest of the American President Woodrow Wilson – eight referendums were held to determine the borders in Europe. Wilson's commitment to self-determination was not – it seems – only a result of a study of the European doctrines espoused in the wake of the French Revolution, still less the ideals of the Italian Risorgimento or the doctrines of Grotius and Pufendorf. Rather Wilson's commitment was also inspired by his early years as a populism campaigner for more direct democracy. These ideals – so it seems – inspired the president in his espousal of national self-determination. Wilson did not – as commonly assumed – mention referendums in his famous Fourteen Points speech to Congress on 8 January 1918. However, it is clear from the context that the 28th president wanted the decisions regarding the borders to be taken by the peoples concerned through plebiscites[44]. As he said in another speech at the time:

> Peoples may now be dominated and governed only by their own consent. Self-determination is not a mere phrase. It is an imperative principle of action, which statesmen will henceforth ignore at their peril. The settlement of every question, whether of territory, of sovereignty, of economic arrangement, or of political relationship [must be decided] upon the basis of the free acceptance of that settlement by the people immediately concerned, and not upon the basis of the material interest or advantage of any other nation which may desire a different settlement for the sake of its own exterior influence or mastery[45].

For all his idealism Wilson was not always true to his word. Indeed, a referendum organised by the council in Tyrol was ignored – at the insistence of the French – despite the fact that more than 90 per cent voted for union with Austria[46].

Not all the votes resolved the matters. However, it is worth noting that, as Bogdanor has pointed out, "It was precisely in those areas where plebiscites were refused (with the exception of Alsace-Lorraine) – Danzig, the Polish corridor and the Sudetenland – that were the subject of revisionist claims by the Nazis in the 1930s"[47].

Tellingly, German revisionist claims were *not* made in areas that were ceded after a referendum, such as North Schleswig where there was a large German-speaking minority. This is possibly because "frontiers that were fixed by plebiscite could not easily be undermined"[48].

However, at the time when Wilson and others espoused direct democracy as a mechanism for resolving nationalist issues the nascent Soviet state and its leader Vladimir Lenin also made some surprising overtures towards a recognition of the people's right to self-determination. In the Bolshevik leader's own words, "all nations dwelling in Russia ... [have] the genuine right to self-determination"[49].

It is beyond the scope of this brief chapter to go into details about this. It should be noted, however, that for Lenin, national self-determination had to be understood from within a Marxist framework and not from the perspective of theories of popular sovereignty. As Lenin made clear in "Critical remarks on the national question: The right of nations to self-determination":

> From the standpoint of national relations, the best conditions for the development of capitalism are undoubtedly provided by the national state. This does not mean, of course, that such a state, which is based on bourgeois relations, can eliminate the exploitation and oppression of nations. It only means that Marxists cannot lose sight of the powerful *economic* factors that give rise to the urge to create national states. It means that "self-determination of nations" in the Marxists' Programme *cannot*, from a historico-economic point of view, have

> any other meaning than political self-determination, state independence, and the formation of a national state[50].

At that stage, referendums on independence borders were relatively rare. Most referendums were about whether certain territories wanted to be part of larger unit. For example, as Table 3.1 shows, referendums in various parts of the Italian peninsula on whether to join the newly unified Italian kingdom were held. Referendums on what we might call "right-sizing" the state were the norm, but as the table also shows, these have become rarer[51].

It was only after the Second World War that the number of independence referendums started to increase. To be sure, there had been the independence referendums in the Confederate states,

Table 3.1 Referendums on territorial transfers to a larger unit

1527 Burgundy	1898 New South Wales	1921 Sopron
1791 Avignon	1899 Western Australia	1938 Austria (Anschluss)
1792 Savoy	1898 Queensland	1947 Brigue
1792 Nice	1898 Victoria	1948 Newfoundland
1793 Moselle	1899 New South Wales	1948 Jungadagh
1798 Mulhouse	1900 South Australia	1949 Chandernagor
1798 Geneva	1909 Natal	1955 Saarland
1848 Lombardy	1919 Aaland (Union with Sweden – not official)	1956 Togoland
1848 Venice	1919 Vorarlberg	1961 Cameroun (two referendums in the two areas on unification)
1857 Moldova	1920 Eupen	1962 Singapour
1860 Parma	1920 South Schleswig	1967 Afars
1860 Tuscany	1920 North Schleswig/Sønderjylland	1975 Sikim
1860 Sicily	1920 Allenstein	1991 Kourilles
1860 Naples	1920 Marienwerder	2014 Crimea
1860 Marche	1920 Klagenfurt	2014 Donbas
1860 Umbria	1921 Upper Silesia	
1860 Savoy	1921 Tyrol	
1860 Nice		
1898 Tasmania		

Source: own study based on Centre for Research on Direct Democracy (2020), www.c2d.ch.

but after these American plebiscites (which we have discussed above) it took a full 44 years before the next referendum on independence was held.

In this case, a vote on whether Norway should secede from Sweden (more than 99 per cent supported the proposition) in a referendum in 1905. In the Norwegian case, the referendum was the brainchild of Norwegian Prime Minister Christian Michelsen, who wrong-footed the Swedish Unionist elite by calling a surprise referendum after the Swedish king had refused to appoint a government that had a majority in the Stortinget (the Norwegian legislature)[52].

In the period between the two world wars, only two independence referendums were held. One in 1933, on whether Western Australia should secede from Australia. A majority voted for secession. However, as the Australian Labor Party (which opposed secession) won the state elections held on the same day, the application for formal independence was never sent to the British parliament for ratification as was required under the rules. Instead, the federal government set up the Commonwealth Grants Commission, which successfully sought to address the grievances, especially regarding equalisation payments. As a result of this, demands for outright independence all but disappeared[53].

Another vote was held in 1935, this time on whether the Philippines should become independent from the United States. A successful referendum was held on a new independence constitution after the Philippine Congress had rejected the US Congress's Hare-Hawes-Cutting Act, which granted independence for the erstwhile overseas dependency. However, it was not until the Second World War that referendums began to be used consistently. This happened when areas seceded from their parent states. Of the over 60 referendums on independence since 1860, 56 have been held after 1944, the vast majority of these – 42 in total – were in Europe[54].

As shown in Table 3.2, there were 14 independence referendums in the four decades after the Second World War.

Table 3.2 Secession referendums, 1944–1989 (those not leading to new states in bold)

Parent country	Seceding country	Year	Turnout	Yes (%)
Denmark	Iceland	1944	98	99
China	Mongolia	1945	98	64
Denmark	**Faroe Islands**	**1946**	**50**	**64**
UK	Newfoundland	1948	52	88
France	Cambodia	1955	100	-
France	Guinea	1958	97	95
New Zealand	Western Samoa	1961	86	77
West Ind Fed	Jamaica	1961	46	60
France	Algeria	1962	99	75
Malaysia	Singapore	1962	71	90
UK	Malta	1964	50	80
USA	Micronesia	1975	52	59
Canada	**Quebec**	**1980**	**85**	**41**
Cyprus	**Northern Cyprus**	**1985**	**78**	**70**

Source: own study based on Centre for Research on Direct Democracy (2020), www.c2d.ch.

One would perhaps have suspected that these referendums would have pertained to decolonisation; that the independence movements would have sought popular approval of their newly gained or espoused freedom. This was not the case.

The elites who fought for and won independence were not, in most cases, willing to risk the political victories gained in negotiations or wars by submitting declarations of independence to an unpredictable electorate. Indeed, the only colonies to submit the declarations of independence to referendums were Cambodia, Western Samoa and Guinea. In the first two cases, the votes were held at the instigation of the parent states, which wanted to show that there was popular support for abandoning the territories[55].

The Guinean referendum was somewhat different. Held on the same day as 11 other referendums in other French colonies, on whether to take part in the newly established Communauté française (established by Charles de Gaulle[56]), the Guineans defied Paris.

Led by the independence leader Ahmed Sékou Touré (an aristocratic member of the Mandinka ethnic group) they voted to become independent. Ninety-five per cent voted in support of secession. France retaliated by withdrawing all aid.

However, within two years Mali, Niger, Upper Volta (now Burkina Faso), Côte d'Ivoire, Chad, the Central African Republic, the Republic of Congo and Gabon became independent states. All territories that had returned huge majorities for maintaining links with France in the referendum in 1958 became independent states *without* a referendum within five years of the 1958 plebiscite. However, none of the new states submitted the decision to become independent to the voters. It was almost as if referendums on independence were anathema to the independence movements[57].

Generally, the reasons for holding referendums in the aftermath of the Second World War were varied. In the case of Mongolia, the vote was held for geopolitical reasons at the instigation of Stalin; the vote in Algeria was held after a lengthy war of independence and negotiations. Overall, it would be difficult to find a general pattern of *when* independence referendums were held after the Second World War[58].

In the 1970s, there was only one referendum on independence: the decision of the Trust Territory of the Pacific Islands to become independent from the United States under the name of the Federated States of Micronesia in 1975.

In the 1980s, there was a similar paucity of independence referendums, the only two being the 1980 vote in the Francophone Canadian province of Quebec and a vote in Northern Cyprus. In the former, 59 per cent (on an 85 per cent turnout) rejected the secessionist Parti Québécois' proposal for "sovereignty association" – a veiled description of independence. The vote in Northern Cyprus on whether to become an independent country in 1985 (formally on a new constitution) passed, but only Turkey recognised the new state[59].

It was only after the fall of communism in Europe starting in 1989 that the floodgates of independence referendums opened. Again, the reasons seem to have been varied. In many cases, referendums were held because the international community – especially the major European powers – insisted upon referendums in order to recognise the new states, particularly the Badinter Commission, set up by the European Communities (soon to become the EU), which stressed that referendums were a *conditio sine qua non* for recognising new states. There is historical and anecdotal evidence to suggest that it was this requirement that prompted a large number of successor-states to hold referendums, especially in the Former Yugoslavia[60].

The referendum was also in many cases a kind of symbolic national manifestation of a newly found freedom. By voting, often almost unanimously, in an independence referendum, the new state made the plebiscite a symbolic representation of the nation itself: a mirror image of the *demos* and the *ethnos* merged into one indivisible unity. Ernest Renan's often cited remark, that a "nation is a daily plebiscite" is perhaps an accurate description of these referendums[61].

As this author has argued at length elsewhere, the referendums were also held for more prosaic reasons, namely when a new elite was under threat from external and internal powers and wanted to prove that it had popular support and the requisite legitimacy to govern[62].

Not all of the states, of course, were recognised and not all of the referendums were conducted in accordance with the internationally recognised standards of free and fair voting.

In addition to referendums in former Soviet and Yugoslav entities, a proliferation of plebiscites was held in sub-national territories such as, for example, Abkhazia in Georgia and Krajina in Bosnia, where minorities sought to win approval for independence from recently declared independent states. None of these sub-national referendums – while the majorities were large – resulted in the establishing of new states.

While most referendums in this period were held in former communist countries, a few were held in Western democracies. In 1995, the voters in Quebec again rejected independence, this time by a whisker[63], and so did voters in Puerto Rico in a multi-option referendum in 1993[64].

In 1998, the voters in Nevis failed to meet the required threshold of 66 per cent necessary to secede from the Federation of St Kitts and Nevis. In the latter case, there were explicit provisions for referendums, albeit with a supermajority which was not reached[65].

Interestingly, the only unsuccessful referendums on independence have been held in countries with established democratic traditions, prompting a scholar (and later politician) to conclude that "secessions are … difficult in established democracies"[66].

During this period, referendums came in different forms and not all followed legal procedures – or indeed any at all. Some referendums were held under legally agreed rules, such as the ones in Scotland (2014), New Caledonia (2018 and again in 2020) and Bougainville (2019), others like the vote in Kurdistan and Catalonia (both 2017) were legally speaking *ultra vires*, i.e. not held in accordance with established and codified legal principles.

In many cases – Catalonia, New Caledonia and Scotland among them – the vote took place in a political culture that was shaped by the precedents of previous referendums. For example, in Catalonia there had been referendums on devolution of powers short of independence in the early 1930s and in the later 1970s. In Scotland, there had been referendums on devolution in 1979 (unsuccessful) and in 1997 (successful). Likewise, there had been votes on independence in New Caledonia, such as, for example, the 1988 vote on the Matignon Accords on devolved powers.

The Catalan referendums had previously only been on devolution. It is a little-known fact, outside the ranks of specialists, that there were early referendums on the transfer of powers to the autonomies in the 1930s. The 1931 constitution of Spain provided that historical nations could hold referendums on further

Table 3.3 Secession referendums, 1991–2020 (those not leading to new states in bold)

Parent country	Seceding country	Year	Turnout	Yes vote (%)
USSR	Lithuania	1991	91	84
USSR	Estonia	1991	77	83
USSR	Latvia	1991	74	88
USSR	Georgia	1991	98	90
USSR	Ukraine	1991	70	85
Georgia	**South Ossetia**	**1991**	**98**	**90**
Georgia	**Abkhasia**	**1991**	**99**	**58**
Yugoslavia	Croatia	1991	98	83
Croatia	**Serbs**	**1991**	**98**	**83**
Yugoslavia	Macedonia	1991	70	75
USSR	Armenia	1991	95	90
Bosnia	**Serbs**	**1991**	**90**	**-**
Serbia	**Sandjak**	**1991**	**96**	**67**
Serbia	Kosovo	1991	99	87
USSR	Turkmenistan	1991	94	97
USSR	**Karabagh**	**1991**	**N.A**	**N.A**
USSR	Uzbekistan	1991	98	94
Macedonia	**Albanians**	**1991**	**99**	**93**
Moldova	**Transnistie**	**1991**	**100**	**NA**
Yugoslavia	Bosnia	1992	99	64
Yugoslavia	Montenegro	1992	96	44
Georgia	**South Ossetia**	**1992**	**NA**	**NA**
Bosnia	**Krajina**	**1992**	**99**	**64**
Ethiopia	Eritrea	1993	99	98
Bosnia	**Serbs**	**1993**	**96**	**92**
USA	**Puerto Rico**	**1993**	**48**	**73**
USA	Palau	1993	64	68
Georgia	**Abkhasia**	**1995**	**96**	**52**
Quebec	**Cris**	**1995**	**95**	**75**
Canada	**Quebec**	**1995**	**49**	**94**
St Kitts and Nevis	**Nevis**	**1998**	**57**	**61**
USA	**Porto Rico**	**1998**	**50**	**71**
Indonesia	East Timor	1999	78	94
Somalia	Somaliland	2001	-	97
New Zealand	**Tokelau**	**2006**	-	**95**

Table 3.3 (Cont.)

Parent country	Seceding country	Year	Turnout	Yes vote (%)
Yugoslavia	Montenegro	2006	55	86
South Sudan	South Sudan	2011	97	98
Britain	**Scotland**	**2014**	**83**	**44**
Iraq	**Kurdistan**	**2017**	**72**	**92**
Spain	**Catalonia**	**2017**	**43**	**92**
France	**New Caledonia**	**2018**	**81**	**43**
PNG	**Bougainville**	**2019**	**87**	**98**
France	**Caledonia**	**2020**	**85**	**46**

Source: own study based on Centre for Research on Direct Democracy (2020), www.c2d.ch (accessed 2–6 October 2020).

autonomy[67]. Pursuant of this, a referendum was held in Catalonia in 1931. After the fall of Franco there was another referendum to restore autonomy for Catalonia. Thus in 1979, 91 per cent of a 59 per cent turnout voted to establish a *Comunidad Autónoma*[68], after a provision for further autonomy (supported by voters in a referendum in 2006) had been rejected by the Constitutional Tribunal. This brought the matter to a head. The secessionist government in Barcelona sought to hold a referendum in 2014 – this time on outright independence.

This was declared *ultra vires* by the *Tribunal Constitucional* in October 2014. In response Artur Mas (the Catalan leader) organised a "consultation", which went ahead despite another ruling by the highest court. On 14 November 2014, 80 per cent of those taking part supported independence, though the turnout (which was never officially provided by the provincial government) was below 41 per cent. This set the scene for the formal referendum on independence in 2017, in which 92 per cent on a 42 per cent turnout voted for independence.

It seems unlikely that this vote would have been held if Madrid had been less aggressive. What is interesting is the role of the courts. Hence, we turn to this matter.

The legal position: what's law got to do with it?

Independence referendums are not a solid part of international law, let alone constitutional jurisprudence, as indeed was proven by the fact that Kosovo became independent although no vote immediately proceeded the declaration of independence, and as Slovakia and the Czech Republic were established without a referendum[69]. As Yves Beigbeder has observed, "the crucial requirement for self-determination plebiscites or referenda is the political will or consent of the countries concerned, their conviction that populations should not be treated as mere chattels and pawns in the game, but that their free vote should be the basis for territorial and sovereignty allocations"[70]. But when is such a vote permitted?

Territories that wish to secede cannot just hold referendums as they please. They must have the legal right to do so under a democratic constitution. To take the example of Scotland, although the SNP won a majority of the vote in 2011, the party was "clearly aware that it would be democratically perverse, as well as politically and legally impossible, to try to override the legal legitimacy of the [Scotland] Act [1998] by way of an extra-constitutional referendum"[71]. This situation is not so different from the situation in Catalonia where the regionalist party *Convergencia i Unió* and its allies won an election to the Parliament de Catalunya on a similar pledge in November 2012 – or even in more recent elections.

Hence, the situation in Catalonia mirrors patterns elsewhere. But in one sense it was unique for the exceptionally prominent role played by the courts. In Spain the judiciary came out squarely against even the most minimal attempt to gauge citizens' opinion towards a referendum on independence and rejected even discussion of the mere possibility of this happening[72].

To be sure, in other countries too, legal arguments were prominent – not least in Canada (see below). Fundamentally, very few countries have freely accepted that referendums on independence take place. The Soviet Union did not accept the secession of Latvia, Lithuania and Estonia through referendums. And the break-up of Yugoslavia, which was preceded by popular votes, was likewise rejected by Belgrade. They were ruled unconstitutional by Yugoslavia's Constitutional Court[73].

True, neither Yugoslavia nor the Soviet Union were democratic states and might not be expected to be committed to the self-determination of the peoples. To be sure, they all had references to self-determination, but this was largely window dressing. Indeed, it is well-established from historical research that communist leaders went to great lengths to give the impression of popular democracy and ditto approval by the voters[74].

Opposition to secession through referendums is not confined to authoritarian states. For example, in 1944 the Danish government did not accept the outcome of a referendum on independence for Iceland. And two years later, the Faroe Islands' vote for independence was rejected. After negotiations, the Danes accepted that the Faroese kept their MPs in Copenhagen, but were granted legislative power in all areas except foreign affairs and defence. In effect, the Faroe Islands got what has in other cases been called "devolution max"[75]. This deal was sealed when the Unionist Parties won the hastily organised general election to the *Lagtinget* (the Faroese legislature) shortly after the referendum[76].

To hold a referendum is not just a political act. It is a legal one. As such it must be held under legally accepted rules. Generally speaking, it has become an accepted norm in international relations that erstwhile colonies should be granted independence after referendums[77]. This was not always the case and this change represents a break with earlier epochs, when "the rules governing the intercourse of states neither demand[ed] nor recognize[ed] the application of the plebiscite in the determination of sovereignty"[78].

Such views notwithstanding, the overall legal position is clear, "there is no unilateral right to secede based merely on a majority vote of the population of a given sub-division or territory"[79]. In an *obiter dicta* in a case about the legality or otherwise of Kosovo's secession from Yugoslavia, the International Court of Justice (ICJ), opined in a passage that deserves to be quoted verbatim:

> In contrast, claims to external self-determination by such ethnically or racially distinct groups pose a challenge to international law as well as to their own State, and most often to the wider community of States. Surely, there is no general positive right under international law, which entitles all ethnically or racially distinct groups within existing States to claim separate statehood, as opposed to the specific right of external self-determination which is recognized by international law in favour of the peoples of non-self-governing territories and peoples under alien subjugation, domination and exploitation. Thus, a racially or ethnically distinct group within a State, even if it qualifies as a people for the purposes of self-determination, does not have the right to unilateral secession simply because it wishes to create its own separate State, though this might be the wish of the entire group. The availability of such a general right in international law would reduce to naught the territorial sovereignty and integrity of States and would lead to interminable conflicts and chaos in international relations[80].

For an entity to hold a referendum on independence it must follow the established rules. The general rule is that referendums either:

- have to be held in accordance with existing constitutions (such a provision exists, for example, in Article 39(3) of the Ethiopian constitution[81]); or
- following an agreement between the area that seeks secession and the larger state of which it is part (this is what happened in the very different cases of Scotland, 2014, and South Sudan, 2011). A provision for such an arrangement exists in Greenland (formally a part of Denmark with devolved powers). According to the Danish law on Greenland: (1) A decision regarding Greenland's independence shall be taken by the people of Greenland. (2) If decision is taken pursuant to subsection (1), negotiations shall commence between the Government [of Denmark] and *Naalakkersuisut* [the government of Greenland] with a view to the

> introduction of independence for Greenland. (3) An agreement between Naalakkersuisut and the Government regarding the introduction of independence for Greenland shall be concluded with the consent of *Inatsisartut* [the Greenland Legislature] and shall be endorsed by a referendum in Greenland. The agreement shall, furthermore, be concluded with the consent of the Folketing [The Danish Parliament].

Following this logic, it was strictly speaking illegal for Catalonia to hold a referendum. As Tom Ginsburg and Mila Versteeg have argued, "when a constitution explicitly prohibits secession, it is difficult for secessionist movements to gain support for their cause, as they have to overcome the prohibition. This, in turn, reduces the bargaining threats that can be used by subordinate units, while strengthening the central authorities, thereby making breakup less likely"[82].

However, there is another rule that can be added to this legal theory. The Catalans might have claimed that they were allowed the right to hold a referendum because other avenues were closed. As Antonio Cassese, a prominent international lawyer, has put it:

> When the central authorities of a sovereign State persistently refuse to grant participatory rights to a religious or racial group, grossly and systematically trample upon their fundamental rights, and deny them the possibility of reaching a peaceful settlement within the framework of the State structure … a group may secede – thus exercising the most radical form of external self-determination – once it is clear that all attempts to achieve internal self-determination have failed or are destined to fail[83].

This is not just the view of an academic lawyer. There is even support for this in *black letter* case law. In the words of Judge Yusuf in *Re Kosovo*:

> Where the State not only denies them the exercise of their internal right of self-determination (as described above), but also subjects them to discrimination, persecution and egregious violations

> of human rights or humanitarian law. Under such exceptional circumstances, the right of peoples to self-determination may support a claim to separate statehood provided it meets the conditions prescribed by international law, in a specific situation, taking into account the historical context[84].

Where does this leave the Catalan case? Premier Carles Puigdemont was not willing to negotiate a constitutional change. His offer of negotiation was solely about an independence referendum[85]. Hence, given that Spain is a democratic state (it scores a top-ranking 1 on Freedom House, for example), the rule summed up by Judge Yusuf in *Re Kosovo* hardly covered Catalonia. Was the referendum in the Spanish *Autonomia* consequently illegal? The answer is in the affirmative, but that does not detract from the impression that the Spanish government was disproportionate in its response.

While the reaction of Madrid was heavy-handed (and a public relations disaster), it took place within the confines of a democratic state. Legally, the Rajoy government was within its constitutional right to follow the course it chose. But it also exacerbated the situation and – speaking as an outsider – it was not conducive to solving the issue.

The Madrid government was inflexible. A bit of forbearance could have solved the conflict. The Canadian Supreme Court's judgement in the famous *Re Quebec* case could serve as an inspiration.

The Canadian Court held that while the "secession of Quebec from Canada cannot be accomplished … unilaterally" a referendum itself was not unconstitutional but a mechanism of gauging the will of the francophone province. Consequently, a referendum, provided it resulted in a "clear majority", "would confer legitimacy on the efforts of the Quebec government"[86]. In other words, a result in favour of secession would require the rest of Canada to negotiate with Quebec. Needless to say, this ruling does not apply in Catalonia; however, the Canadian example suggests that other countries' courts have shown flexibility and appreciation of nuances that are conducive to compromises.

Conclusions

The history of referendums on self-determination have had an uneven history. It is a genealogy rather than a linear narrative. The original ideas – as espoused by autocratic kings – bear little resemblance to the present-day practice. Yet, there are resemblances. Some of the ideas that were first articulated by the early proponents of self-determination referendums (the likes of Grotius and Pufendorf among others) can be detected even now, several hundred years later.

Referendums are about politics as well as about law. Winning a plebiscite does not give a territory the right to establish an independent state. And winning an election does not give a Party the right to hold a referendum.

Yet such reasoning can become stale and legalistic, especially when it is being pursued inflexibly and with political motives – as was arguably the case when Mariano Rajoy used force to prevent the referendum in Catalonia in 2016 and when the Spanish government employed the law (and harsh police tactics) in pursuit of their goals.

Admittedly, there was a similar lack of flexibility on the other side. Confrontation suited both sides politically. But, as far as finding a solution, referendums on independence are not always conducive to this. In the words of Clifford Geertz, a social anthropologist:

> It is the very process of formation of a sovereign civil state … that among other things, stimulates elements of parochialism, communalism, racialism, and so on, because it introduces into society a valuable new prize over which to fight and a frightening new force with which to contend[87].

Maybe John Stuart Mill was right that "free institutions are next to impossible in a country made up of different nationalities"[88]. The recent experience in Catalonia seem to suggest this. However, other referendums have been conducted peacefully, the one in Scotland in 2014 being a case in point. Maybe, the Catalan referendum resulted in strife because the different sides did not heed another one of Mill's maxims, namely that:

> One of the most indispensable requisites in the practical conduct of politics, especially in the management of free institutions, is conciliation; a readiness to compromise; a willingness to concede something to opponents, and to shape good measures so as to be as little offensive as possible to persons of opposite views; and of this salutary habit, the mutual give and take[89].

Notes

1 J. S. Mill, "Considerations on representative government", in J. Gray (ed.), *On Liberty and Other Essays* (Oxford: Oxford University Press, 1991), pp. 205–467 (p. 431).

2 See M. Guidi and M. Casula, "The Europeanization of the Catalan debate", in C. Closa, C. Margiotta and G. Martinico (eds), *Between Democracy and Law: The Amorality of Secession* (London: Routledge, 2019), pp. 173–192; see also W. Husar-Poliszuk, "A political corrida: Spanish-Catalan parallels", *Review of Nationalities* 9(1) (2019), pp. 149–164.

3 T.W. Waters, *Boxing Pandora: Rethinking Borders, States, and Secession in a Democratic World* (New Haven: Yale University Press, 2020), p. 124.

4 T. Ginsburg and M. Versteeg, "From Catalonia to California: Secession in constitutional law", *Alabama Law Review* 70(4) (2019), pp. 923–985 (p. 929).

5 BBC World News, 12 May 2014.

6 Ronald J. Hill and Stephen White, "Referendums in Russia, the former Soviet Union and Eastern Europe", in M. Qvortrup (ed.), *Referendums Around the World: The Continued Use of Direct Democracy* (Basingstoke: Palgrave, 2014), pp. 19–45 (p. 26).

7 Ibid.

8 E. Giuliano, *Constructing Grievance: Ethnic Nationalism in Russia's Republics* (Ithaca: Cornell University Press, 2014), p. 122.

9 S. Wambaugh, *The Doctrine of Self-Determination Vol. 1: A Study of the Theory and Practice of Plebiscites* (Oxford: Oxford University Press, 1919), p. xxiii.

10 In the following, a referendum is defined as a vote by the whole electorate on a policy issue. The words referendum and plebiscite will be used interchangeably.

11 M. Foucault, "Nietzsche, genealogy and history", in Paul Rabinow (ed.), *The Foucault Reader: An Introduction to Foucault's Thought* (London: Penguin, 1986), p. 81.

12 Ibid.

13 Emer de Vattel, *Le droit des gens* (1758), Liber 1, Chapter 21, Para. 263. A contemporary statement by the authorities cited by Vattel reads: "that, having never been subject but to the crown of France, they would die subject to it; and that, if the king abandoned them, they would take up arms, and endeavour to set themselves at liberty, rather than pass into a new state of subjection."

14 Wambaugh, *The Doctrine of Self-Determination*, p. xxiii.

15 Desiderius Erasmus, *Erasmus Against War*, ed. J.W. Mackail (Boston: The Merrymount Press, 1907 [1517]), p. 51.

16 Wambaugh, *The Doctrine of Self-Determination*, p. xxiv.

17 Eugène Solière, *Le Plébiscite dans l'annexion. Étude historique et critique de droit des gens* (Paris: L. Boyer, 1901), p. 26.

18 Ibid.

19 Jean Bodin, *Six Books of the Commonwealth* (Oxford: Basil Blackwell, 1967), p. 133.

20 Hugo Grotius, *De Jure Belli ac Pacis* (1625), Liber 2, Cap. 6, Sec. 5.

21 Samuel Pufendorf, *De jura naturae et gentium* (1672), Liber 8, Chapter 5, Para. 9.

22 Vattel, *Le droit des gens*, Liber 1, Chapter 21, Para. 263–264. In the light of these frequent references to the people, and the stated legal position as expressed by some of the foremost legal minds, it is perhaps instructive to note that modern lawyers are less convinced about the people's right to be consulted. Indeed, as Peter Radan has shown in a careful analysis, "that there is no rule in international law that requires a referendum" (Peter Radan, "Secessionist referenda in international and domestic law", in M. Qvortrup (ed.), *Nationalism, Referendums and Democracy* (London, Routledge, 2014), p. 12).

23 See, *inter alia*, W. Danspeckgruber, "Self-determination, self-governance and security", *International Relations* 15(1) (2000), pp. 11–21.

24 Cited in J.B. Duvergier (ed.), "Collection complète des lois, décrets, Vol. 1", *Bulletin des lois de la République française* (1824), p. 191.

25 Archives Parlementaires 1 Series, Vol. 25 (Paris: P. Dupont, 1875), p. 425.

26 Cited in G.F. von Martens, *Recueil de Principaux traits d'alliance de paix* (Göttingen: J.C. Dieterich, 1801), pp. 400–401.
27 M. Griffiths, "Self-determination, international society and world order", *Macquarie Law Journal* 3(1) (2003), pp. 29–49 (p. 38).
28 E.D. Weitz, "From the Vienna to the Paris system: International politics and the entangled histories of human rights, forced deportations, and civilizing missions", *The American Historical Review* 113(5) (2008), pp. 1313–1343.
29 Fyodor Dostoevsky, *Notes from the Underground. 2nd Edition*, translated and edited by Michael R. Katz (New York: W.W. Norton & Co., 2008), p. 19.
30 Lord Palmerston cited in Lytton Strachey, *Queen Victoria* (London: Penguin, (1971) [1921]), p. 185.
31 J. Mattern, *The Employment of the Plebiscite in the Determination of Sovereignty* (Baltimore: Johns Hopkins University Press, 1921), p. 171.
32 Ibid., p. 120.
33 Quoted in ibid., p. 123.
34 Cited in ibid., p. 123.
35 Ibid., p. 123.
36 *Texas* v. *White*, 74 U.S. 700, 726 (1868).
37 *Kohlhaas* v. *Alaska* 147 P.3d 714 (Alaska 2006).
38 Di Camillo, Cavour to Villamarina, Minister of Sardinia at Naples, March 1860, *Lettere edite ed inedite di Camillo Cavour* (Torino: Roux, 1883), Vol. 3, p. 211.
39 Wambaugh, *The Doctrine of Self-Determination*, p. xxxiii.
40 Palmerston to von Bunsen, 24 June 1848, *British and Foreign State Papers*, Vol. 40, p. 1321.
41 Graff von Bunsen to Palmerstone, 24 June 1848, *British and Foreign State Papers*, Vol. 40, p. 1321.
42 Bernsdorff, in *Conference of London*, Protocol No. 10, 1864.
43 See M. Qvortrup, *Referendums and Ethnic Conflict* (Philadelphia: University of Pennsylvania Press, 2014), p. 22.
44 J.L. Snell, "Wilson on Germany and the Fourteen Points", *Journal of Modern History* 26(4) (1954), pp. 364–369.
45 Woodrow Wilson quoted in Lawrence T. Farley, *Plebiscites and Sovereignty: The Crisis of Political Legitimacy* (Boulder: Westview Press, 1986), p. 3.
46 See *New York Times*, "French try to stop Tyrol plebiscite: Vote on annexation to Germany set for April 24 strongly opposed by Paris", 11 April 1921, A6.
47 Vernon Bogdanor, "Referendums and separatism II", in Austin Ranney (ed.), *The Referendum Device* (Washington, DC: The American Enterprise Institute, 1981), p. 145.
48 Ibid.

49 Lenin quoted in U.O. Umozurike, *Self-Determination in International Law* (Hamden: Archon, 1972), p. 162.
50 Vladimir I. Lenin, "Critical remarks on the national question: The right of nations to self-determination", in *Lenin: Collected Works* (Moscow: Progress Publishers, 1972), Vol. 20, p. 393.
51 On this concept see: B. O'Leary, I. Lustick, T. Callaghy and T.M. Callaghy, *Right-Sizing the State: The Politics of Moving Borders* (Oxford: Oxford University Press, 2001).
52 T. Bjørklund, *Om Folkeavstemninger: Norge og Norden 1905-1994* (Oslo: Universitetsforlaget, 2003), p. 66.
53 N. Warren, "Reform of the Commonwealth Grants Commission: It's all in the detail", *University of New South Wales Law Journal* 31(2) (2008), pp. 530–552.
54 M. Qvortrup, "Introduction: Nationalism, referendums and democracy: Independence, recognition and voting", in M. Qvortrup (ed.), *Nationalism, Referendums and Democracy: Voting on Ethnic Issues and Independence* (London: Routledge, 2020), pp. 3–8.
55 J. Laponce, *Le Référendum de Souveraineté: Comparaisons, Critiques et Commentaires* (Québec City: Les Presses de l'Université Laval, 2010), p. 35.
56 F. Simonis, "L'administration coloniale et le référendum du 28 septembre 1958 dans les fédérations d'AOF et AEF", *Outre-Mers. Revue d'histoire* 95(358) (2008), pp. 59–73.
57 Laponce, *Le Référendum de Souveraineté*, p. 52.
58 L.T. Farley, *Plebiscites and Sovereignty: The Crisis of Political Illegitimacy* (London: Westview, 1986), p. 36.
59 D. Lockhart and S. Ashton, "Tourism to Northern Cyprus", *Geography* 75(2) (1990), pp. 163–167 (p. 163).
60 P. Radan, "Post-secession international borders: A critical analysis of the opinions of Badinter", *Melbourne Law Review* 1 (2000), p. 50.
61 Renan quoted in A. Roshwald, "The daily plebiscite as twenty-first-century reality?", *Ethnopolitics* 14(5) (2015), pp. 443–450 (p. 443).
62 M. Qvortrup, *Referendums and Ethnic Conflict* (Pittsburgh: University of Pennsylvania Press, 2014).
63 R. Nadeau, P. Martin and A. Blais, "Attitude towards risk-taking and individual choice in the Quebec referendum on sovereignty", *British Journal of Political Science* 29(3) (1999), pp. 523–539.
64 J.O. Diaz, "Puerto Rico, the United States, and the 1993 referendum on political status", *Latin American Research Review* 30(1) (1995), pp. 203–211.
65 T. Nisbett, "Will St. Kitts and Nevis break up?", *Federations* 4(2) (2004), pp. 10–11 (p. 10).
66 S. Dion, "Why is secession difficult in well-established democracies? Lessons from Quebec", *British Journal of Political Science* 26(2) (1996), pp. 269–283 (p. 269).

67 Constitución española de 1931, Art. 12.
68 M. Guibernau, "Spain: Catalonia and the Basque Country", *Parliamentary Affairs* 53(1) (2000), pp. 55–68.
69 M. Fabry, *Recognizing States: International Society and the Establishment of New States since 1776* (Oxford: Oxford University Press, 2010).
70 Y. Beigbeder, *International Monitoring of Plebiscites, Referenda and National Elections: Self-Determination and Transition to Democracy* (Dordrecht: M. Nijhoof, 1994), p. 160.
71 S. Tierney, *Constitutional Referendums: The Theory and Practice of Republican Deliberation* (Oxford: Oxford University Press, 2012), p. 147.
72 Tribunal Constitucional Pleno (2010) *Sentencia 31/2010, de 28 de junio de 2010*, BOE núm. 172, de 16 de julio de 2010.
73 B. Bagwell, "Yugoslavian constitutional questions: Self-determination and secession of member republics", *Georgia: Journal of International and Comparative Law* 21(4) (1991), pp. 489–523.
74 J.A. Getty, "State and society under Stalin: Constitutions and elections in the 1930s", *Slavic Review* 50(1) (1991), pp. 18–35.
75 M. Keating, "Rethinking sovereignty: Independence-lite, devolution max and national accommodation", *Revista d'estudis autonòmics i federals* 16(1) (2012), pp. 9–29.
76 H.A. Sølvará, "Færøernes Statsretlige Stilling i Historisk Belysning – Mellem selvstyre og Selvbestemmelse", *Faroese Law Review* 3(3) (2003), pp. 156–173 (p. 156).
77 United Nations Secretary-General (2008), SG/SM/11568, GA/COL/3171.
78 Mattern, *The Employment of the Plebiscite in the Determination of Sovereignty*, p. 171.
79 J. Crawford, *The Creation of States in International Law* (Cambridge: Cambridge University Press, 2006), p. 417.
80 International Court of Justice, *Re Kosovo. ICJ Advisory Opinion per Judge Yusuf*, International Law Materials (2010), pp. 621–622.
81 *Constitution of the Federal Democratic Republic of Ethiopia* (21 August 2005), www.wipo.int/edocs/lexdocs/laws/en/et/et007en.pdf (accessed 6 October 2020).
82 Ginsburg and Versteeg, "From Catalonia to California", p. 928.
83 A. Cassese, *Self-Determination of the Peoples: A Legal Reappraisal* (Cambridge: Cambridge University Press, 1995), p. 120.
84 International Court of Justice, *Accordance with International Law of the Unilateral Declaration of Independence in Respect of Kosovo (Request for Advisory Opinion)*, General List No. 141, International Court of Justice (ICJ), 22 July 2010, p. 622.

85 Guidi and Casula, "The Europeanization of the Catalan debate", p. 185.
86 Canadian Supreme Court (2008), *Re Quebec*, 161 DLR (4th), p. 385.
87 C. Geertz, "The integrative revolution: Primordial sentiments and politics in the new states", in Clifford Geertz (ed.), *Old Societies and New States: The Quest for Modernity in Asia and Africa* (New York: The Free Press 1963), pp. 105–157 (p. 120).
88 Mill, "Considerations on representative government", p. 428.
89 Ibid., p. 385.

Part III

Regulation

Chapter 4

The regulation of referendums: campaign spending

After the referendum in Schleswig-Holstein in 1920, Sarah Wambaugh, an American expert on referendums, concluded:

> Democracy cannot be served by faulty plebiscites [we would call them referendums]. If we are to keep the tool, we must learn how to use it. Therefore, we must study those already held so that we may discover the errors as well as perfect our technique[1].

As we saw in the previous chapter, the Catalan plebiscite in 2017 was not a model to be emulated. While the referendums Wambaugh had studied in the 1920s were mostly the results of negotiations and compromises, the one in Catalonia almost a century later was the very opposite. We still have not learned from the "errors", and, in the Spanish case, the two sides did not seem anxious to "perfect" the "technique" of democracy. This is not just true for when to hold referendums, it is also true for *how* to hold them.

As we saw in Chapter 2, there has been a shift towards more referendums. Perhaps reflecting citizens' demand for more choice, this has even been described as "on demand" direct democracy[2]. But sometimes these referendums have been characterised by deception and fake news of the worst kind. The most conspicuous fact associated with modern politics, it has been said, is that "the very concept of objective truth is fading out of the world"[3]. The aim of this chapter is to determine if there are ways in which regulation can (and has) helped rescue the "objective truth".

Referendums should be about deliberation, about open debate before a vote is taken. In short, to quote the legal scholar Ron Levy, "widespread citizen involvement is therefore only a starting point"[4]. For politics to function, we cannot *just* look at the exciting parts, the campaign rallies, the eloquent speeches, the cheering crowds, and so on, but we must also look at the more tedious elements; the proverbial devils in the detail, and the regulatory small print.

This aspect of referendums has received a somewhat limited attention in the academic literature. While there have, to be sure, been studies such as Andrew Ellis' compendium *Administration of Referendums*[5] and other reports on referendum regulation in recent years[6], these were largely based on secondary data. By contrast, the present chapter is based on a survey of practitioners and analysis of primary and secondary legislation in democratic countries (as defined by Freedom House). Hence the present book deals with the legal regulation of referendums in a way that hasn't been done before.

But, of course, the law is not always a reflection of political practice. Sometimes, as Alexis de Tocqueville famously noted, political practice is shaped more by political culture and depends on what modern scholars call "social capital", and less on constitutional prescriptions. As he famously noted, "Mexico, which is as fortunately situated as the Anglo-American Union, has adopted these same laws but cannot get used to a democratic form of government"[7]. For him, therefore, democratic governance was not the result of rules and articles in constitutional documents, still less institutions, but "the habits and conceived ideas", which "gradually permeated … customs, opinions, and social mores"[8].

Still, as nations have developed legal systems (and courts to police these regimes), statutory rules and legislation have become increasingly important and it is now the general consensus in political science that formal rules constrain actors and have an impact on public policy-making[9]. This is not the place for a learned exposition of political theory, rather, the aim of this book is merely to map the landscape and to record the facts. The aim of the chapter is to determine which countries regulate referendums. The hope, above all, is that this chapter may provide those organising a referendum with an overview of how these institutions of direct democracy are administered and regulated in other jurisdictions.

In such endeavours it is always important to compare like with like. It makes no sense to compare democratic norms between countries that fall short of the ideals of free and fair elections. Hence, in carrying out this survey we have included only countries that are categorised as "Free" by Freedom House. Admittedly, we could have used other measures, however, the Freedom House Scores are perhaps the most commonly used measure of democratic freedom, and it was concluded that this is sufficient reason for using it as our benchmark.

Operationally we sent surveys to the London embassies of 37 countries and experts to map the level of regulation of referendums and direct democracy. Of these countries, we received answers from 30. Hence the survey is not universal, yet still large enough for us to draw valid conclusions.

This chapter covers issues such as campaign spending limits, media objectivity, regulation of government involvement, regulation of online campaigning, grants to campaigns to ensure a level playing field, and mechanisms to increase the participation and involvement of marginalized groups. In addition, the chapter develops an Index of Referendum Regulation (IRR).

Campaign spending

The risk that the richer side will win a referendum by outspending the poorer is one of the main concerns in direct democracy campaigns. In an editorial arguing for regulation of the process ahead of a planned referendum on the Japanese constitution, *The*

Japan Times expressed concern that "the side with more funding can have a big impact on the voters' decisions"[10]. In an official report by the Venice Commission (formally European Commission for Democracy Through Law) it was stressed that "the principle of equality of opportunity applies to public funding; equality should be ensured between a proposal's supporters and opponents"[11]. For this reason, one would have expected rules ensuring parity of contributions in several countries.

Yet, based on the legislation analysed from 30 democracies for this book, only a small minority of seven countries (23 per cent) have limits on campaign spending. The situation in Austria is typical of many countries. A country-expert reports:

> In Austria, there are no limits on campaign spending in referendums. The relevant laws on binding referendums (*Volksabstimmungsgesetz*) and consultative referendums (*Volksbefragungsgesetz*) contain no material provisions on the way the campaigns should be conducted. The lack of a campaign spending limit is even more remarkable as there is one in place for elections. The law on party finance (*Bundesgesetz über die Finanzierung politischer Parteien*) dictates that political parties may not spend more than seven million euros during the campaign for local, regional, national or European elections. There is no mention of referendums in this law[12].

The countries that have limits on campaign spending have little in common. They include Brazil, Canada, Lithuania, New Zealand, Portugal, Slovenia, Taiwan and the United Kingdom. In addition to these countries, some Australian states have limits on how much can be spent in ballot campaigns.

The United Kingdom is an example of a country where there are the strictest limits on how much money each side can spend. The Political Parties, Elections and Referendums Act 2000 (the Act is also known as PPERA) provides that any individual or organisation wishing to spend more than £10,000 during the designated

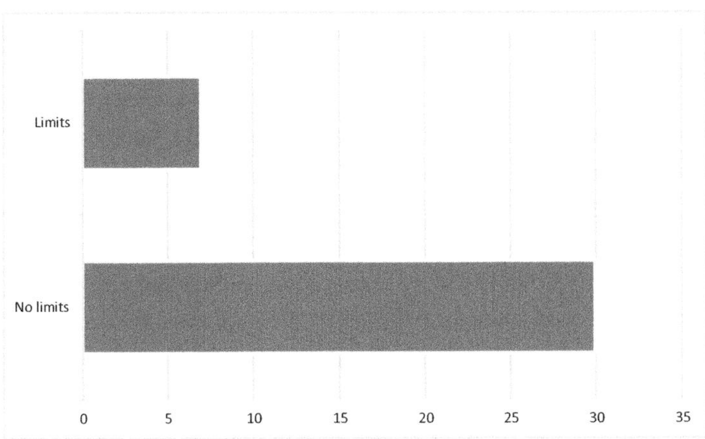

Figure 4.1 Limits on campaign spending.

ten-week "referendum period" must register with the Electoral Commission.

The Act also provides the two designated groups on either side of the referendum can spend up to £5,000,000, and that political parties taking part have limits worked out in proportion to the votes they received at the last general election. The absolute limit for any political party is £5,000,000.

These relatively strict limits on campaign spending, which were first used in the referendums on a regional assembly in the North East in 2004[13], are in sharp contrast to the rules introduced for the 1975 referendum, in which the "Remain" side outspent their opponents by a factor of 10:1[14]. The new regime under PPERA, which in a modified form was applied in Scotland's 2014 independence referendum, provided for a level playing field. In that contest, the two official campaigns, *Better Together* (which represented the status quo) and *Yes Scotland* (which advocated independence), spent a total of £1,422,602 and £1,420,800, respectively[15]. Thus, while the PPERA rules do not guarantee strict mathematical parity, they ensure that both sides have an opportunity to put their respective cases to the voters.

Because smaller organisations can spend money in addition to that spent by the two designated campaigns, there can be some disparity between the two sides notwithstanding the restrictions in campaign spending. Thus, it is instructive to note that, according to official data by the Electoral Commission, "registered participants" supporting Remain spent £19,309,588, whereas those supporting Leave only spent a total of £13,332,569[16] in the 2016 Brexit referendum.

Perhaps, surprisingly, other established democracies have far fewer rules limiting campaign spending in referendums. The Scandinavian and Nordic countries often pride themselves on being model democracies[17]. In terms of direct democratic regulation, they are not. Neither, Denmark, Finland, Iceland nor Norway have restrictions on campaign spending, and none of the countries have rules prohibiting foreign donors from contributing (unlimited) funds to campaigns[18]. Though it should be noted that in Denmark there is a similar ban on foreign donations. Thus *Partiregnskabsloven* ("The Law on Party Budgets") contains a ban on anonymous contributions of over Dkr 20,900 ($2,000)[19].

In Sweden, "it is unclear whether the new laws of campaign financing of parties apply at times of referendums. As long as the financing of referendum campaigning is channelled through parties, the rules apply. But it is unclear if this is true for campaign organizations", wrote a country expert[20].

Other countries with a reputation of high levels of democracy are likewise unregulated as regards limits on campaign spending and donations. And some have even gone in the other direction. Australia is a case in point. The cap on campaign spending was repealed in 1980 – perhaps interestingly as the voters had recently approved four constitutional amendments in a country where most referendums are lost. Yet, unlike the Scandinavian countries, Australia is not completely unregulated. Thus, The Referendums (Machinery Provisions) Act 1984 (Cth) places obligations on entities which spend above $13,800 (indexed annually, as per the Commonwealth Electoral Act 1918 (Cth)) in promoting referendum matters. The latter are defined as any matter which is calculated to affect the result of a referendum. Henceforth, entities spending more than $13,800 in promoting a referendum matter must include the name of the person promoting the material, the relevant town of the entity and the name of the natural person responsible for giving effect to the authorisation.

However, while there are no longer limits on campaign spending in federal referendums in Australia, there is an extensive regime to ensure parity of expenditure in state referendums[21].

In the United States, attempts to introduce limits on campaign spending in referendums and initiative campaigns have been reversed by the courts[22]. The lack of limits on campaign spending is thus a result of judicial review, not a consequence of lacking political will.

In 1976, the Massachusetts legislature enacted the Massachusetts General Laws, which disallowed the use of "corporate funds to purchase advertising to influence the outcome of referendums elections unless the corporation's business interests were directly involved"[23]. This legislation was challenged in the courts. While the plaintiffs were initially unsuccessful at the Supreme Court of Massachusetts[24], the US Supreme Court ruled in their favour in *First National Bank of Boston* v. *Bellotti*[25]. Writing for a 5–4 majority, Justice Lewis F. Powell Jr. held that limits to campaign spending introduced by the Massachusetts legislature were unconstitutional and that they,

> Cannot be justified by the State's asserted interest in sustaining the active role of the individual citizen in the electoral process and preventing diminution of his confidence in government. Even if it were permissible to silence one segment of society upon a sufficient showing of imminent danger, there has been no showing that the relative voice of corporations has been overwhelming or even significant in influencing referenda in Massachusetts, or that there has been any threat to the confidence of the citizenry in government[26].

This ruling was repeated in 1981 in *Citizens Against Rent Control* v. *City of Berkeley*, in which the US Supreme Court overruled a decision by the Californian Supreme Court permitting local authorities to introduce limits on campaign spending. Writing for the majority, Chief Justice Rehnquist – who had been a dissenting voice in *First National* – held that "there is no significant state or public interest in curtailing debate and discussion of a ballot measure". And he added that "the integrity of the political system will be adequately protected if contributors are identified in a public filing revealing the amounts contributed"[27].

Thus, in America campaign contributions are treated as a First Amendment right, a freedom of speech issue, and the only restrictions on campaign spending permitted are those rules that require participants to be transparent about their donations and contributions.

Despite some academic literature suggesting that "voting intentions coincide with disparities in campaign spending"[28], the courts have allowed richer contributors to outspend their opponents. However, it should be noted that increased campaign spending is not always successful. It has even been argued that too much campaign spending can have detrimental effects. Shaun Bowler and Todd Donovan found, "when a group such as the *Philip Morris Company* [a tobacco manufacturer] … finances a yes-campaign and media attention emphasizes the source of the funds, many voters are given a cue about who's behind it"[29].

The same situation exists in the Federal Republic of Germany. While there have been no federal referendums under the 1949 constitution, there have been an increased use of (and provisions for) referendums and initiatives in Germany after the fall of the Berlin Wall[30].

So, apart from the United Kingdom, the list of countries that have introduced spending limits is low. In the following, the countries will be analysed in turn, and in alphabetical order. We begin with Brazil.

The largest country in South America is also the only country in Latin America to have limits on campaign spending. Countries with many more referendums, such as Uruguay (with no less than 12 referendums since 1989) and Bolivia (seven referendums since 1989), are, of course, more frequent users of direct democracy, yet neither of these countries have introduced limits on the amount of money spent in ballot campaigns. The reason for this could be that the issues put before voters in Brazil were extremely controversial. (Though the same could be said for the 1989 referendum on the amnesty for crimes committed by the military junta in Uruguay which also dealt with a thorny and divisive issue!)

In any case, after a divisive referendum on a partial ban on firearms was rejected by 63 per cent of the voters in 2005, legislation was introduced to prevent the richer side from bankrolling a referendum. Henceforth, the Brazilian electoral authority (Justiça Eleitoral) was to decide the limits for campaign costs for each new election, referendum or plebiscite[31].

While the Brazilian legislation has not been used at the federal level, it has been used in local or state referendums. Thus, in a referendum held on 11 December 2011, the voters of the state of Pará were asked to vote on proposals to split it into three parts: Carajás in the southeast, Tapajós in the west, and a rump Pará in the northeast. The proposal to create Carajás was defeated by a 67–33 margin, and the proposal to create Tapajós was defeated by a 66–34 margin. In the referendum, the Superior Electoral Court (Tribunal Superior Eleitoral) ruled that each parliamentary front (known as *frente parlamentar*) could spend up to R$10 million (the equivalent US$2.6 million) in campaign costs[32].

In addition to this case, the Brazilian Supreme Court (Supremo Tribunal Federal) declared rules that allowed companies to donate to election campaigns unconstitutional in 2015[33]. At present, political parties can donate to parliamentary campaigns, and voters can donate up to 10 per cent of their individual annual income in the previous year to referendum campaigns[34].

Canada is another country where a controversial referendum led to legislation. While the number of referendums in Canada on the provincial level is much lower than in its southern neighbour, the 1992 federal law on referendums[35] went much further than the legislation introduced in any of the US states. The statute limited the amounts that could be spent by each referendum committee, "No person or group, other than a registered referendum committee, shall incur referendum expenses during a referendum period that, in the aggregate, exceed five thousand dollars"[36].

However, this limitation came with a caveat, which was, perhaps, more than an oversight. Thus, there was no limit on the number of referendum committees that could be created on each side[37]. As a result, the richer side (the one advocating a "yes" to the Charlottetown Agreement) could consequently outspend the other[38]. And it did, "the YES committees spent 13 times as much as the NO committees"[39]. In spite of this, the yes side lost by a 10 per cent margin (55–45 per cent) on a 75 per cent turnout[40].

By contrast, in Ireland, "there are no limitations on campaign spending at referendums", but "strict limits on donations to candidates, political parties and other groups involved in campaigns". In the Republic of Ireland, "donations within legal limits can be accepted and must be declared in annual statements. This legislation applies to political campaigns at referendums"[41].

However, although the Electoral Act 1997 put in place prohibitions on donations from abroad "to protect against interference by foreign individuals or entities in Ireland's domestic political processes", including elections and referendums, these have often been criticised for not taking into account developments of the digital age. For example, the Irish Standards in Public Office Commission issued a report in 2017, in which it expressed concern that "Facebook campaigns are not regulated by this legislation – meaning individuals or groups from anywhere can pay for Facebook advertising targeting certain demographics of Irish voters"[42].

This is very different from the situation in Lithuania, which has one of the most comprehensive regimes for regulating referendums and initiatives (and is one of the highest users of direct democracy instruments[43]). With 12 referendums since independence it is has held more popular votes than all its neighbouring countries combined. The Republic of Lithuania Law on Funding of, and Control over Funding of, Political Parties and Political Campaigns 2004[44] provides, in Article 3, that only "Independent and represented political campaign participants" may contribute to referendum campaigns. These are defined, per Section 2 of the Act, as, "1) a political party; 2) a potential candidate; 3) a self-nominated candidate; 4) referendum initiators; 5) referendum opponents; 6) a public election committee"[45]. Article 10 of the Act states further:

> Each independent political campaign participant [may make a] donation which does not exceed the amount of 10 average monthly earnings valid in the fourth quarter of the previous calendar year. During a calendar year the total amount of donations by one natural person for independent political campaign participants may not exceed 10 per cent of the amount of the annual income declared by the natural person for the previous calendar year[46].

The Act also provides that "[a] political campaign participant shall not have the right to use for funding the political campaign the received monetary donations which are not entered on the accounting records of political campaign funding and sets lower limits under which donations need not be declared"[47].

Perhaps, interestingly, the Act further stipulates that "not more than 10 per cent of the fixed maximum permitted amount of political campaign expenses may be funded with small donations". Further, only citizens of Lithuania and residents in the country may contribute to campaigns[48].

Like Britain and Israel, New Zealand does not have a written constitution. This means that parliament is supreme and that all referendums are advisory only. Since the 1990s, there have been a number of changes to the constitutional system in the country. The change from a first-past-the-post to a mixed-member electoral system in the 1990s coincided with the introduction of the Citizens Initiated Referendum Act 1993[49]. Since then, there have been ten referendums (of which four were citizen-initiated, covering wildly different issues ranging from the wages of fire fighters to criminal justice).

Despite the relatively high number of referendums, the regulation of campaign finance has not been consistent. Thus, recent referendums in New Zealand have had their own enabling legislation passed, for example, the New Zealand Flag Referendums Act 2015 and the Electoral Referendum Act 2010. These rules "included regulation of advertising, but there is not a standing status quo that would apply to all referendums. Hence, the voting system referendum [in 2011] had restrictions on campaign spending, but the flag referendums [held in two stages in 2015 and 2016, respectively] did not"[50].

Unlike New Zealand, Portugal is an example of referendum regulation by default. The so-called Legal Regime Governing Referenda (known as LORR)[51], provides that expenditures of less than €435.76 do not need to be declared. In elections, each candidate is allowed to spend a maximum of €20,916. In referendums, this figure is multiplied by the number of possible candidates in a national legislative election, typically by 320 (or 328 in cases where Portuguese electors living abroad can vote). The maximum expenditure thus is €6,693,120[52].

Slovakia has a very light regime of referendum regulation, despite this being one of the countries that has used mechanisms of direct democracy relatively frequently – a total of eight since independence in 1992[53].

Yet, the "Slovak legislation does not directly regulate pre-referendum campaigns and therefore the situation is rather ambiguous"[54]. Thus, while "there are no explicitly mentioned spending limits for political parties during the pre-referendum campaign (even though the limits for various pre-electoral campaigns are set)", the "legislation also recognizes third parties (i.e. registered subjects willing to conduct a political campaign before the elections or the referendum) for which the spending limit is set to 100,000 Euros"[55].

Arguably, one of the most democratic countries in Asia[56], Taiwan has become one of the most frequent users of referendums, initiatives, and recalls since the country became democratic in 1987. Beginning with the Election and Recall Act 1989 and continuing with the Referendum Act 2003 (which introduced the initiative[57]), a total of 15 nationwide polls have been held[58].

Article 20 of the Referendum Act sets out a relatively detailed regulation of campaign spending. While there is no limit on how much inhabitants can spend, the amount spent by foreigners is strictly limited. Not surprisingly, given Taiwan's status and its relations vis-à-vis the People's Republic of China, the Referendum Act stipulates that campaign groups,

> May not accept donations from foreign associations, juridical persons or individuals, or associations or juridical persons mainly composed of foreign members, individuals, juridical persons, associations or other institutions in the People's Republic of China, or the juridical persons, associations or other institutions mainly composed of the citizens of the People's Republic of China[59].

It is also stipulated that "public enterprises or incorporated foundations receiving donations from the government" are prohibited from making donations. While there are no upper limits to donations, contributions of more than NT$2,000 must be declared[60].

However, all these countries are exceptions. Overall, very few countries meet the requirement of the Venice Commission that "equality should be ensured between a proposal's supporters and opponents"[61]. One can be outraged by this. But, in fairness, whether this is a problem is widely debated. Limits of campaign spending are, as one classic study from the early 1980s put it,

"More heavily criticized than any other form of regulation. Their critics make two main charges. First the limits are almost always set far below what is necessary to mount even what most campaign organizers feel is a minimum campaign ... Second, the more effectively ceilings are enforced the more they favour ... the status quo in referendums"[62].

Whether this argument can be sustained today is questionable. Indeed, there were no expressions from senior politicians that the limits were too low in the Brexit campaign, and there is no clear empirical evidence to support the second charge that effective ceilings maintain the status quo. The Brexit referendum, to use the same example, resulted in an outcome that was *very* different from the status quo!

The only major argument against campaign spending limits or limits on donations is that it is debatable if money makes a difference. There are, as we saw, several examples of campaigns that lost despite having the lion's share of the financial resources. However, gross disparities would seem to run counter to natural justice and the deep sense of fair play that is essential for running a credible democracy.

The United Kingdom, Brazil, Lithuania and Canada are the only democratic countries to have strict limits on campaign spending. Of these, the Canadian system is undermined by the rule that spending is limited for each of the participants and not for each of the sides, and the Lithuanian and Brazilian systems are arguably unfair as contributions are limited to a percentage of the donor's income – something that gives richer individuals an advantage. Based on this survey, the rules regulating campaign spending remain unfair. A much-cited study stated that "the most frequently heard criticism of the referendum is the role that big money plays in direct democracy campaigns"[63]. The evidence in this chapter suggests that little has changed.

Subsidies to campaigns

Democracy requires a level playing field. If extreme disparities are in place, there is a danger that the poorer side loses access to the media and to advisors with expertise in referendum campaigns. To limit this danger, some countries have introduced grants to ensure that referendum campaigns are not unduly dominated by those with the deepest pockets.

Whereas restrictions in campaign spending might in some countries be perceived to impinge on the freedom of speech, government grants to ensure parity have not, according to the responses to this survey, been ruled to be inconsistent with First Amendment rights or the equivalent in non-American jurisdictions. There are strong reasons for providing public subsidies or expenditure floors. Austin Ranney noted,

> The absence of parties and party labels in referendum campaigns means that voters enter campaigns with less information and fewer guideposts than in candidate elections, and the campaigns are therefore significantly more important as suppliers of information and arguments that make for interested voters and informed votes. Accordingly, the prime object of government regulation of referendum campaigns should be to ensure that both the proponents and opponents of each proposition should have enough resources to make at least adequate presentations of their cases[64].

Yet, while a few countries provide grants for campaigns in referendums, most countries do not. And there are fewer now than in the 1980s. Back then, 11 countries "provided some form of assistance"[65], now the number is only eight.

In contrast to the rules limiting campaign spending, the three Scandinavian countries (Denmark, Norway and Sweden) provide grants to both sides during referendum campaigns. The same is true for the Netherlands and Japan (although the latter has yet to hold its first nationwide referendum). In Germany there are provisions for reimbursements of some expenditure incurred during state-level referendums, and in France and Australia there has been ad-hoc funding for campaigns to provide a level playing field. Each country will be analysed in turn.

In Australia there is nothing to prevent the government from appropriating funds to support referendum campaigns – conversely, there is nothing that forces governments to do so. Before the referendum on the monarchy, in 1999, there were no public grants to either side. However, to inform the public of the two positions, the Liberal government headed by John Howard allocated 7.5 million AUD to, respectively, the YES and the NO umbrella organisations. However, as these commissions are not provided for by legislation, they were not required by statute to meet minimum levels of fairness, accountability or objectivity[66].

Bulgaria is a relative newcomer to the world of referendums. While there were dubious plebiscites during the years of communism (two constitutional votes were held in respectively 1947 and 1971), the country had fewer than the average number of referendums in the years immediately after the fall of the Iron Curtain.

It was not until 2013 that the first referendum was held[67]. After this there have been a further four referendums (on two different occasions). Partly as a consequence of this, regulations of the process of direct democracy have been introduced. One of the regulations is a provision for (partial) government funding of direct democracy campaigns. Thus, the Direct Citizen Participation in State and Local Government Act states that, "The Election Code shall apply in respect of information and explanatory campaign, where equal opportunities shall be guaranteed for the different opinions on the referendum subject to be presented"[68]. However, the Act does not specify if the money can be given to umbrella organisations. Thus, the recipients of government grants are parties, and not campaign organisations. This creates a problem as referendums do not always have the opposition pitted against the government.

Denmark is one of the most frequent users of referendums in Europe. Despite this – or critics will say because of this – different governments have been reluctant to introduce regulatory legislation. But some exist. Thus, in an answer to a written question by the MP Alex Ahrendtsen (from the Danish People's Party) the Danish Ministry of the Interior and Economics (Indenrigs og Økonomiministeriet) responded that "while generic legislation did not exist", funds had been allocated to referendums on an ad-hoc basis. Thus, in,

> The 2015 referendum … the Folketinget had granted DKr 20.8 million for a public information. This grant was raised to Dkr 15 million, with a view to distribution among the parties elected to the Folketing and the European Parliament, and Dkr 10 million to information activities, which were distributed after organisations applied for funds. In addition, the Ministry of Justice distributed a further Dkr 3.5 million for information activities[69].

France, like Denmark, is one of the more frequent users of referendums. In addition to mandatory referendums on constitutional changes (Article 89), the president may "submit policy issues to referendums" (Article 11), as de Gaulle did frequently (see Chapter 2). This provision has been used eight times. There has only been one constitutional revision referendum under the Fifth Republic, namely the 2002 referendum on reducing the presidential term from seven to five years. In addition, France has the "Shared initiative", which allows "one-fifth of the members of Parliament, supported by one-tenth of registered voters"[70]. This provision has hitherto not been used[71].

Despite these relatively extensive provisions for referendums, the process is somewhat unregulated. As noted in the previous section, there are no limits on campaign spending. Further, grants to individual campaigns were unknown until the beginning of the twenty-first century. In the words of Laurence Morel, the foremost expert on French referendums, "at the last referendum (2005) for the first time the government provided for some financial help to parties and groups allowed to campaign. But this was an ad hoc decision"[72].

Italy provides a bit of a special case as most referendums are initiated by the people. At the national level, the Italian constitution stipulates that referendums can be held either:

1. to repeal legislation or sections thereof (known as *Referendum Abrogativo*), upon proposal of at least 500,000 voters or of five regional councils (Article 75) or;
2. when a constitutional revision is not approved by a majority of two-thirds of the members of each House of the Parliament or five regional councils ask to hold a referendum within three months of parliament voting for a change of the constitution (Article 138).

In the case of the former, there are mechanisms for reimbursement of expenditures, though there are limits to these. These are set out in Article 1(4) of Law No. 157 of 1999[73] and are linked to the number of signatures collected to validly present a proposal for a referendum.

A committee established to promote a constitutional referendum or a referendum aiming to repeal legislation get a reimbursement equal to €1 per the number of signatures collected up to the maximum threshold of €2,582,285. A committee promoting a referendum to repeal legislation gets the reimbursement only if two requirements are met: (1) the Constitutional Court has declared admissible the question(s) to be put to a vote in the referendum; and (2) the quorum for the validity of the referendum is reached. By contrast, no quorum of participation nor admissibility check by the Constitutional Court are required for the validity of constitutional referendums.

Between 2015 and 2019, the voters in the Netherlands could request a referendum on an already enacted law. According to the Advisory Referendum Act (Wet raadgevend referendum), the Referendum Committee (De referendumcommissie) provided subsidies of a total of €600,000 for the pro-agreement camp, the same amount for opponents and a total of €800,000 for neutral information activities. In addition, individuals could apply for a maximum of €5,000 and organisations for a maximum of €50,000[74].

Germany provides a special case. Like in the United States, direct democracy is exclusively a state and a local matter. (The Federal Constitution currently only provides for referendums on the changing of state borders – such as the successful referendum on the amalgamation of Baden and Württemberg in 1951 or the failed referendum on a merger of Berlin and Brandenburg in 1996.) In a pithy summary by a German scholar the situation is as follows:

> Since its founding in 1949, the German political system has rested firmly on the principles of representative democracy … Today, however, the concepts of representative democracy and the "the party state" are under stress and participatory concepts are gaining ground. Although there is no direct democratic experience at the national level, the situation looks quite different at the level of states and municipalities. Since the 1990s all German federal states (*Bundesländer*) have introduced referendums at the state and local levels that can be launched by, respectively, authorities and citizens[75].

One of the main developments in these *Länder* is reimbursements of campaign expenditure – in effect a retrospective grant. Thus, in the city-state of Hamburg and in the state of Schleswig-Holstein, costs for a referendum campaign are reimbursed. In Hamburg, €0.10 per vote (limited to €40,000) will be reimbursed, in neighbouring Schleswig-Holstein significantly more (€0.28 per yes vote)[76].

In other states, it is even possible to reimburse expenditure at the earlier stages of a petition drive. Thus, the state of Lower Saxony refunds €0.10 per valid signature for a petition for a referendum that has been concluded. And, in Rheinland-Palatine, a state currently governed by a coalition of the Social Democrats, the Greens and the centre-right FDP, there is reimbursement of both the expenses incurred during the signature gathering and during the actual campaign.

Purdah rules: limits on government spending in referendum campaigns

Governments have to provide information to the people. But sometimes – especially during elections and referendum campaigns – there is a risk that the administration (ab)uses its position and uses tax-payers' money on what is essentially advertising for the side they favour to win. This was famously the case in Ireland in 1995. At the time the voters were asked to vote on an amendment to the constitution that would make divorce legal. The government decided to spend £500,000 to inform the voters about a yes-vote, but without spending anything to explain the no-position. Patricia McKenna, a Green MEP – who supported the amendment – found this unfair and undemocratic. She challenged the legality of the decision to promote one side only. The Supreme Court found in favour of the plaintiff. The Court held that the constitution required equal treatment of each side in a referendum, and that,

> Such expenditure also had the effect of putting the voting rights of those citizens in favour of the amendment above the voting rights of those citizens opposed to it [and that] as well as representing a breach of the constitutional right to equality [it] also represented an infringement of the constitutional right to freedom of expression and the constitutional right to a democratic process in referenda[77].

In other countries there are similar rules that limit the involvement of governments. In the United Kingdom, the word *purdah* is used to signify the time between the announcement of an election and the final election result[78].

Thus, in relation to referendum campaigns, Britain is one of the countries with the most extensive rules of government regulation during campaigns. In Britain too there are limits on what the government can say during the referendum period and it must observe a strict parity in its spending. However, the British system does not entirely preclude the government from using its resources to influence the result. Thus, "there is not a specific prohibition on amount spent by government. But the 2000 Act precludes local government and central government from issuing publishing 'promotional material' in connection with the referendum in a period of 28 days prior to the referendum"[79]. Moreover, the government can spend money before the referendum begins.

Like with most other things pertaining to referendum campaigns, the role of the government and spending of tax-payers' money is largely unregulated. Austria's referendum on EU membership is not an untypical example. The government spent 47 million shillings (roughly four million dollars) on a media campaign – roughly ten times that of the opposition. The campaign worked, and even the Austrian chancellor admitted it was money well spent, "the work of the advertising agency has obviously not been wasted"[80]. This is still the case in Austria. In answer to the question, "Are there limits on how much money the government can spend during the referendum campaign?" the country's leading authority on referendums curtly responded, "Not at all"[81].

Thus, overall, a mere 23 per cent of countries have rules that limit spending by the government. A couple of examples will suffice. In Japan, "the government can spend the cost of public relations of TV and newspaper concerning the referendum by the national referendum law"[82]. Likewise, in Germany, government spending during referendum campaigns "is not regulated in any federal state. There are no limits or regulations"[83].

The few countries that have provisions that limit or regulate the amount spent by governments are Australia, Ireland, Latvia, Lithuania, the Netherlands, Poland, Switzerland, Taiwan and the United Kingdom. Though, as is inevitable, some countries have stricter rules than others.

Hence, Switzerland and the Netherlands have only limited regulations. In the case of the former, there are "not exact limits, but the Governments (at both national and cantonal level) are bound by the principle of proportionality and there are numerous court rulings that clarify what/when/how/who may"[84], and in the Netherlands, the information campaign was outsourced but there were no formal upper limits on government information activity[85].

The countries with the most thorough regulations are – once again – Latvia and Lithuania. In the case of the latter country, the Law on National Referendum, Legislative Initiative and European Citizens' Initiative is very detailed and serves as a good example. Article 30 of the Act reads:

> Chapter VI: Campaigning before a National Referendum, Campaigning for a Legislative Initiative and Campaigning for the Initiative to Revoke the Saeima, section 30: (1) The broadcasts on campaigning before a national referendum, campaigning for a legislative initiative and campaigning for the initiative to revoke the Saeima may not be included in the form of advertising in the news broadcasts of electronic mass media[86].

The same level of regulation exists in Australia, where the federal government is limited to providing a text-based, 2,000-word information booklet for the No and Yes sides[87]. Further, the Referendum (Machinery Provisions) Act 1984 (Cth) prevents any spending with respect to the delivery of pamphlets outside of that envisioned by the Act[88]. This includes any positive advertising for either side[89].

As we have seen, Taiwan has held many referendums, and these have been relatively regulated.

According to Article 20 of the Referendum Act, the government in what is officially known as the Republic of China can only spend money on holding referendums and the related presentations or debates. However, the regulation is in some ways patchy. Thus, there are no other rules that regulate how much money the government can spend providing "the representatives of positive and negative opinions with time to present their opinions or debate through national broadcast TV channels"[90]. The competent authority is only required to:

> Make the following matters known to the public through public notice 28 days before the day of the referendum:
>
> 1. The date of voting for the proposal of a referendum and the times of commencement and termination of voting.
> 2. The serial number, main text, and statement of reasons for the proposal of the referendum.
> 3. The position papers raised by the government agencies on the proposal of the referendum.
> 4. The scope and method of executing the right of referendum[91].

While there are no cases of lawsuits and litigation to test the correct interpretation of these rules, the consensus seems to be that the government is prohibited from using public money in pursuit of its policies during referendum campaigns[92].

While Australia, Britain, Latvia and Taiwan have statutory limits on campaign spending, other countries, most notably Ireland, have limits on government spending as a result of litigation. The main case is the aforementioned McKenna judgment of 1995. The situation in Ireland has been summed up as follows by Theresa Reidy:

> The government may not use public funds in support of either side in a political campaign at a referendum. This requirement is the result of a Supreme Court decision known as the McKenna judgment which dates from 1995. The government makes a financial allocation to establish a Referendum Commission for each referendum and this statutory body is responsible for providing information on the referendum question and promoting turnout[93].

Yet, while rules exist, they are sometimes circumvented. This is what the David Cameron government (controversially) did before the 2016 Brexit referendum. Only two days before the campaign period began, HM Treasury spent "more than £9m on … a leaflet to every UK household setting out the case for remaining in the European Union"[94].

Overall, the limits on government spending during referendum campaigns is, at best, patchy. The result of a referendum can be questioned if the administration is able to spend tax-payers' money on an outcome they seek. There is an urgent need to introduce rules that regulate and limit this practice.

But perhaps these regulations are beginning to become obsolete. Increasingly, referendum campaigns (like elections) are fought online and on social media. This was certainly the case with the Brexit referendum. And more recent referendums have followed the same pattern. This is an area that has received even less attention. The next section hopefully can begin to rectify this gap in the literature.

Online campaigning regulation

The revelation of Cambridge Analytica's controversial and very successful use of personal data during the 2016 Brexit referendum campaign showed that the company had harvested the personal data from millions of Facebook users without their consent and used it for political advertising purposes. This caused understandable concern. At one level, it was a watershed moment for the public's understanding of the abuse of personal data, and it caused a decline in Facebook's stock price[95].

Using state-of-the-art technology, the Leave-campaign effectively targeted swing voters and citizens who rarely voted but who would be likely to vote for leaving the European Union. While there was some controversy over the involvement of Cambridge Analytica[96], Vote Leave did not break the law. There was a simple reason for this, there was not much of a law to be broken. According to the English contemporary historian Andrew Blick:

> In the period since the 2000 [Political Parties, Elections and Referendum] Act was passed, online campaigning has become far more important and sophisticated, leaving the legislative framework out of date. There is currently a widely voiced view that the 2000 Act needs to be amended to reflect this development, but at present regulations in this area are considered inadequate. While within the UK, it is subject to the EU GDPR regime, something that the UK intends to preserve … when it leaves the EU[97].

This is not a unique situation, though out of the 30 countries, nine (or 29 per cent) have rules and regulations that pertain to online campaigning. Australia is a good example of the dearth of regulation, a fact that has been mentioned by local experts[98]. It has been argued that,

> The *Referendums (Machinery Provisions) Act 1984* (Cth) famously seldom has been updated. In outline it is roughly unchanged from the early part of the 20th century. In particular, the legislation does not reflect the current prevalence of the internet. In 2013, the Act was amended to allow the Electoral Commissioner to email commissioned pamphlets to voters, however, the Act does not otherwise directly regulate online campaigning[99]. The only reference to online campaigning is a reference by exclusion – online communication falls under "other communication" as per s110C(5) item 2. Moreover, none of its provisions bear on the use of personal data. This area of law is also left unaddressed by the *Privacy Act 1988* (Cth)[100].

This lack of regulation is pronounced even in countries where almost everyone is online. Although Japan is a country where over 90 per cent of the population uses the Internet[101], there is no regulation. As Mitsuhiko Okamoto has noted, "The national referendum law also does not cover on-line campaign. The law does not assume on-line (internet) campaign[s]"[102].

Once again, countries which often pride themselves on – and score highly in league tables of – the quality of their democracies fare badly. Thus Canada, Denmark, the Netherlands, Norway and Sweden have no regulation of online campaigning in referendums.

However, this absence of regulation is not universal. A number of smaller countries have regulations. These include the Baltic countries (Estonia, Latvia and Lithuania), Slovakia, Iceland and New Zealand, as well as larger countries like France and Brazil.

In addition to these countries, there is some regulation of online campaigning in Switzerland, though this is due to the court's interpretation of existing statute law regarding general advertising[103]. The Federal Act on Political Rights (Bundesgesetz über die politischen Rechte), Article 11(2), contains a "disclaimer" with regard to the official explanatory pamphlet (in which the initiative or referendum committee is allowed to place some information of its own). It reads:

> References to electronic sources may be included in the explanatory statement only if the author of the references declares in writing that none of the content of the sources is illegal and that the sources are not linked to electronic publications with illegal content[104].

This regulation has been followed up by recent explanatory guidance by the government. Thus, generally speaking, the Federal Council is of the opinion that existing regulation is sufficient also for the use of social media in referendum campaigns[105].

The Baltic states are some of the countries with the most up-to-date regulation of online campaigning[106]. This is not surprising as Estonia, Latvia and Lithuania reportedly have been targets in cyber-attacks that are believed to have come from Russia[107]. However, this vulnerability is especially considerable in the first two of these countries due to their large Russian-speaking populations (26 per cent in Estonia and 24 per cent in Latvia).

In recent years, Lithuania has also become a victim of cyber-attacks from – it is believed – its larger eastern neighbour[108]. It is not clear whether this perception is directly responsible for the legislation in the country, but it is noteworthy that the regulations were introduced after a major attack on the Lithuanian banks. In the country there is not a complete ban on online campaigning but many of the issues that caused concern during the Brexit referendum have been regulated in this country. According to a country expert,

> [The rules are set out in] Law No. 13,488 of 2017 and the Superior Electoral Court ruling discipline on-line campaigning. Parliamentary Parties can have websites, blogs or profiles in social media. Content boosting in social media and others is allowed, but the use of fake profiles or robots is illegal. The use of personal data in campaigning is also illegal. Companies, upon users' consent, can only collect data that is related to their services and cannot transfer users' personal data to third parties with only a few exceptions[109].

A similar level of regulation exists in Estonia. As far back as 2008, the *Riigikogu*, the unicameral parliament of the country, introduced The Advertising Act, which bans political advertising on the internet, including "subliminal techniques"[110]. This regulation has been updated yearly since its promulgation.

While legislation in Estonia is comprehensive, the rules pertaining to online advertising are even more detailed in Latvia, where the Law on National Referendum, Legislative Initiative and European Citizens' Initiative has been continuously updated to take into account new developments in online advertising[111]. Chapter VI of the Act provides a ban on "hidden campaigning", and explicitly cites advertising on the "Internet". To wit, "Hidden campaigning before a national referendum, hidden campaigning for a legislative initiative or hidden campaigning … is prohibited"[112].

Other countries have similarly sought to regulate online campaigning. One of these countries is Iceland. Until the financial collapse of the island nation's economy in 2008, there had been no nationwide referendums since 1944 when the country voted to sever its ties with Denmark.

As a consequence of the political crisis caused by the massive debt following the bankruptcy of the IceSave and Kaupthing banks,

Ólafur Ragnar Grímsson, the Icelandic president at the time, took the unusual and unprecedented step of vetoing the agreement the government had made with the country's international creditors[113]. This resulted in two referendums in, respectively, 2010 and 2011, in which the government's plans were rejected by over 90 per cent of the voters. Following these referendums, the voters approved six amendments to the constitution in a non-binding referendum in 2012.

This upsurge in the use of the referendum in Iceland was accompanied by detailed set of regulations of online campaigning. While not as detailed as that of the Baltic states, "the Icelandic government recently implemented law on online anonymous campaigning. Political bodies are prohibited from financing or taking part in the publishing of any campaign-related material without making their affiliation public"[114].

In Portugal, similar legislation pertaining to the use of the internet is subject to the same regulations as in other media. These regulations are laid down in Lei n.° 72-A/2015, which, according to its preamble, "establishes the legal regime for journalistic coverage in the electoral period, regulates electoral propaganda through commercial advertising". According to the Act, the media must ensure "balance, representativeness and equity in the treatment of news, reporting of facts or events of informative value"[115]. This is not restricted to the traditional media. Thus, according to the Act, "in the use of the Internet, the media observe, with due adaptations, the same rules to which they are obliged by this law, in relation to the other means of communication"[116].

While all actors "shall at all times enjoy full freedom of use of social networks and other means of expression through the Internet", there are limits[117]. Thus it is illegal to use these media "for the dissemination of campaign content on the eve of election day (reflexion day)", and there is a ban on "the use of commercial advertising". In cases of violation of these regulations, there is a sanctioning regime, laid down in Article 12 of the Act, according to which breach of rules pertaining to commercial advertising may result in fines of between €15,000 and €75,000.

Slovakia is another European country that has seen an explosion in the use of referendums[118]. In this Central European country, "a referendum can be initiated either by a petition signed by at least 350,000 citizens, that is, around 8 per cent of all eligible citizens, or by a resolution adopted by the national parliament. This allows both political parties and civic initiatives to pursue a referendum"[119].

As a consequence of the political salience of the referendum, the *Národná rada* (Parliament) has enacted legislation to prevent abuse of online campaigning. This "legislation stipulates that every single element of political advertising (including on social media) must clearly mention that it belongs to a political campaign"[120]. In Slovakia, all political advertisements are prohibited 48 hours before a referendum or an election is held. However, unlike the detailed legislation in the Baltic states and Iceland, country experts have expressed concerns that the legislation still allows campaigners to circumvent the legislation so that posts on "social media which are not sponsored … but still can be released by campaigning parties"[121].

Traditionally France had a low level of regulation of referendums. This has changed in recent years (see above). The recognition that referendums do not take place in a vacuum has led to updating of legislation pertaining to online campaigning, thus, "Regulations of internet campaigns have been introduced for elections after the last referendum (2005) and should thus apply to referendums when applicable. They mainly reproduce however the regulations of traditional campaigns. With the addition of norms for personal data"[122].

As noted earlier, Brazil has an exceptionally high level of referendum regulation. This is also true for legislation of online campaigning. This is largely detailed in Law No. 13,488 of 2017 and the Superior Electoral Court's (Tribunal Superior Eleitoral) rulings on online campaigning[123].

While parliamentary parties can have websites, blogs or profiles in social media, the legislation and subsequent judgments limit their scope. Thus, while content boosting in social media and others is allowed, it is prohibited to use fake profiles or bots. Furthermore, the use of personal data in campaigning is also illegal. Companies, upon users' consent, can only collect data that is related to their services and cannot transfer users' personal data to third parties[124].

Cambridge Analytica used a loophole to influence the outcome of the Brexit referendum in a way that was considered to be unethical by many. Could this happen again? Based on the data and the legislation analysed in this chapter, there is reason to believe that it could. This is especially true for developed democracies, such as Britain, the Scandinavian polities and the Low Countries. The almost complete lack of regulation of online campaigning makes this an urgent concern. Other countries should follow the lead of the Baltic countries and Brazil and introduce tighter control of online campaigning.

Traditional media

It is commonplace to argue that all campaigning after 2016 has taken place on the internet and that old-fashioned news outlets such as television, and, indeed, newspapers are obsolete. There is a tendency in that direction, but the evidence suggests that the "old" media are still important parts of the process of agenda-setting[125].

A survey carried out by BMG Research on behalf of the Electoral Reform Society ranked the BBC as one of the three most valued sources on the Brexit debate[126]. A total of 34 per cent found the BBC to be the most important source of information (with the figure being 41 per cent for those over the age of 64). This was far ahead of other broadcasters (17 per cent) and social media (16 per cent). For those aged 18–24, BBC (at 24 per cent) was less important than social media (33 per cent). Notwithstanding the differences between the cohorts, television is still a very important source

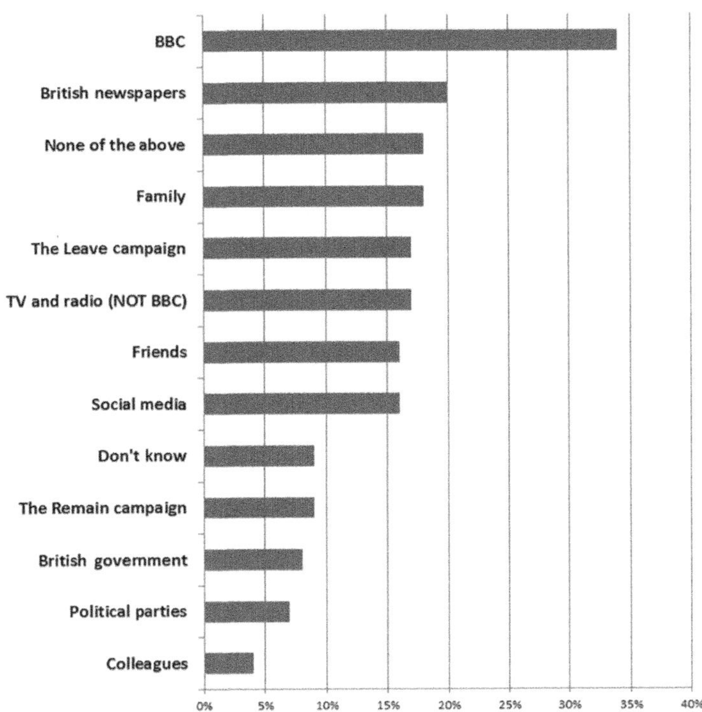

Figure 4.2 Information sources in the British Brexit referendum, 2016.

Source: BMG Research, N: 1638, available at www.bmgresearch.co.uk/bbc-important-referendum-information/

of information. While one cannot extrapolate from the EU referendum, television also helped set the agenda in the 2014 Scottish independence referendum[127].

Despite this, in most countries broadcast media are not statutorily required to provide equal time and space to all sides in the referendum. Roughly one-third (11 countries) require balance or equal airtime to both sides in referendum campaigns by law. These include Australia, Brazil, Bulgaria, Estonia, Iceland, Japan and Poland. A further six (France, Finland, Sweden, Switzerland, Romania and Hungary) require, by law, that the mass-media provide opportunities for a fair presentation of the views of each side.

Once again, Austria is a good example. In response to the question, "Are print, broadcast or online media required to provide equal time and space to all sides in the referendum?" Stefan Vospernik responded, "there are no regulations or laws in this regard, as there are no such provisions for elections".[128]

Referendums are treated by the media in a similar way as elections, with the parliamentary parties having the main say in the media coverage[129]. A few countries provide regulations to ensure a level playing field. For example, in Bulgaria, the Direct Citizen Participation in State and Local Government Act states, "The Election Code shall apply in respect of information and explanatory campaign, where equal opportunities shall be guaranteed for the different opinions on the referendum subject to be presented"[130].

Portugal is a country with some regulation of referendums, but relatively few opportunities for engagement in direct democratic processes[131]. However, there is extensive regulation of the mass-media in the country. According to the Lei Orgânica do Regime do Referendo, media are required to observe the core "principles of equal opportunities and treatment of campaigners"[132]. This is set out in the Act, which stipulates that "the parties and groups of registered electors that are campaigning in a referendum have the right to equal opportunities and treatment, in order to undertake their campaign activities freely and under the best conditions"[133]. More specifically, the Act provided "access to specific resources", which include,

> The use, in accordance with the present Law, of news publications, broadcasts by public and private radio and television stations with a national or regional scope, and public buildings or enclosed spaces, shall be free of charge to parties and groups of registered electors that intervene in a referendum[134].

As regards radio and television stations, the Act specifies that these are "obliged to give equal treatment to the parties and groups of registered electors that … in the referendum"[135] and that these, during the campaign period, radio and television stations shall reserve "fifteen minutes between seven p.m. and ten p.m.; on Saturdays and Sundays – thirty minutes between seven p.m. and ten p.m." to presenting their views ahead of the vote[136]. These rules also apply to "private radio stations with a national scope"[137]. According to these broadcasts shall,

> Be divided up between the entities that are intervening in the referendum equally in two blocks: one part between the parties for which one or more Members of the Assembly of the Republic were elected in the last legislative elections, to be allocated jointly when parties ran in coalition; and another part between the other parties and groups of registered electors that have been lawfully formed for the purpose[138].

Further, "in the case of a popular referendum initiative, the group of registered electors that initiated the referendum shall share the first block of broadcasting time in a position equivalent to that of the parties referred to in the first half of the previous paragraph"[139]. In addition, the National Electoral Commission "shall distribute radio and television broadcasting times by lottery at least three days before the campaign begins and shall communicate the result of the distribution to the broadcasting stations within the same time limit"[140]. While extensively regulated, the Portuguese provisions do not provide mathematical parity of views.

The same is true for Estonia. The Estonian Public Broadcasting Act 2007 specifies that "Broadcasting shall be politically balanced", that is,

> Public Broadcasting shall give equal opportunities to all the candidates participating in the elections … Similarly to the elections of local governments, equal opportunities shall be created in the event

> of referendums. The rules for reflecting elections in the programme services of Public Broadcasting shall be approved by the Public Broadcasting Council and such rules shall be disclosed not later than within a week after the date of announcement of the elections[141].

However, in practice this does not mean equal opportunities for presenting views. According to an expert, "there is no absolute requirement of equal time for each [of the] political forces which results from the multiplicity of various political options. Public media should provide time for as many political forces as possible"[142].

Other countries have less detailed legislation. To name but a few, in Iceland, there are rules intended to ensure parity, however, "This only applies to the only publicly owned media, RÚV [the national broadcaster]. RÚV is obliged to ensure equal representation of all sides of a referendum"[143].

Similar rules exist in other jurisdictions. For example, in the Czech Republic, there is a "general requirement for news is that it must provide space to all involved parties. If it fails to do so, the media outlet can be fined"[144].

In Spain, the Organic Law on the Regulation of the Different Modalities of Referendum states that public media must offer free information spaces to each political group represented in regional or national parliament (depending on the referendum), but it explicitly excludes groups not represented[145]. This is odd as the rationale of the referendum is that it allows people a say when they potentially disagree with their representatives. Further, these "have to be proportional to the number of seats of each political group in parliament". However, in the latter case, there is no guarantee that these will give proportional voice to parties that are outside parliament. Thus, in the 2005 referendum on the European Constitution both of the larger parties, PP and PSOE, were in favour while only Izquierda Unida, the successor of the Communist Party, campaigned for a "no".

In Romania, the regulation is left to judicial bodies. Thus, Decision no. 441/2018 of the National Audio-visual Council

(CNA) on the coverage of the national referendum on the revision of the constitution on radio and television stations on 6 and 7 October 2018 held that the media must provide balanced coverage[146]. However, in Romania there is also a considerable body of statutory legislation. This was repeated in a court decision, which said:

> In the debates, the broadcasters must ensure equal opportunities between supporters and opponents of the referendum; if one of the guests does not participate, this must be mentioned on the post; the absence of the point of view of one of the parties does not exonerate the creator / moderator from ensuring impartiality[147].

Further, the same ruling noted that "broadcasters must ensure a balance in reflecting the campaign activities of the partisans and opponents of the issue subject to the referendum". As stated in primary legislation, which provides that, "in order to encourage and facilitate the pluralist expression of opinion streams, broadcasters have the obligation to reflect electoral campaigns in a fair, balanced and impartial manner"[148].

Overall, there are several countries that provide mechanisms for ensuring a fair balance of views. However, the problem is that many regulations are assuming that the parties in the respective parliaments reflect the sides in referendums. This is far from always the case. It would be far better to adopt rules like those in Iceland where the public broadcaster, RÚV, must ensure a fair and balanced representation of rules. However, to require parity in privately owned media may not be desirable as it is likely to infringe free speech.

Overall levels of regulation of referendums

As the foregoing sections show, the levels of regulation of referendums differ considerably. Some countries have virtually no regulations (even countries with strong democratic traditions such as Denmark and Uruguay). Conversely, there are strong regimes of regulation in other countries including polities with a chequered democratic history (such as Brazil). Overall, and based on the previous sections, we can establish a crude ranking of referendum regulation by giving one point for each of the areas that are regulated. We call this measure the Index of Referendum Regulation (IRR). Thus, a country like France gets the score "3" as there are regulations of three out of the five areas.

As the index shows, three countries score the highest, Poland, Brazil and Lithuania – all polities that have recently become democratic. Thus, in general, there is a slight negative correlation between the number of years a country has been democratic and the levels of regulation, though this is not statistically significant. Further, there is no significant correlation between the number of referendums held and the levels of regulation.

The big question, then, is what accounts for this. Perhaps due to the small number of cases, it is difficult to discern a statistical pattern. Neither the number of referendums, nor provisions for citizen-initiated referendums are statistically significant variables (respectively, Pearson's correlation coefficients of, R:0.10 (p=0.58) and 0.20 (p=0.21).

When we carried out a regression analysis, we only found that the dummy variable for parliamentary systems was statistically

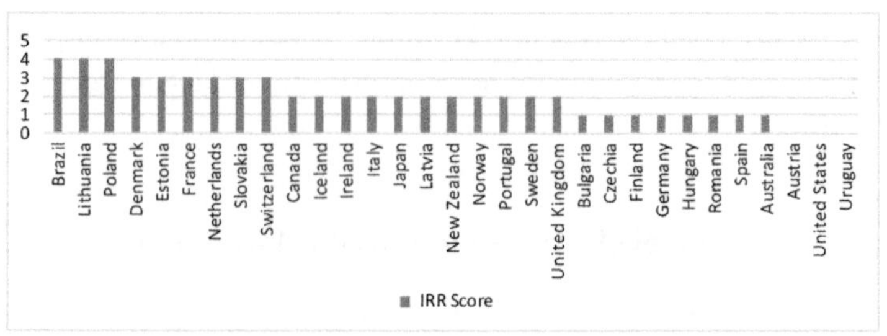

Figure 4.3 Index of Referendum Regulation score.

Table 4.1 Index of referendum fairness and institutional variables (standard errors in brackets)

Variable	B
Total number of referendums	0.091
	(0.078)
Parliamentarism	-2.142*
	(0.707)
Ideology (right)	0.011
	(0.051)
Effective number of parties	0.145
	(0.200)
Constant	2.524
	(3.365)

Dependent variable: index of referendum fairness, R-Squared: 0.82. * p>0.1

significant but in a negative direction. It is difficult to explain this. It could be speculated that referendums are less likely to be regulated as parliamentary systems tend to be more consensus orientated, and that the parties have a shared interest in maintaining the status quo as referendums tend to be held on issues over which there is a shared consensus across the political spectrum. Thus the consensus in Britain in 1975 might explain why there was no regulation in that year's referendum, whereas the opposite was the case when the British government passed the Political Parties, Elections, and Referendums Act in anticipation of a divisive battle over a referendum on the Euro that was never held.

In any case, what the chapter has shown is that the regulation of referendums is patchy, and that the aim of ensuring a fair outcome – one that reflects the views of the voters – has not always been a top priority when countries have introduced legislation. Thus, it is perhaps telling that some of the most regulated countries are places where there is a real (and justified) fear of outside interference.

Notes

1 S. Wambaugh, *Plebiscites Since the World War* (Washington, DC: Carnegie, 1933), p. ix.
2 Dorota Maj, "Direct democracy in Lithuania", in Maria Marczewska-Rytko (ed.), *Handbook of Direct Democracy in Central and Eastern Europe after 1989* (Opladen: Barbara Budrich Publishers, 2018), pp. 146–163 (p. 150).
3 George Orwell, *Fascism and Democracy* (London: Penguin, 2020), p. 32.
4 R. Levy, "'Deliberative voting': Realising constitutional referendum democracy", *Public Law* 47(4) (2017), pp. 555–574 (p. 556).
5 Andrew Ellis, "Administration of referendums: A comparative study of independence referendums" (Port Moresby: National Research Institute, PNG, 2018).
6 See e.g. Independent Commission on Referendums, *Report of the Independent Commission on Referendums* (London: The Constitution Unit, 2018). Earlier studies include A. Ranney, "Regulating the referendum", in A. Ranney (ed.), *The Referendum Device* (Washington, DC: The American Enterprise Institute, 1981), pp. 89–98.
7 Alexis de Tocqueville, *Democracy in America* (London: Penguin, 2003), p. 359.
8 Ibid., p. 360.
9 See for example, G. Helmke and S. Levitsky, "Informal institutions and comparative politics: A research agenda", *Perspectives on Politics* 2(4) (2004), pp. 725–740.
10 "Editorial: Campaign ads for referendums", *Japan Times*, 23 May 2019.
11 European Commission for Democracy Through Law – Venice Commission (2007) Code for Good Practice on Referendums Study No. 371/ 2006CDL-AD, p. 20.
12 Stefan Vospernik, written evidence, 28 August 2019.
13 K. Knock, "The north east referendum: Lessons learnt?" *Parliamentary Affairs* 59(4) (2016), pp. 682–693.
14 B. Seyd, "Regulating the referendum", *Representation* 35(4) (1998), pp. 191–199.
15 www.bbc.co.uk/news/uk-scotland-scotland-politics-32735695 (accessed 20 July 2019).
16 www.electoralcommission.org.uk/find-information-by-subject/political-parties-campaigning-and-donations/campaign-spending-and-donations-at-referendums/campaign-spending-at-the-eu-referendum (accessed 16 July 2019).
17 David Arter, *Scandinavian Politics Today* (Manchester: Manchester University Press, 2013).

18 Personal communication with Steen Sauerberg (Denmark), Markku Suksi (Finland), Hildur Margrét Jóhannsdóttir (Iceland) and Tor Bjørklund (Norway). On file with the Westminster Foundation for Democracy.
19 Partiregnskabsloven (om private bidrag til politiske partier og offentliggørelse af politiske partiers regnskaber) Lovbekendtgørelse nr. 139 af 7. februar 2019.
20 Personal communication, Professor Henrik Ekengren Oscarsson (Sweden), March 2019. See also https://partiforskning.gu.se/english/partyfinancing (accessed 16 July 2019).
21 The following section draws on personal communication with Professor Ron Levy, Australian National University.
22 America is one of a handful of democracies never to have held a nationwide referendum (others include India, Israel and Japan). Yet, at the state level, referendums and initiatives are common and, in some states, they are held even more frequently than in Switzerland. See T.E. Cronin, *Direct Democracy: The Politics of Initiative, Referendum, and Recall* (Cambridge, MA: Harvard University Press, 1999).
23 Massachusetts General Laws 1976, Chapter 55, Para 8.
24 *First National Bank of Boston* v. *Attorney General*, 359 N.E.2d 1262 (Mass. 1977).
25 *First National Bank of Boston* v. *Bellotti*, 435 U.S. 765 (1978).
26 Ibid.
27 *Citizens Against Rent Control* v. *City of Berkeley*, 454 U.S. 290 (1981).
28 David B. Magleby, *Direct Legislation: Voting on Ballot Propositions in the United States* (Baltimore: Johns Hopkins University Press, 1984), p. 150.
29 Shaun Bowler and Todd Donovan, *Demanding Choices: Opinion, Voting and Direct Democracy* (Ann Arbor: Michigan University Press, 1998), p. 150.
30 See Brigitte Geissel, "Direct democracy and its (perceived) consequences: The German case", in Saskia P. Ruth, Yanina Welp and Laurence Whitehead (eds), *Let the People Rule* (Colchester: ECPR Press, 2017), pp. 155–167.
31 Law No. 13,488 of 2017.
32 Res. No. 23,348 of 2011.
33 Personal communication, Professor Octavio Amorim Neto, Brazilian School of Public and Business Administration at the Getulio Vargas Foundation, Rio de Janeiro, March 2019.
34 Law No. 13,165 of 2015.
35 Referendum Act (S.C. 1992, c. 30). There have only been three federal referendums in Canada. In 1898 on Alcohol Prohibition, in 1942 on entering the Second World War, despite a manifesto commitment by Liberal PM McKenzie King to stay out of the conflict, and in 1992 on a new constitution. Only McKenzie King's referendum passed. See M. Mendelsohn, "Introducing deliberative direct democracy in Canada: Learning from the

American experience", *American Review of Canadian Studies* 26(3) (1996), pp. 449–468.

36 Referendum Act S.15(1).

37 Personal communication, Professor Louis Massicotte, L'Université Laval.

38 See L. Massicotte, "A deal which leaves all parties unhappy: The Canadian constitutional referendum of 1992", *Zeitschrift für Kanada-Studien* 13(1) (1993), pp. 125–140; R. Johnston, E. Gidengil, N. Nevitte and A. Blais, "La dynamique référendaire: pourquoi les Canadiens ont-ils rejeté l'Accord de Charlottetown?", *Revue française de science politique* 46(5) (1996), pp. 817–830.

39 Personal communication, Professor Louis Massicotte, L'Université Laval.

40 Lawrence LeDuc, *The Politics of Direct Democracy: Referendums in a Global Perspective* (Toronto: Broadview Press, 2003), p. 56.

41 Personal communication, Dr Theresa Reidy. See www.sipo.ie/en/reports/register-of-third-parties/explanatory-note-for-third-parties.pdf (accessed 10 June 2020) for further information.

42 www.thejournal.ie/kanto-vote-referendum-3914073-Mar2018/ (accessed 20 July 2019).

43 There have been 14 initiatives and referendums since 1991. See also D. Auers, J. Ruus and A. Krupavicius, "Financing referendums and initiatives in the Baltic states", in K.G. Lutz and S. Hug (eds), *Financing Referendum Campaigns* (London: Palgrave Macmillan, 2010), pp. 81–106.

44 Republic of Lithuania Law on Funding of, and Control over Funding of, Political Parties and Political Campaigns, 23 August 2004 No. IX-2428, as amended 6 December 2011 – No XI-1777.

45 Ibid., Art. 2.

46 Ibid., Art. 10.

47 Ibid., Art. 10 (s) 11.

48 Ibid., Art. 12.

49 See C. Morris, "Improving our democracy or a fraud on the community? A closer look at New Zealand's citizens-initiated referenda act 1993", *Statute Law Review* 25(2) (2004), pp. 116–135.

50 Personal communication, Benjaman Baker, NZ Electoral Commission, May 2019.

51 Law no. 15-A/98 of 3 April 1998 (amended several times).

52 See Article 19.° and 20.° of the law on the Financing of Political Parties and Electoral Campaigns (LORF). Further, accounts are submitted to the National Election Commission (CNE) by each party or group of electors within a maximum time limit of 90 days after the results have been proclaimed (Article 74 of the LORF).

53 Eleven issues were put to a public vote on seven occasions since the country split from Czechoslovakia in 1992.

54 Personal communication, Miroslav Nemčok, Masaryk University.
55 Ibid.
56 Taiwan has a Freedom House rating of 97 – marginally ahead of Japan (96) and significantly higher than South Korea (83). See Freedomhouse.org.
57 Shauna Reilly, *Direct Democracy: A Double-Edged Sword* (London: Rienner, 2018), p. 56.
58 The recall is used more sparingly. An attempt to recall President Chen Shui-bian – the first non Kuomintang president – got one million signatures but parliament (with a Democratic Progressive Party majority) did not authorise the recall. In 2015 Kuomintang (KMT) representative Alex Tsai faced a recall. Although 97 per cent of those voting supported the recall, the turnout of 24 per cent fell well short of the 50 per cent turnout requirement. "Editorial: Alex Tsai vote reveals recall flaws", *Taipei Times*, 15 February 2015.
59 Referendum Act stipulates, Art.20(1–2).
60 Regulations of Licensing and Management on Funding for Referendums (lately amended date: 2018–05–11), Article 8.
61 European Commission for Democracy Through Law – Venice Commission, Code for Good Practice, p. 20.
62 Ranney, "Regulating the referendum", p. 92.
63 Charles Bell and Charles Price, *Californian Government Today: Politics of Reform* (Chicago: University of Chicago Press, 1988), p. 103.
64 Ranney, "Regulating the referendum", p. 95.
65 Ibid.
66 Paul Kildea and George Williams, "Reworking Australia's referendum machinery", *Alternative Law Journal* 35(1) (2010), pp. 22–26 (n 11, p. 25).
67 Petia Gueorguieva, "Les élections européennes en Bulgarie de 2014. Élections en crise, Studia Politica", *Romanian Political Science Review* 14(3) (2014), pp. 377–394.
68 Petia Gueorguieva, written evidence, 3 May 2019.
69 Sagnr 2019–1780 Økonomi- og indenrigsministeren, Spørgsmål nr. 430. Information provided by Alex Ahrendtsen, MF (11th April).
70 Art. 11, Loi constitutionnelle n° 2008–724 de modernisation des institutions de la Ve République.
71 An attempt to block the privatisation of airports was underway as this book was being written. See www.monde-diplomatique.fr/2019/06/ENDEWELD/59940 (accessed 20 July 2019).
72 Personal communication, Professor Laurence Morel, University of Lille.
73 The title of the law is Legge 3 giugno 1999, n. 15 "Nuove norme in materia di rimborso delle spese per consultazioni elettorali e referendarie e abrogazione delle disposizioni concernenti la contribuzione volontaria ai

movimenti e partiti politici. Gazzetta Ufficiale n. 129 del 4 giugno 1999" (in English, "New rules on the reimbursement of expenses for electoral and referendum consultations and repeal of the provisions concerning the voluntary contribution to political movements and parties").

74 www.referendum-commissie.nl/subsidie/subsidieregeling (accessed 19 July 2019).
75 Geissel, "Direct democracy and its (perceived) consequences", p. 155.
76 Personal communication, Caroline Vernaillen, Democracy International.
77 *Patricia McKenna* v. *An Taoiseach and Others* (No. 2) [S.C. Nos. 361 and 366 of 1995].
78 The word comes from the Urdu word purdah which translates as "curtain" or "veil".
79 Andrew Blick, written evidence, 12 June 2019.
80 Franz Vranitzky quoted in M. Qvortrup, *A Comparative Study of Referendums* (Manchester: Manchester University Press, 2005), p. 154.
81 Stefan Vospernik, written evidence, 28 August 2019.
82 Mitsuhiko Okamoto, written evidence, 12 June 2019.
83 Caroline Verneilen, written evidence, 11 June 2019.
84 Personal communication, Uwe Serdühlt, June 2019.
85 Saskia Hollander, written evidence, 3 June 2019.
86 Likum par tautas nobalsošanu, likumu ierosināšanu un Eiropas pilsoņu iniciatīvu (Law on National Referendum, Legislative Initiative and European Citizens' Initiative), adopted on 31 March 1994.
87 Referendum (Machinery Provisions) Act 1984 (Cth) s 11(b)(i)-(ii).
88 Ibid., s 11(4)(a).
89 *Reith* v. *Morling* (1988) 83 ALR 667.
90 Ruichuan Yu, written evidence, 12 May 2019.
91 Referendum Act, Art. 17 (1–4).
92 Ruichuan Yu, written evidence, 12 May 2019.
93 Theresa Reidy, written evidence, April 2019.
94 www.bbc.co.uk/news/uk-politics-eu-referendum-35980571 (accessed 26 August 2019).
95 Though it should be noted that the stock recovered the value. See www.cbsnews.com/news/facebook-stock-price-recovers-all-134-billion-lost-in-after-cambridge-analytica-datascandal/ (accessed 28 September 2020).
96 See www.theguardian.com/uk-news/2019/jul/30/cambridge-analytica-did-work-for-leave-eu-emails-confirm (accessed 22 August 2019).
97 Andrew Blick, written evidence, 7 June 2019.
98 Kildea and Williams, "Reworking Australia's referendum machinery", pp. 22, 26.
99 Referendum (Machinery Provisions) Amendment Act 2013 (Cth) s 4.

100 Ron Levy, written evidence, 21 May 2019.
101 https://data.worldbank.org/indicator/IT.NET.USER.ZS (accessed 22 August 2019).
102 Mitsuhiko Okamoto, written evidence, 12 June 2018.
103 I am grateful to Uwe Serdühlt for this information.
104 For an English translation of the Federal Act on Political Rights, see: www.admin.ch/opc/en/classified-compilation/19760323/201511010000/161.1.pdf.
105 Bericht des Bundesrates vom 10.5.2017, Rechtliche Basis für Social Media: Erneute Standortbestimmung.
106 On direct democracy in the Baltic states see, respectively, Dorora Maj, "Direct democracy in Lithuania", "Direct democracy in Latvia" and "Direct democracy in Estonia", all in Maria Marczewska-Rytko (ed.), *Handbook of Direct Democracy in Central and Eastern Europe after 1989* (Opladen: Barbara Budrich Publishers, 2018), pp. 96ff, 131ff and 146ff.
107 www.rand.org/pubs/research_reports/RR1577.html (accessed 28 September 2020).
108 www.reuters.com/article/us-lithuania-russia-cyber/russian-hacking-threatens-lithuanias-banks-survey-idUSKBN18X29T (accessed 5 May 2020).
109 Dorota Maj, written evidence, 10 May 2019.
110 Advertising Act, 12.03.2008, "Riigi Teataja" I 2008, 15, 108, Art. 11.
111 Originally, Likum par tautas nobalsošanu, likumu ierosināšanu un Eiropas pilsoņu iniciatīvu "Latvijas Vēstnesis" [Latvian Journal of Law], 47 (178), 20.04.1994.
112 Law on National Referendum, Legislative Initiative and European Citizens' Initiative, Art. 31(3).
113 K.A. Curtis, J. Jupille and D. Leblang, "Iceland on the rocks: The mass political economy of sovereign debt resettlement", *International Organization* 68(3) (2014), pp. 721–740.
114 Ms. Hildur Margrét Jóhannsdóttir, written evidence, The Icelandic Embassy in London, May 2019.
115 Lei n.º 72-A/2015, Art. 6.
116 Ibid., Art. 11.1.
117 Ibid., 11(3).
118 On referendums in Slovakia see Miroslav Nemčok and Peter Spáč, "Referendum as a party tool: The case of Slovakia", *East European Politics and Societies* 33(3) (2018), pp. 755–777.
119 Ibid., p. 759.
120 Miroslav Nemčok, PhD, written evidence, 26 March 2019.
121 Ibid.
122 Laurence Morel, written evidence, 3 May 2019.

123 We have only touched upon electoral courts in passing. However, their role cannot be underestimated. The composition of them can be a cause for controversy. The Tribunal Superior Eleitoral strikes a fair balance and might be a candidate for the best practice model. The composition of the court is ruled by Article 119 of the Brazilian constitution. This stipulates that the court shall be composed by seven members. Three of them shall be elected by secret vote from among the Justices of the Supreme Federal Court and two other judges shall be elected by secret vote from among the Justices of the Superior Court of Justice. The remaining two shall be appointed by the Federal President from among six lawyers of notable juridical knowledge and good moral reputation nominated by the Supreme Federal Court.

124 Professor Octavio Amorim Neto, written evidence, 16 May 2019.

125 Ece Özlem Atikcan, *Framing the European Union: The Power of Political Arguments in Shaping European Integration* (Cambridge: Cambridge University Press, 2015).

126 N: 1638, www.pressgazette.co.uk/eu-referendum-bbc-must-important-source-for-voters-but-social-media-trumps-journalism-for-the-young/ (accessed 26 August 2019).

127 Marina Dekavalla, *Framing Referendum Campaigns in the News* (Manchester: Manchester University Press, 2018), p. 58ff.

128 Vospernik, S. (2014). *Modelle der direkten Demokratie.* Baden Baden: Nomos Verlagsgesellschaft mbH & Co. KG.

129 Stefan Vospernik, written evidence, 28 August 2019.

130 Direct Citizen Participation in State and Local Government Act, Art. 16 (1).

131 Pedro Tavares de Almeida, "Portugal", in Dieter Nohlen and Philip Stöver (eds), *Elections in Europe: A Data Handbook* (Oxford: Oxford University Press, 2010), pp. 1525–1577.

132 Tiago Tibúrico and Pedro Tavares de Almeida, written evidence, 27 March 2019.

133 Lei Orgânica do Regime do Referendo, Art. 44.

134 Ibid., Art. 46.

135 Ibid., Art 57.

136 Ibid., Art. 58.

137 Ibid., Art. 57.2c.

138 Ibid., Art. 61(1).

139 Ibid., Art. 61(2).

140 Ibid., Art. 62.

141 Eesti Rahvusringhäälingu seadus (Estonian Public Broadcasting Act 2007), Art. 6.

142 Dorota Maj, written evidence, 10 May 2019.

143 Ms. Hildur Margrét Jóhannsdóttir, written evidence, The Icelandic Embassy in London, May 2019.
144 Miroslav Nemcok, written evidence, 10 May 2019.
145 Ley Orgánica 2/1980, de 18 de enero, sobre la regulación de las distintas modalidades de referendum, Art. 14.
146 Dr Veronica Anghel, written evidence, 13 May 2019.
147 See Decision of the National Audiovisual Council no. 220/2011 on the Audiovisual Content Regulatory Code. Art. 3.
148 General Audio-visual Law No. 54/2002 Art. 42. Further, in national referendums in Romania, both public and private radio and television stations must according to Law no. 3/2000 (Legea nr. 3/2000 privind organizarea şi desfăşurarea referendumului) and according to the subsequent Audiovisual Law (Legae nr. 504/2002) provide a fair balance of views.

Part IV

Improving direct democracy

Chapter 5
Referendums and deliberative democracy

"We need a referendum based on facts", wrote a commentator in an op-ed after the Brexit referendum in the United Kingdom[1]. The question addressed in this chapter is how or, indeed, if, referendums can be compatible with this ideal; in other words, if a large-scale direct democratic exercise grounded in "facts" is possible. In the concrete case, the question will be framed more narrowly, can referendums be compatible with the ideals of deliberative democracy? And, more particularly, if mechanisms can be put in place to facilitate this ideal[2].

In this section, the practice of referendums will be contrasted with other mechanisms such as mini-publics or citizens' juries (also known as citizens' assemblies) to see if these can improve the process. The latter analysis will largely be based on recent Irish experiences. The overall hypothesis – though not stated in Popperian terms – is that the often-criticised aspects of referendums can – in part – be remedied by institutional mechanisms for "discussion[s] aimed at producing reasonable, [and] well informed opinions"[3].

Referendums and deliberation

There has been a recent increase in the number of referendums held per decade in democratic countries. One of the reasons for this is likely to be a result of the fact that "a shift in political attitudes has taken place, the effect of which has been to make citizens more confident in their ability to make key policy decisions or less confident in the ability of elected representatives to do so"[4]. Moreover, "[Polls suggest that] elected officials are often seen to be out of touch", and as a result, "ordinary citizens feel an increasing sense of political powerlessness and express little trust in the ability of political institutions to address their concerns"[5].

Indeed, it is a general and global trend. At a global level, an average of 66 per cent of those polled by Pew Research Centre described as "good" or "very good" a "democratic system where citizens, not elected officials, vote directly on major national issues that become law"[6]. And, generally speaking, majorities in all countries polled show support for more referendums (see also Chapter 1)[7].

This public enthusiasm for referendums is in sharp contrast to the established canon of representative democratic theorists of Western political philosophy. *The Federalist* was opposed to referendums on the ground that "the public voice, pronounced by representatives of the people, will be more consonant to the public good than if pronounced by the people themselves"[8]. John Stuart Mill found that "if the good of the governed is the proper business of government, [then] it is utterly impossible that the people should directly attend to it. The utmost they can do is to give some of their best men [and women] a commission to look after it"[9].

In the last century, Spanish philosopher José Ortega y Gasset, in a similar elitist vein, opined that direct democracy was undesirable as "the mass crushes beneath it everything that is different, everything that is excellent, individual, qualified and select"[10]. More contemporary scholars have followed suit. Giovanni Sartori postulated that referendums give citizens responsibility to decide issues they do not understand[11]. Haskell's observation, that "only representative institutions can fill the need for informed deliberation, consensus and compromise, all of which are necessary for good government in the public interest"[12], seems to be widely shared. Indeed, Bernard Manin, in his *The Principles of Representative Government*, excluded discussion of referendums, apparently on the grounds that these were incompatible with his ideal of representative government[13]. Others have taken a different view. "Can democracy be saved?" asked the noted scholar Donatella della Porta, and found the answer in part in "participation, deliberation and social movements"[14].

Yet, much as representative government provides the (theoretical) conditions conducive to deliberation, this system is subject to *logrolling*, *pork-barrelling* and various forms of *rent-seeking*. As Irish playwright, critic, polemicist and political activist George Bernard Shaw pessimistically put it in a play from 1903, "Democracy substitutes election by the incompetent many for appointment by the corrupt few"[15]. That is, we are caught between the Scylla of a demagogical form of direct democracy and the Charybdis of rent-seeking representative democracy. How do we overcome this?

One answer has been to engage in deliberative democratic practices. Maija Setälä, for example, has suggested that referendums can be complemented by mechanisms of deliberation, "Supporters of deliberative and participatory democracy … point out the developmental potential of political participation and argue that initiatives and referendums encourage public debate on issues, which increases people's competence"[16].

Although sceptics might – with some justification – object that this "does not … address the capacity issue"[17], deliberative theorists (and practitioners) may answer with the late Benjamin Barber's often cited words, "democracy is best taught by practicing it"[18]. We shall return to this below in the section about Ireland. Before doing so, however, it is necessary to outline what is meant by deliberative democracy and how different strands of this might be made compatible with the practice of referendums.

Deliberative democracy: a basic overview

Beginning in the 1970s, but accelerating in the 1990s, there was a growing literature on deliberative democracy. The research was (and is) heterogeneous, to say the least. Spanning from philosophical writings of Jürgen Habermas[19], through the mid-level theories of deliberative ethics of Fung[20], to more practical writings on citizens' juries[21] and democratic mini-publics[22], by writers like John Drysek[23] and James Fiskin[24], deliberative democracy has more recently entered legal theory and touched upon constitutional politics of referendums in the work of Ron Levy[25] and Hoi Kong's work on republican deliberation[26], and in work on divided societies and deliberation by Ian O'Flynn[27].

The aim of mini-publics and citizens' assemblies or juries is to find a way for a representative sample of citizens to reach informed decisions on contentious and controversial policy issues. Yet, as practically all of the foremost writers within this area of research admitted, there were limits to this approach. As Jane Mansbridge and colleagues wrote, "No single forum, however ideally constructed, could possess deliberative capacity sufficient to legitimate most of the decisions and policies that democracies adopt"[28].

Under ideal circumstances, a referendum (provided the turnout is high) can be a legitimate mechanism for making decisions, as it "has the potential to facilitate the 'voice' of groups in such a way that they share constitutional authorship"[29]. However, as the quote by Grayling, at the beginning of this chapter, suggests, the Brexit referendum (and perhaps others) was deficient in other ways as especially the "leave-side" – so it was alleged – deliberately distorted assertions, made oversimplifications and used arguments that were based on pure fabrication (see the previous chapter).

Given these limitations on the part of deliberative democracy (lack of representativeness) and some of the perceived shortcomings of referendums (i.e. it being prone to distortions of facts)[30], can we devise a way of strengthening both by combining them?

Can we extract the best of both worlds in practical politics? Given that we cannot have large-scale deliberation, is there a minimal requirement for how referendums can be conducted to meet the normative ideal?

At the prescriptive level, this chapter accepts *a priori* the contention that in a democracy the participants have "the duty to become informed, to get the facts, to listen to expert advice and arguments, to discuss, to deliberate, to form a judgment, and to act strictly and always in the best interests of their country"[31].

As we have seen, recent referendums (and we have covered some of them in this book already) have been criticised for reducing complex issues into oversimplified dichotomies, which lend themselves to emotional arguments[32], "referendums, come in for particular criticism, [as they are] often blamed for exacerbating polarisation and facilitating misrepresentation and disinformation". As a result of this, "elitists might suggest that this simply means that 'the people' cannot be trusted with policy choices"[33]. Yet, other scholars have stressed that referendums can be compatible with the normative ideal (see Tierney's analysis of the Scottish referendum on independence[34]).

The question, then, is if, and under which conditions, such a debate can be established in a time of heightened political tension, such as during a referendum campaign.

Deliberative forums in referendums

As noted above, there has been an increased interest in combining referendums and mechanisms of direct democracy among theoreticians in recent years. At the more theoretical end, Goodin and Dryzek have discussed the "macro-political impact of minipublics"[35]. More recently, these proposals have been further developed into concrete plans for improving the information available for citizens[36]. For example, David Altman has proposed the establishment of "Deliberative Citizens Commission[s]" in "which a stratified random sample of eligible voters are convened for the purpose of discussion, deliberating and offering a policy question that will be decided upon in a future popular vote"[37]. And, Irish scholar Jane Suiter has analysed the deliberative forum in Ireland before the 2018 referendum as an example of this[38]. A recent study by Alan Renwick and Michela Palese suggests it has almost become the consensus that "citizens assemblies" provide a mechanism for public deliberation, have played a "very positive role" and have been "used to good effect … to provide a statement of what a representative sample of citizens think about an issue"[39].

Yet, the experience with mini-publics in resolving actual political issues remains patchy. Admittedly, experiences with citizens' assemblies on electoral reform in Canada suggested that these "have the potential to provide impartial, independent deliberation on the law of democracy, including the rules for redistricting, campaign finance, political party funding or future consideration of electoral reform"[40]. Yet, these issues are not a high-salience and they are not contentious in the same way as highly partisan issues like Brexit, same-sex marriage and abortion. This makes the Canadian case unsuitable for comparison as electoral reform is an issue that does not cause division – at least not among the general public. (Among political scientists and other anoraks, of course, this is different!)

In Ireland, however, the citizens' assemblies pertained in three cases to long-standing, controversial and divisive issues such as marriage equality, the ban on blasphemy in the constitution and, above all, abortion. Given the high profile and the contentious nature of the issues debated at the Irish citizens' assembly, it provides a good test case for assessing the suitability of this deliberative process for controversial issues such as peace agreements, EU membership and other divisive issues. In the words of a recent study, "Ireland … not only stands out internationally as the first country in the world to hold two constitutional mini-publics in quick succession, but also as a world leader in the linking of deliberative democracy (mini-publics) and direct democracy (referendums)"[41].

This glowing reference, it should be noted, is tempered by the fact that the authors were advocates for introducing this mechanism into the Irish political system. Does their conclusion stand up to closer scrutiny? To answer this question, it is necessary to understand the context.

Following the financial crisis, trust in the political class in Ireland was at an all-time low, and a group of scholars and activists established the forum We the Citizens, which advocated the use of mini-publics. The "aim was to demonstrate the virtue of deliberative approaches by holding our own (pilot) citizens' assembly"[42]. Following this, almost by accident, the idea of mini-publics was taken up by the opposition party Fine Gael before the election in 2011.

Following the historic defeat of Fianna Fáil in the 2011 general election, Fine Gael and its new coalition partner, Labour, agreed to establish a Constitutional Convention in late 2012. This, in part, operated as a citizens' jury. Comprised of 66 randomly selected members of the public and 33 politicians, the Convention met over 15 months to debate major constitutional issues, one of which was the contentious issue of marriage equality. We will focus on this issue as it was the most controversial one and hence a good way of gauging whether deliberative forums can be useful in resolving divisive subjects.

First, it is necessary to understand how the process worked. The format of the deliberation was as follows:

> The Convention discussed this [marriage equality] issue in its third session held on the weekend of 13–14 April 2013. As per its standard practice, the Convention members' deliberations were informed by expert briefing documents and presentations, submissions from advocacy groups and individuals (an unprecedentedly large number of submissions were made for this topic – amounting to over one thousand pieces of varying lengths), and presentations by a number of advocates (included in the mix a Catholic Bishop, the grown-up children of same-sex couples, and a gay man opposed to marriage equality)[43].

Two years later the referendum was called, which resulted in a 62 per cent majority for legalising same-sex marriage[44]. In their study of the Constitutional Convention, Reidy and colleagues found:

> The contribution of the Constitutional Convention to this referendum process was threefold. In the first instance, the fact that the Convention members voted so overwhelmingly in favour of the recommendation and the intense media interest that surrounded its debate and recommendations somewhat forced the hand of the Taoiseach. As someone who is instinctively socially conservative and who up till then had resisted requests to express a view on marriage equality Enda Kenny moved quite quickly to endorse the Convention's recommendation. It would have been easy enough for him to forestall demands for a referendum on this matter given that it was not included in the Programme for Government.

However, this upbeat assessment was in sharp contrast to the cynicism that characterised the public – and to a degree the academic – debate before the Constitutional Convention. Legal scholar Conor O'Mahony dismissed the forum as the "so-called constitution", and described it as a "joke"[45]. Likewise, commentator Fintan O'Toole lamented that the new government's promises of "radical root and branch reform" merely had resulted in "piecemeal reform, beginning with trivialities"[46].

At a more systematic level, these perceived shortcomings about the process were analysed in the wake of the referendum. Thus Carolan found that the virtues of the Constitutional Convention had "been oversold", and that the "process in fact suffered from a number of serious limitations that undermine its claims to either representative or deliberative legitimacy"[47]. In particular he questioned the representativeness of the participants. Yet, despite his concerns, he concluded that the Constitutional Convention had,

> Been a positive and engaging experience for participants. As has been the experience with other experiments in participatory deliberation. [T]he Irish experience confirms once again—if confirmation was

> needed—that citizens are capable of engaging in a serious manner with complex questions of constitutional or political reform[48].

As a result of these – largely constructive – criticisms the Fine Gael–Independent minority government, which took office in 2016, committed itself to repeating the format of a deliberative forum, though this time with one major difference. In the government's statement before it took office, it committed itself to establishing "a Citizens' Assembly, within six months, and *without* participation by politicians"[49].

Having learned from the criticisms of the Constitutional Convention, all the 99 members of the citizens' assembly were selected by representative criteria included gender, age, location and social class[50].

Although not explicitly mentioned in the government programme, abortion was the first issue to be discussed by the citizens' assembly. That this issue was debated is noteworthy and significant. Again, a bit of context is necessary. Unlike most other North European countries, where over 80 per cent support a pro-choice stance[51], Ireland has always been the odd one out and – at least until recently – markedly more socially conservative than any other West European country. This was reflected in voting behaviour. In 1983, the Irish voters supported a pro-life amendment to the constitution by 67 per cent[52], and this opposition to abortion was reaffirmed in 1992, when it was made illegal to travel to terminate a pregnancy[53]. The votes were divisive, and Ireland was subsequently split over this contentious issue[54]. Yet, while abortion was a controversial issue throughout the period after 1992, it only rose to the top of the political agenda in 2012, when the Indian-born Savita Halappanavar died after University Hospital Galway denied her request for an abortion following an incomplete miscarriage in October 2012. Her death led to renewed debate about abortion.

In light of this, it was not surprising that the Taoiseach Enda Kenny – though personally unconvinced about the matter – sought to diffuse the issue by referring it to a citizens' assembly. While the citizens' assembly discussed other matters apart from abortion, including blasphemy, an ageing society and climate change, there were only referendums on the termination of pregnancies and blasphemy[55].

However, abortion was the most contentious issue and we will therefore focus on this subject. The citizens' assembly met under the chairmanship of Mary Laffoy (a Supreme Court judge) and discussed abortion at five day-long meetings between October 2016 and April 2017. During this time the Assembly received more than 13,000 emails and submissions and listened to testimonies, presentations and evidence from pro-life and pro-choice organisations, as well as from the Catholic Church, humanist societies and medical and legal experts[56].

The Assembly was concluded by holding a number of indicative votes. The delegates voted for a proposal that allowed the Oireachtas (parliament) to legislate regarding "[the] termination of pregnancy, any rights of the unborn, and any rights of the pregnant woman"[57]. Following this gate-keeper vote, the members spent the following day narrowing down the options. These votes suggested that abortion should be available in the case of "risk to the life of the woman"[58].

Following the conclusion of the citizens' assembly, the new Taoiseach, Leo Varadkar of Fine Gael, announced the government would bring forward legislation to hold a referendum, which would give the Oireachtas the right to legislation on abortion. This referendum was held in May 2018. Sixty-six per cent of the voters supported the proposal to remove the Eighth Amendment from the Irish Constitution (which had banned abortion *tout court*). In December 2018, the Oireachtas passed the Health (Regulation of Termination of Pregnancy) Act 2018 by 90 votes to 15 – with 12 abstentions[59]. The Act permitted termination of pregnancies under medical supervision, up to 12 weeks, and later if pregnancy poses a serious health risk to the mother or in cases of fatal foetal abnormality.

In the wake of the referendum, several commentators and academics praised the process and the way in which the citizens' assembly had facilitated a compromise[60].

Can – and should – the Irish experience be emulated? There is reason to be sceptical. For starters, it would seem the participants had too little time to debate the issues. With 13,000 submissions and only a week to debate them, the process hardly provided for deliberation or discussion[61]. In the word of one study (about the Constitutional Convention), "the tight timelines ... meant that very little time could be spent on a discussion of broader principles or values because a lot of essential and sometimes technical information needed to be covered"[62].

Yet, despite this, the members of the citizens' assembly overwhelmingly agreed with the statement, "I did feel free to raise my opinions"[63]. Moreover, and perhaps equally important, 62 per cent of the members of the Constitutional Convention "felt sufficient time had been devoted to each issue"[64]. Further, according to the evaluation carried out by Suiter and colleagues, "only 21 per cent [of Convention members] disagreed or completely disagreed that they had changed their view"[65]. One critic of the citizens' assembly admitted to changing his mind:

> The establishment of assemblies in advance of the referendum has an impact on the deliberative nature of the referendum in the wider community. In both referendums [in 2018 – abortion and blasphemy] there is a positive and statistically significant effect on the probability of voting Yes by those who felt they fully understood the issues[66].

These positive responses are in sharp contrast to the verdict on the Brexit referendum. Of course, it ought to be noted that in a democracy "voting yes" is not necessarily a desirable outcome. Nevertheless, the process in Ireland was seen as one that provided for a more balanced debate – something that is even acknowledged by the opponents of abortion such as Archbishop Michael Jackson, who spoke about the positive debate and "the telling and listening to stories". And he continued, in a paragraph that sums up the spirit of democratic deliberation:

> Telling and hearing stories builds relationships of understanding across seemingly unbridgeable divides. People have found in the stories of lives lived for others the outworking of friendship and compassion with people who experience crisis and vulnerability. These are people like any of us – people who hold strong opinions, people whose values infuse their consciences while they continue to agree to disagree agreeably with one another[67].

This is in sharp contrast to the British Brexit referendum where most commentators – irrespective of their attitude to the European Union – were critical of the referendum process and the public deliberations that went before it[68].

Summing up

"If the Brexit referendum had been preceded by such a dignified and humble exercise in listening and thinking, it would surely have been a radically different experience". Thus, wrote Fintan O'Toole, a one-time critic of deliberative assemblies[69]. There are no "correct" results in referendums. The process of democracy – provided it takes place within the limits of a Rawlsian "Overlapping Consensus"[70] – is a neutral one. But to be legitimate, the process must be based on evidence, a balanced debate and without undue influence by the government or those with the deepest pockets. Many referendums have not lived up to this.

The question is if this can be remedied through mini-publics or deliberative assemblies? While the examples of citizens' assemblies are too small to draw statistically valid conclusions, the evidence from Ireland, provided in this chapter, suggests that the use of a citizens' assembly before a referendum can lead to a more balanced debate.

The recent experiences with deliberative assemblies before, respectively, the referendum on same-sex marriage (2015) and the abortion referendum (2018) suggest that citizens' assemblies can play an important and positive role in framing the debate on a controversial political issue[71].

Needless to say, this institutional innovation cannot stand alone and is not the only factor behind the discursive nature of a debate. But the experience from the Republic of Ireland is according to all reports a positive one. The referendum process in Eire is far from ideal, and there is still a legitimate concern that one-sided campaign spending may have an impact on the outcome of referendums in the Republic of Ireland (see the previous chapter).

Ireland too needs reform, but the evidence from that country suggests that referendums can be made more democratic, more legitimate, and resolve long-standing political conflicts if the vote is preceded by a deliberative assembly. John Dryzek once wrote that, "the essence of democratic legitimacy should be sought … in the ability of all individuals subject to a collective decision to engage in authentic deliberation about that decision"[72]. The Irish process of citizens' assemblies is still a far cry from this ideal, but it does provide an answer to Grayling's request for a "referendum based on facts".

Excursus: participatory budgeting in Mexico and Brazil

Participatory budgeting is another kind of deliberative democracy that has gained a lot of attention in recent years. Under this system, citizens are involved in the process of deciding how public money is spent. The system was first pioneered in the Brazilian City of Porto Alegre in Brazil in the late 1980s.

As a result of the involvement of the citizens, the local government has become better at supporting the poorest parts of the city, has improved service and infrastructure, has strengthened governance and increased citizen participation. Those evaluating the process deemed it a success. It was a real success in terms of involving people typically left outside of the political process. The money allocated to the participatory budget in Porto Alegre was 21% of the total social budget[73].

A similar institution has recently been introduced in Mexico. Following the elections in 2018, the new left-of-centre government was (officially) keen to introduce mechanisms of direct democracy. Hence, they proposed to introduce the Civic Participation Law, which allowed for participatory budgeting at the local level, including in Mexico City. The process is as follows:

Mexico City's Congress is composed of 66 representatives who work in committees to prepare bills. Once a committee has reached agreement on a bill, the proposal goes to the full Congress to be voted on in a plenary session. If the bill is approved by a simple majority of votes, it becomes a law. The Civic Participation Law regulates, among other things, the participatory budgeting (pb) and the citizen councils (cc) mechanisms. The first one gives citizens the opportunity to propose and vote for projects on how to spend 3 per cent of the city's public budget. The latter allows neighbourhood representatives to work as a liaison between the municipal authorities and the citizens[74].

As Greta Rios, an activist, reported, the government suddenly began to drag their feet, and delay the implementation of plan. Indeed, it was only after a lawsuit and intensive lobbying by civil society groups that the law was enacted. Was it all a show? Was it cynical window-dressing? Not entirely. According to Rios, who initiated the lawsuit:

"This law is far from perfect, but it is undoubtedly better than having no law at all. For me, it has been a very tiring and long road, but in the end, I have the satisfaction of having proved several points. For one, the democratic system does protect your rights if you are willing to actively fight for them. It also became very clear that individual citizens have much more power than authorities want us to know"[75].

Notes

1 www.theneweuropean.co.uk/top-stories/ac-grayling-second-referendum-based-on-facts-1-5846989 (accessed 19 January 2019).
2 For an overview see, John Dryzek, *Deliberative Democracy and Beyond: Liberals, Critics, Contestations* (Oxford: Oxford University, 2002).
3 Simone Chambers, "Deliberative democratic theory", *Annual Review of Political Science* 6(1) (2003), pp. 307–326 (p. 309).
4 Matthew Mendelsohn and Andres Parkin, "Introduction", in Matthew Mendelsohn and Andres Parkin (eds), *Referendum Democracy: Citizens, Elites and Deliberation in Referendum Campaigns* (Basingstoke: Palgrave, 2001), p. 6.
5 Laurence LeDuc, *The Politics of Direct Democracy: Referendums in Global Perspective* (Toronto: Broadview Press, 2003) p. 11.
6 www.pewglobal.org/2017/10/16/democracy-widely-supported-little-backing-for-rule-by-strong-leader-or-military/pg_2017-10-16_global-democracy_2-02/ (accessed 18 March 2019).
7 Ibid.
8 The Federalist [James Madison] [1787] "Federalist Paper No. 10", in Clinton Rositer (ed.), *The Federalist Papers* (New York: Signet Classics, 2003), pp. 71–79 (p. 77).
9 John Stuart Mill [1861] "Considerations on representative government", in John Gray (ed.), *John Stuart Mill: On Liberty and Other Essays* (Oxford: Oxford University Press, 1991), pp. 205–470 (p. 456).
10 José Ortega y Gasset, *The Revolt of the Masses* (New York: W.W. Norton, 1964), p. 18.
11 Giovanni Sartori, *The Theory of Democracy Revisited* (Washington, DC: CQ Press, 1987), p. 120.
12 John Haskell, *Direct Democracy or Representative Government? Dispelling the Populist Myth* (London: Westview Press, 2001), p. 11.
13 See Bernard Manin, *Principles of Representative Government* (Cambridge: Cambridge University Press, 1997).
14 D. Della Porta, *Can Democracy be Saved? Participation, Deliberation and Social Movements* (Oxford: John Wiley & Sons, 2013).

15 George Bernard Shaw, *Man and Superman* (London: Penguin, 2000), p. 212.
16 M. Setäla, "On the problems of responsibility and accountability in referendums", *European Journal of Political Research* 45(4) (2006), p. 717.
17 Stephen Tierney, *Constitutional Referendums: The Theory and Practice of Republican Deliberation* (Oxford: Oxford University Press, 2012), p. 35, n. 49.
18 Benjamin Barber, *Strong Democracy: Participatory Politics for a New Age* (Berkeley: University of California Press, 1984), p. 235.
19 Jürgen Habermas, *Theorie des Kommunikativen Handelns I-II* (Frankfurt: Suhrkamp Verlag, 1981).
20 Archon Fung, "Deliberation before the revolution: Toward an ethics of deliberative democracy in an unjust world", *Political Theory* 33(3) (2005), pp. 397–419.
21 G. Smith, *Democratic Innovations: Designing Institutions for Citizen Participation* (Cambridge: Cambridge University Press, 2009).
22 See M. Setälä, *Deliberative Mini-Publics: Involving Citizens in the Democratic Process* (Colchester: ECPR Press, 2014); R.E. Goodin and J.S. Dryzek, "Deliberative impacts: The macro-political uptake of mini-publics", *Politics & Society* 34(2) (2006), pp. 219–244.
23 John S. Dryzek, *Discursive Democracy: Politics, Policy, and Political Science* (Cambridge: Cambridge University Press, 1994).
24 James Fiskin, *Democracy and Deliberation: New Directions for Democratic Reform* (New Haven: Yale University Press, 1991).
25 Ron Levy, "The law of deliberative democracy: Seeding the field", *Election Law Journal* 12(4) (2013), pp. 355–371.
26 Hoi Kong, "Towards a civic republican theory of Canadian constitutional law", *Review of Constitutional Studies* 15(2) (2010), pp. 249–279. See also Tierney, *Constitutional Referendums*.
27 Ian O' Flynn, "Divided societies and deliberative democracy", *British Journal of Political Science* 37(4) (2007), pp. 731–751.
28 Jane Mansbridge, James Bohman, Simone Chambers, Thomas Christiano, Archon Fung, John Parkinson, Dennis F. Thompson and Mark E. Warren, "A systemic approach to deliberative democracy", in John Parkinson and Jane Mansbridge (eds) *Deliberative Systems: Deliberative Democracy at the Large Scale* (Cambridge: Cambridge University Press, 2012), pp. 1–26 (p. 1).
29 Joanne McElvoy, "Letting 'the people(s)' decide: Peace referendums and power-sharing settlements", *Democratization* 25(5) (2018), pp. 864–881 (p. 866).
30 For critique of referendums, see David S. Broder, *Democracy Derailed: Initiative Campaigns and the Power of Money* (New York: Harcourt, 2000).
31 www.theneweuropean.co.uk/top-stories/ac-grayling-second-referendum-based-on-facts-1-5846989 (accessed 19 January 2019).
32 Michael Bruterand and Sarah Harrison, "Understanding the emotional act of voting", *Nature: Human Behaviour* 1 (2017), pp. 1–3.

33 Jane Suiter, "Deliberation in action: Ireland's abortion referendum", *Political Insight* 9(3) (2018), p. 30.
34 Tierney, *Constitutional Referendums*.
35 Robert E. Gooding and John S. Dryzek, "Deliberative impacts: The macro-political uptake of minipublics", *Politics and Society* 34(2) (2006), pp. 219–220.
36 See Matt Qvortrup, "Citizenship and contemporary direct democracy", *Perspectives on Politics* 17(3) (2019), pp. 909–911.
37 David Altman, *Citizenship and Contemporary Direct Democracy* (Cambridge: Cambridge University Press, 2019), p. 183.
38 Suiter, "Deliberation in action".
39 Alan Renwick and Michela Palese, *Doing Democracy Better: How Can Information and Discourse in Election and Referendum Campaigns in the UK be Improved?* (London: The Constitution Unit, 2019), p. 237.
40 Michael Pal, "The promise and limits of citizens' assemblies: Deliberation, institutions and the law of democracy", *Queen's Law Journal* 38(2) (2012) pp. 259–294 (p. 290).
41 David M. Farrell, Jane Suiter and Clodagh Harris, " 'Systematizing' constitutional deliberation: The 2016–18 citizens' assembly in Ireland", *Irish Political Studies* 34(1) (2019), pp. 113–123.
42 David Farrell, Eoin O'Malley and Jane Suiter, "Deliberative democracy in action Irish-style: The 2011 we the citizens' assembly", *Irish Political Studies* 28(1) (2013), pp. 99–113 (p. 102).
43 Johan A. Elkink, David M. Farrell, Theresa Reidy and Jane Suiter, "Understanding the 2015 marriage referendum in Ireland: Context, campaign, and conservative Ireland", *Irish Political Studies* 32(3) (2017), pp. 361–381 (p. 362).
44 See Yvonne Murphy, "The marriage equality referendum 2015", *Irish Political Studies* 31(2) (2016), pp. 315–330.
45 Cited in Renwick and Palese, *Doing Democracy Better*, p. 192.
46 Fintan O'Toole, "We ourselves are fit to make a new republic", *Irish Times*, 11 September 2012, A12.
47 Eoin Carolan, "Ireland's constitutional convention: Behind the hype about citizen-led constitutional change", *International Journal of Constitutional Law* 13(3) (2015), pp. 733–748 (p. 733).
48 Ibid., p. 745.
49 The Government of Ireland, *A Program for a Partnership Government*, 11 May 2016, p. 153 [italics added].
50 www.rte.ie/news/2016/0910/815628-citizens-assembly/ (accessed 19 May 2019).
51 See www.pewforum.org/2018/10/29/eastern-and-western-europeans-differ-on-importance-of-religion-views-of-minorities-and-key-social-issues/pf-10-29-18_east-west_-00-05/ (accessed 15 May 2019).

52 Brian Girvin, "Social change and moral politics: The Irish constitutional referendum 1983", *Political Studies* 34(1) (1986), pp. 61–81.
53 Richard Sinnott, "Cleavages, parties and referendums: Relationships between representative and direct democracy in the Republic of Ireland", *European Journal of Political Research* 41(6) (2002), pp. 811–826.
54 Siobhán Mullally, "Debating reproductive rights in Ireland", *Human Rights Quarterly* 27(1) (2005), pp. 78–104.
55 In the referendum on abolishing the blasphemy clause in the Irish constitution, 64 per cent supported deleting the prohibition against blasphemy.
56 www.rte.ie/news/2016/1222/840774-assembly/ (accessed 17 May 2017).
57 www.citizensassembly.ie/en/Meetings/Ballot-4-Results-Tables.pdf (accessed 16 May 2019).
58 www.citizensassembly.ie/en/Meetings/Ballot-4-Results-Tables.pdf (accessed 19 May, 2019).
59 www.irishtimes.com/news/politics/oireachtas/bill-providing-for-access-to-abortion-passes-in-the-d%C3%A1il-1.3722206 (accessed 19 May 2019).
60 Luke Field, "The abortion referendum of 2018 and a timeline of abortion politics in Ireland to date", *Irish Political Studies* 33(4) (2018), pp. 608–628.
61 www.rte.ie/news/2016/1222/840774-assembly/ (accessed 16 May 2019).
62 Jane Suiter, David Farrell and Clodagh Harris, "The Irish constitutional convention: A case of 'high legitimacy'", in Min Reuchamps and Jane Suiter (eds), *Constitutional Deliberative Democracy in Europe* (Colchester: ECPR Press, 2016), pp. 33–51 (p. 44).
63 Quoted in Renwick and Palese, *Doing Democracy Better*, p. 190.
64 Suiter et al., "The Irish constitutional convention", p. 44.
65 Ibid.
66 Suiter quoted in Renwick and Palese, *Doing Democracy Better*, p. 196.
67 Archbishop Michael Jackson, "Lessons from the emphatic yes in referendum", *The Irish Times*, 30 May 2018.
68 John Curtice, "Brexit: Behind the referendum", *Political Insight* 7(2) (2016), pp. 4–7.
69 Fintan O'Toole, "If only Brexit had been run like Ireland's referendum", *The Guardian*, 29 May 2018.
70 John Rawls, "The idea of an overlapping consensus", *Oxford Journal of Legal Studies* 7(1) (1987), pp. 1–25.
71 On "framing", see D. Chong and J.N. Druckman, "Framing theory", *Annual Review of Political Science* 10 (2007), pp. 103–126.
72 John Dryzek, *Deliberative Democracy and Beyond: Liberals, Critics and Contestations* (Oxford: Oxford University Press, 2000), p. v.

73 Y. Sintomer, C. Herzberg and A. Röcke, "From Porto Alegre to Europe: Potentials and limitations of participatory budgeting", *International Journal of Urban and Regional Research* 32(1) (2008), pp. 164–178.
74 Greta Rios, "Mexico: How democracy can be the power of one" (2019), https://twentythirty.com/mexico-how-democracy-can-be-the-power-of-one/ (accessed 12 October 2020).
75 Ibid.

Chapter 6

The recall as a mechanism for increasing accountability: an American case study

"The rulers should be accountable to the ruled; they should in other words be obliged to justify their actions to the ruled and be removable by the ruled", wrote the political scientist Jack Lively in a classic text about democracy[1]. This chapter is about the last part of the sentence, about being "removable by the ruled"; about the institution of "the recall". Very little has been written about this, even though this is an important aspect of democracy[2].

A political scientist has defined the recall as "a form of direct democracy that allows voters to limit an elected official's term in office"[3]. To be a proper recall, the "process begins with an application to circulate a petition for a recall", and, if "the proponents gather the requisite number of signatures, then a special election is held for the recall of that official"[4].

The contention by proponents of the recall is it "keeps office-holders ... more responsive and accountable"[5]. The question is if this hypothesis can be verified.

Political science is often a highly abstract business. The members of the author's profession often focus on the general pattern, and often do so to the exclusion of the very human stories that most voters associate with public affairs. But sometimes the two worlds intersect. The trial *People* v. *Turner* in 2015 was a case in point. In this year, a judge handed down what many regarded as an unduly lenient sentence of six months' imprisonment for sexual assault and attempted rape. This would later have political implications.

The crime that started the whole sorry tale was committed by Stanford student Brock Turner, a frat boy and member of the prestigious university's swimming team – and, as it happens, someone who bore a striking resemblance to the Hollywood actor Zac Efron. It was not an unusual night for the privileged upper middle-class student and Olympic hopeful. He went to an alcohol-fuelled party. One of the other guests was Zhang Xiao Xia, a first generation Chinese American, known by her anglicised name Chanel Miller.

Ms Miller drank too much. She lost consciousness. Mr Turner seized the opportunity and sexually assaulted her. Unfortunately for him, he was discovered. He tried to flee but was caught by the police. The case caused a sensation. All major news outlets across America reported the incident. The trial case was seen as the beginning of the Me Too movement.

There was never much doubt that the defendant was guilty. The usual sentence for this crime was six years. Yet, Judge Aaron Persky – himself also a Stanford graduate – took pity upon the delinquent and declared that "a prison sentence would have a severe impact on him"[6].

But a sentence would arguably have an equally "severe impact" on any young man and the statistical fact is that judges were less concerned about this "impact" if the felon was from an ethnic minority. Indeed, at the time of the offence criminologists found that the sentences for whites were about a third shorter than those for African Americans[7]. That could have been the end of the story. It was not.

Shortly after the trial, citizens gathered signatures with a view to recalling Judge Persky. In California, judges are elected just like politicians and can be removed from office by a vote of the citizens in the Golden State. On 6 June 2018, the *Los Angeles Times* reported that "California voters made history Tuesday, recalling a judge for the first time since 1932"[8].

The question is if this type of democratic procedure is defensible – desirable even. To determine that we will look at the practice of the recall. But before we turn to the empirics, it is useful to consider the history of the device in general, but in particular in America where the procedure has been most common, though it originates from elsewhere and has a very long pedigree.

The history of the recall

Charles de Montesquieu, the famous French nobleman, wine merchant(!) and philosopher was not generally enamoured by popular government. "The people", he insisted, "should not enter the government except to choose their representatives". However, Montesquieu, elitist though he occasionally was, found it indispensable that the representatives "should be accountable to those that have commissioned them"[9]. In other words, the people should be allowed to recall their representatives, if these did not live up to the trust placed in them.

In the history of political theory, this is far from being a radical position. A decade later, Jean-Jacques Rousseau took a similar view in *The Social Contract*, and wrote, "the holders of executive office are not the people's masters but its officers [and] the people can appoint them and *dismiss* them as it pleases – *les diśituer quant il lui plait*"[10].

In the eighteenth century, this was a rather common view. But it wasn't even a novelty then. Indeed, the recall first appeared in the Roman Republic where, in 133 BC Tribune Octavius – according to Plutarch's account – was recalled after he had vetoed a senate Bill[11].

In the middle ages, the prominent philosopher Marsilius of Padua (1275–1342) acknowledged the citizens' right to "remove rulers from office who betrayed their trust"[12]. And, a few hundred years later, the radical Levellers in England, in the seventeenth century, espoused the device – some even believed members of the House of Commons should be subject to revocation[13]. Thus, in the *Agreement of the People* (1647), the Levellers mentioned the power of "removing and calling to account magistrates"[14] (though in the end these ideas came to naught).

When America seceded from Britain in 1776, the idea of the recall – perhaps inspired by Montesquieu – found its way into *The Articles of Confederation* (1781–1789). These provided for the "Recall and replacement of delegates even within their one-year term"[15].

The mechanism was even included in James Madison's first draft of the US constitution. The so-called Virginia Plan stated unequivocally that "members of the National Legislature [should be] subject to recall"[16]. When this draft was rejected, the lack of a recall provision in the US constitution was one of the main objections raised by the anti-Federalists. "Brutus", one of the most celebrated opponents of the Philadelphia constitution, wrote: "It seems an evident dictate of reason, that when a person authorises another to do a piece of business for him, he should retain the power to replace him"[17].

Likewise, in the heated debates in the New York ratifying convention, Melancton Smith – believed to be Brutus' alter ego – again defended the recall, noting that it would be used sparingly, "the power of the recall would not be exercised as often as it ought. It is highly improbable that a man, in whom the state has confided, and who has an established influence, will be recalled, unless his conduct has been notoriously wicked"[18]. This was to no avail, the proposal for a recall was rejected as too radical.

Discussions about it were not revived until after the American Civil War. In the 1880s, as a result of what was perceived as the corruption of the political system and the undue influence of the Party-Machine, so-called Populists championed the use of referendums, initiatives, direct elections of US Senators, primary elections and the recall from the 1880s. The movement in favour of these reforms had a distinct left-wing tenor. To wit, "Populist and Socialist Labor parties [in the United States] urged the adoption of the recall in several of their national and state platforms in the 1890s"[19].

It is relatively well established that these ideas were inspired by the Swiss experiences. For example, the American Labour leader J.W. Sullivan's *Direct Legislation by the Citizenship* was explicitly based on the author's impressions from a trip to Switzerland and he wrote enthusiastically about how "the people may recall their servants at brief intervals"[20].

Sullivan – like other Americans advocating the use of the recall – were almost exclusively basing their advocacy on the Swiss practice, they were not revolutionaries in the Marxian sense. Theirs was an argument for establishing more efficient checks and balances. Or, as William B. Monro, another American Populist, suggested, "the chief argument in favour of the recall as advanced by friends of this expedient, is its efficacy as an agent of unremitting popular control over men in public office"[21].

In a creative analogy which was later cited in court cases supportive of the recall[22], Munro found that the institution was an,

> Application, in the wider sense of the principle of ministerial responsibility, which is a feature of the English government, and which enables the course of public policy to be altered at any moment by the recall of the Cabinet at the hands of the House of Commons[23].

The recall was "a means of keeping officials responsible and responsive to public opinion"[24]. Using another metaphor, Thomas A. Davies wrote of the recall in terms of contract law, "if a man employs an agent for a term if years by contract, and the agent betrays his principal, the principal may terminate the contract and get rid of the faithless one"[25].

Or, in the words of Delos F. Wilcox, another activist and advocate, the representative was to be compared to an ambassador; "a diplomat", he wrote, "is a servant with power but he has specific instructions or is presumed to be acquainted with his master's will. If he fails to recognize his responsibility or if he misinterprets his instructions he may be recalled at any time"[26].

Not surprisingly, the established politicians were severely critical of the recall. President William Taft was one of the strongest critics of the device. Indeed, the 27th president of the United States made a point of vetoing the proposed constitution for Arizona in 1911 (the year before the territory became the 48th state) because the document contained a provision for the recall[27]. The provision was removed from the draft and immediately instated once statehood had been granted[28].

It is a measure of the importance attached to – and the dangers associated with – the recall that Taft continued his crusade against the device after he left the White House. In a series of lectures delivered at Yale University, the former president criticised the recall, which – in his view – would create a "nervous condition of resolution as to whether he [the representative] should do what he thinks he ought to do in the interest of the public"[29].

Of course, this potential for keeping politicians in check, for preventing legislative activism, was the chief reason behind the Populists' espousal of the device. "The recall", noted William A. White, the editor of *Emporia Gazette* and a defender of populist causes, "should make ... statesmen nervous"[30]. The Kansas City based journalist was no mere country-town hack. He later won the Pulitzer Prize. Thus, in America, the supporters of the recall won the day and it was implemented in many states at the instigation of politicians and advocates on the left. The same was not uniformly the case in Europe at the same time.

In Europe, too, it was the left side of politics who promoted the recall. But there was – as we shall see – an ideological gulf between the pragmatic and bourgeois conception of the recall as it developed in America and the socialist and Marxist advocacy of the institution in Europe at the same time. In the old continent, the recall was more broadly associated with revolutionaries than with those advocating piecemeal reform. Karl Marx, Vladimir Lenin, Rosa Luxemburg and Antonio Gramsci were all advocates of the recall[31].

The recall in Marxist theory and practice

No less a figure than Karl Marx made a case for recalling elected representatives in his book on *The Civil War in France.* Marx wrote approvingly about the system under which all the elected representatives' mandates were "at all times revocable" (*"jederzeit absetzbar"*)[32]. Inspired by Marx, Vladimir Lenin made a case for a "fuller democracy" in which all officials should be "fully elective and subject to recall"[33], as this was the only way of overcoming what Karl Marx had considered to be the problem of parliamentarianism, namely "deciding once in three or six years which member of the ruling class was to represent people in parliament"[34]. And, to complete the picture, Antonio Gramsci, the imprisoned leader of the Italian Communist Party (PCI), wrote at length about the recall in his *Prison Notebooks.* Gramsci argued that the recall would solve the problem of accountability while at the same time ensuring that decisions were taken after deliberations. In a democratic state, Gramsci wrote, "the delegate is elected ... imperatively mandated, and instantly recallable ... Since the mandate is imperative and revocable it can also be assumed that the delegates' assembly represent the opinions of the mass of the workers at all times"[35]. That the recall was a central plank, perhaps even the lynchpin, of Lenin's theory of representation is also evidenced by a short essay he wrote weeks after the Revolution. Drawing on the tenor of the argument in *State and Revolution,* Lenin went on, "Democratic representation exists and is accepted under all parliamentary systems, but this right of representation is curtailed by the fact that the people have the right to cast their votes once in every two years, and while it often turns out that their votes have installed those who oppress them, they are deprived of the democratic right to put a stop to that by removing these men"[36]. Lenin cited "cantons in Switzerland and some States of America" as places where "this democratic right of recall has survived". But, perhaps more interestingly, he also suggested that the recall could have made the revolution less violent and that the right of recall held out the prospect of a peaceful means of resolving political problems. Rather than "a rather stormy revolution" – his description of the storming of the Winter Palace – there could have been a peaceful change of power; "if we had had the right of recall [of the Provisional government headed by Alexander Kerensky] a simple vote would have sufficed"[37]. Rosa Luxemburg, who warned against Lenin's centralist tendencies, nevertheless agreed with the Russian on one matter. She also believed in the "right of immediate recall by the local workers' and soldiers' councils and replacement of their representatives in the central council, should these not act in the interests of their constituents"[38]. In practical politics, the recall remained part of the formal institutions in the Soviet Union, but it was not used before the last decade of communist rule when the citizens were allowed to use the provisions during the *Glasnost* period under Mikhail Gorbachev when two deputies were recalled in Sverdlovsk[39].

The attempts to introduce the recall into practical politics mostly failed. True, several German cities and nine of the *Länder* adopted the recall during the years of the Weimar Republic (often at the instigation of moderate socialist politicians). But the provision was of little practical importance[40]. The mechanism disappeared after the Russian Revolution and fell into disuse in America. This began to change in the latter part of the twentieth century. A quick look at its history in the USA is warranted.

The recall in America today

The recall was first introduced in the new city charter for Los Angeles in 1903[41]. It spread to other Californian municipalities, and by 1911 a total of 25 cities had adopted the device. The first state to adopt the recall was Oregon in 1908. Soon thereafter several other states followed suit. By 1914 nine states had adopted the recall for state-wide elected officials. The states were Arizona (1912), California (1911), Colorado (1912), Nevada (1912), Washington (1912), Michigan (1913), Kansas (1914) and Louisiana (1914). In most states the recall was introduced at a time when neither of the two parties were strong and often by the minority party[42]. Nine other states had adopted the device after the populist era.

At present, 18 states, and the District of Columbia, Guam and the Virgin Islands provide for recall of elected officials. At least 36 states permit the recall of various local officials. According to the National Civic and the ICMA Municipal Form of Government Survey, 60.9 per cent of US cities have recall provisions, exceeding the percentages for initiative (57.8 per cent) and popular referendum (46.7 per cent).

Hardly surprising, especially in a litigious society such as the United States, the recall has been challenged in the courts. On the whole, however, these have been sympathetic to the recall at the local and state level but have had serious – and well

Table 6.1 US states with recall provisions for assembly members and governors (signature threshold in brackets)

Alaska (25%)	Kansas (40%)	New Jersey (25%)
Arizona (25%)	Louisiana (33%)	North Dakota (25%)
California (12%)	Michigan (25%)	Oregon (15%)
Colorado (25%)	Minnesota (25%)	Rhode Island (15%)
Georgia (15%)	Montana (15%)	Washington (25%)
Idaho (20%)	Nevada (25%)	Wisconsin (25%)

Source: www.constitution.org/cons/usstcons.htm

founded – reservations about its use at the federal level. Thus, when the New Jersey constitution gave the people "the power to recall, after at least one year of service, any elected official in this State or representing this State in the United States Congress"[43], the New Jersey Supreme Court struck it down as unconstitutional[44]. The court found that the wording of the US constitution ruled out the recall. To wit, each House is to determine "the rules of its proceedings … and with concurrence of two thirds, expel a member"[45]. As the recall allows the people – not "each House" – to "expel a member", the provision in the New Jersey Constitution was clearly a violation of this.

Further, the Court argued that earlier litigation supported this view. Thus, in an earlier ruling the US Supreme Court held that "[a] senator's term can only become vacant by his death … expiration of his term, or by some direct action on the part of the Senate". Hence, any attempt to remove an elected member of the Senate by the people would be a violation of the US Constitution[46]. These legal considerations notwithstanding the recall has been actively used in the United States. Based on this we can consider the effects of the recall and determine if the institution is as destabilising as the critics maintain.

The recall in Britain

The idea of the recall was discussed several times in the United Kingdom. The radical chairman of the Labour Party, Harold Laski, had proposed it in the 1930s in his book *A Grammar of Politics*. He described it as a "valuable addition to our electoral machinery"[47]. But nothing came of this until almost a century later. Following the outrage over expenses paid to Parliamentarians in 2009, demands for reform welled up. The recall was back on the agenda, albeit in a diluted form. While all the major parties had championed the recall before the 2010 election, the version that was passed was, it seemed, rather tame. The Recall of MPs Act 2015 (c. 25) stipulated that, henceforth, voters would be able to recall their constituency Member of Parliament, but only if the MP was found guilty of a wrongdoing that fulfilled certain criteria. This was seen as a major shortcoming. Zac Goldsmith, a Conservative MP supporting the actual recall, believed the act to be ineffective and too vague to have any effect[48].

However, to the surprise of many, the British act proved effective. Three recall processes have been initiated at the time of writing. Ian Paisley Jr., a member of the Democratic Unionist Party, survived after he had been suspended from the Commons. Labour MP Fiona Oluyinka Onasanya was recalled after she had been found guilty of perverting the course of justice in 2019 (27 per cent of her constituents had signed the petition – but Labour retained the seat). And, in the same year, Conservative MP Christopher Davies incurred the wrath of the voters after he was accused of forging invoices. He too was booted out by the voters.

In America, proponents as well as opponents of the recall had expected that the device would be used predominately against judges. This turned out not to be the case. Between 1910 and 1940 only two judges were recalled. This happened in, respectively, 1913 and 1921, and both concerned judges who had given lenient sentences to rapists[49]. It is noteworthy that the California Bar Association was sufficiently concerned about the damage the judges were doing to the legal profession to support the recall[50].

But overall the recall is used sparingly. The Californian Governor Gray Davis – in 2003 – became the first governor to be recalled since the defeat of North Dakota governor Lynn Frazier in 1921[51].

Table 6.2 Successful state-wide recalls in the United States, 1911–2018

1911 recall of Hiram Gill, Mayor of Seattle, Washington
1921 recall of Lynn Frazier, Governor of North Dakota
1983 recall of Michigan state senators Phil Mastin and David Serotkin
1995 recall of California State Assemblyman Paul Horcher
1995 recall of California State Assembly Speaker Doris Allen
1996 recall of Wisconsin State Senator George Petak
2003 recall of Gray Davis, Governor of California
2003 recall of Wisconsin State Senator Gary George
2011 recall of Wisconsin State Senator Randy Hopper
2011 recall of Wisconsin State Senator Dan Kapanke
2011 recall of Arizona State Senator Russell Pearce
2011 recall of Michigan State Representative Paul Scott
2012 recall of Wisconsin State Senator Van H. Wanggaard
2013 recall of Colorado Democratic State Senator John Morse
2013 recall of Colorado Democratic State Senator Angela Giron
2018 recall of California State Senator Josh Newman over his vote to raise the gas tax

After this there were several cases, and there has been an upturn since then, but the device has been used sparingly. The aforementioned case of Judge Aaron Persky of Santa Clara County over his sentencing decision in *People* v. *Turner* is an exception – and powerful because of that. Since the device was introduced, only 16 state representatives throughout the United States have been recalled – ten of which were recalled in the twenty-first century. Four of these have been from California.

Since 1911 there have been 156 recall-petitions at the state level in California. However, only half a dozen reached the ballot paper[52]. In the words of Arnold Schwarzenegger (who became governor after a recall in 2003), "like ballot initiatives, gubernatorial recalls had a long and colourful history. Pat Brown, Ronald Reagan, Jerry Brown, and Pete Wilson had all faced attempts but none of their challengers had ever collected enough signatures to get anywhere"[53]. At the time of writing, the Governor Gavin Newsom is facing a recall.

One of the outcomes of recall elections is often the paradoxical one that the incumbent has been strengthened. Indeed, Ronald Reagan, who faced three recall attempts (in 1967, 1968 and in 1972), was arguably strengthened by the failure of his opponents to unseat him[54].

The same is arguably true for San Francisco Mayor Dianne Feinstein. In 1982 she pushed for the adoption of a strict handgun control measure, which was adopted by the San Francisco Board of Supervisors. In response a left-of-centre pro-gun group, the White Panthers, began to gather signatures for a recall election. The group easily met the 10 per cent signature threshold.

Mayor Feinstein argued that the recall election was a waste of money (it cost $450,000)[55]. But she won a staggering majority of 81 per cent of the votes in the recall election[56]. Feinstein went on to win a seat in the US Senate a few years later. In both cases, the exposure to the media – and the lack of substantial allegations – was able to bolster the incumbent[57]. The same is true for recalls of elected representatives. In only 8 per cent of the votes that were actually held, the sitting representative was recalled. The recall arguably proved the validity of Nietzsche's dictum: "What doesn't kill you makes you stronger"[58].

The question of whether the recall has made elected representatives more responsive to the views of the voters cannot be answered conclusively. However, a number of factors point in this direction. In an interview with political scientist Tom Cronin, a local judge said, "I think the recall keeps officeholders a bit more responsive and accountable"[59].

This view was also supported in an opinion by the Massachusetts Supreme Judicial Court which held that the recall is "a device to make elected officials responsive to the opinions of the voters on particular issues. The implication of the recall under the statute is not of misconduct, but only that the voters prefer not to have the recalled official continue to act"[60].

Chinese democracy

There was no doubt that Mayor Han Kuo-yu was a rising star in Taiwanese politics. For a while anyway. His emphatic victory in the 2018 mayoral election in Kaohsiung made him first head of a special municipality – a powerful position similar to that of a governor in a US state. His popularity made him an obvious choice as a presidential candidate for the Kuomintang Party. He was energetic, as well as ambitious. And delivered results. For example, he met Hong Kong's Chief Executive, Carrie Lam, and signed a trade memorandum of understanding worth 2.3 billion Taiwanese dollars ($77 million) with Hong Kong. But the problem was that this happened at a time of growing tensions between the People's Republic of China and Taiwan. The incumbent President Tsai Ing-wen (of the Democratic Progressive Party) was able to portray Han as a soft touch; as someone who was too close to Beijing. She won the presidential election in a landslide. But this was not the only loss for the once so promising Kuomintang politician. Two days after the presidential election, citizens in Kaohsiung began to gather signatures to trigger a vote to recall Mayor Han. Under the rules in Taiwan, a vote for recalling a mayor will be held if the initiators are able to gather a specified number of signatures in two rounds. First, they must gather petitions by 1 per cent of the eligible voters, and then subsequently by 10 per cent. Those organising the recall vote had to gather 22,814 signatures, and they got 28,000. This triggered the second round where they had to gather a further 377,000. They got 406,000 signatures in April 2020. The electoral commission duly began to organise the vote. On 6 June of the same year 97 per cent voted for Han's recall on a 42 per cent turnout. (The mayor had urged his supporters to boycott the vote – which required a minimum turnout of 40 per cent to be valid[61].) The vote was a rare example of a *recall*, which this chapter is about.

Total recall?

Advocates of the recall (and other forms of direct democracy) argue that these mechanisms improve the quality of representative democracy, as politicians, allegedly, become more representative if faced with the threat of being recalled.

The recall, though rarely used, is an example of a mechanism that has proved successful in holding politicians to account. But it is difficult to claim, in fairness, that the recall has altered politics, let alone had a discernible effect on political life. It is an emergency break, a mechanism, which can be used *in extremis*, as indeed it was in Arizona in 1988 (when the governor resigned just before a recall election was to be held[62]) and in California in 2003. If the recall is to be introduced it is necessary that the threshold is sufficiently high, that the mechanism is not abused, but it is also necessary to ensure that the threshold is low enough to ensure that the recall remains a potent threat.

Further, considerations should be given to the cost of the device. California's recall election in 2003, after all, cost the taxpayer a total of $66 million, including approximately $11 million to provide California's 15.3 million registered voters with the state voter information guide[63]. This sounds like a lot. Still, it is minuscule compared to the total budget of $202 billion for the Golden State. Democracy costs money! And it is worth it!

On balance, the recall provides the voters with a potent last-resort weapon against politicians who are out of touch with the voters, have shown arrogance towards the electors, or acted incompetently. Maybe the Oregon Supreme Court was right when it concluded that the recall is "a wholesome means to the preservation of responsible government"[64].

Benjamin Constant, the French liberal writer, concluded in his famous essay *The Liberty of the Ancients Compared to that of the Moderns*, that "the people, who in order to employ the liberty that suits them, resort to the representative system, must exercise an active and constant surveillance over their representatives and reserve for themselves … the right to discard them if they betray their trust"[65]. The recall is nothing more than putting this into practice.

Notes

1 Jack Lively, *Democracy* (Oxford: Basil Blackwell, 1975), p. 30.
2 An exception to this is the excellent work by Yanina Welp and Whitehead. See Y. Welp and L. Whitehead, "Recall: Democratic advance, safety valve or risky adventure?" in *The Politics of Recall Elections* (London: Palgrave Macmillan, 2020), pp. 9–27.
3 Shauna Reilly, *Direct Democracy: A Double-Edged Sword* (London: Rienner, 2018), p. 37.
4 Henry S. Noyes, *The Law of Direct Democracy* (Durham, NC: Carolina Academic Press, 2014), p. 31.
5 Thomas Cronin, *Direct Democracy: The Politics of Initiative, Referendum and Recall* (Cambridge, MA: Harvard University Press, 1989), p. 145.
6 Judge Persky quoted in *The Cut*, www.thecut.com/2019/06/the-survivor-from-the-brock-turner-case-is-writing-a-memoir.html (accessed 21 January 2020).
7 S.R. Gross, M. Possley and K. Stephens, "Race and wrongful convictions in the United States" (2017), https://repository.law.umich.edu/other/122/ (accessed 11 November 2020).
8 www.latimes.com/local/lanow/la-me-brock-turner-recall-20180606-story.html (accessed 16 July 2020).
9 Charles de Montesquieu, *The Spirit of the Laws* (Cambridge: Cambridge University Press, 1989), p. 160.
10 Jean-Jacques Rousseau, "Du Contrat Social", in B. Gagnebin and M. Raymond (eds), *Oeuvres complètes. Vol. 3: Du contrat social: Écrits politiques* (Paris: Gallimard, 1959), pp. 349–470.
11 Plutarch, *The Parallel Lives, Vol. X* (Cambridge: Loeb Classical Library, 1921), p. 16.
12 Marsilius of Padua, *The Defender of Peace* (Cambridge: Cambridge University Press, 1988), p. 45.
13 Rachel Foxley, *The Levellers: Radical Political Thought in the English Revolution* (Manchester: Manchester University Press, 2013), p. 43.
14 Ibid., p. 179.
15 Cronin, *Direct Democracy*, p. 129.
16 James Madison, *The Constitutional Convention* (New York: Modern Library Classics, 2005), p. 179.

17 Brutus quoted in Ralph Ketcham, *The Anti-Federalist Papers* (New York: Signet Books, 2003) p. 356.
18 Melancton Smith in quoted in ibid., p. 377.
19 Cronin, *Direct Democracy*, p. 130.
20 J.W. Sullivan, *Direct Legislation by the Citizenship* (New York: Twentieth Century Publishing Company & Co, 1892), p. 39.
21 W.B. Munro, *The Initiative, Referendum and Recall* (New York: Appleton, 1912), p. 46.
22 See, for example, *Hilzinger* v. *Gillman* 56 Washington 228 (Washington Supreme Court 1909), 233.
23 Munro, *The Initiative, Referendum and Recall*, p. 46.
24 Ibid., p. 47.
25 Davies in ibid., p. 314.
26 Delos Wilcox, *Government by All the People: The Initiative, the Referendum and the Recall as Instruments of Democracy* (New York: Macmillan Co, 1912), p. 171.
27 Congressional Record, August 15, 1911, 3964.
28 Joseph F. Zimmerman, *The Recall* (New York: Praeger, 1997), p. 16.
29 Taft quoted in Munro, *The Initiative, Referendum and Recall*, p. 83.
30 W.A. White, *The Old Order Changeth: A View of American Democracy* (New York: Macmillan, 1910), p. 60.
31 See M. Qvortrup, *The Referendum and Other Essays on Constitutional Government* (Oxford: Hart, 2019), pp. 180ff.
32 Karl Marx, "Der Bürgerkrieg in Frankreich" (1871), in *Marx-Engels Werke, Vol. 17* (Dietz Verlag, Berlin, 1953), p. 339.
33 Vladimir I. Lenin, *The State and the Revolution* (New York: Kessinger Publishing, 2004 [1917]), p. 39.
34 Ibid., pp. 36–37.
35 A. Gramsci, *Selections from Political Writings 1921–1926*, trans. and ed. Quintin Hoare (New York: International Publishers, 1978), p. 50.
36 V. I. Lenin, "Report on the right of recall", in *Collected Works* (Moscow: Progress Publishers, 1917), pp. 338–339 (p. 339).
37 Ibid., p. 338.
38 R. Luxemburg, "What does the Spartacus League want?" in Peter Hudis and Kevin B. Anderson (eds), *The Rosa Luxemburg Reader* (New York: New York University Press, 1984), pp. 312–374 (p. 354).
39 Stephen White and Ronald. J. Hill, "Russia, the former Soviet Union and Eastern Europe: The referendum as a flexible political instrument", in Michael Gallagher and Pier V. Uleri (eds), *The Referendum Experience in Europe* (London: Palgrave Macmillan, 1996), pp. 153–170 (p. 158).
40 R.H. Wells, "The initiative, referendum and recall in German cities", *National Municipal Review* 18(1) (1929), pp. 29–36 (p. 33).
41 F.L. Bird and F.M. Ryan, *The Recall of Public Officer: A Study of the Operation of the Recall in California* (New York: Macmillan, 1930), p. 22.

42 For a discussion of the debate surrounding the implementation of the device, see T. Goebel, *A Government by the People: Direct Democracy in America, 1890–1940* (Chapel Hill: The University of North Carolina Press, 2002), pp. 68–90.
43 New Jersey Constitution, Art. I, Section 2(b).
44 *Committee to Recall Robert Menendez from the Office as U.S. Senator* v. *Wells*, 7 New Jersey Supreme Court (2010), 720.
45 US Constitution, Art. 1, Sec 5, Clause 2.
46 *Burton* v. *United States* 202 US (1906) 344 at 369.
47 Harold Laski, *A Grammar of Politics* (London: Allen & Unwin, 1938), p. 320.
48 House of Commons Debates, 27 September, 2014, Col. 74.
49 See Anonymous, "Recall of judges", *St. Louis Law Review* 6 (1921), p. 129.
50 Goebel, *A Government by the People*, p. 151.
51 Interestingly Lynn Frazier was elected to the US Senate in the year after he had been recalled. See J.F. Zimmerman, *The Recall: Tribunal of the People* (Westport: Praeger, 1997), p. 59.
52 Cronin, *Direct Democracy*, p. 125.
53 Arnold Schwarzenegger, *Total Recall: My Unbelievable True Life Story* (New York: Simon & Schuster, 2021), pp. 479–480.
54 M.C. Bligh, J.C. Kohles and R. Pillai, "Crisis and charisma in the California recall election", *Leadership* 1(3) (2005), pp. 323–352.
55 Cronin, *Direct Democracy*, p. 140.
56 Ibid., p. 141.
57 This assessment is based on University of California, Berkeley Institute of Governmental Studies San Francisco, Californian Election, 1983 (April 26), recall of Mayor Dianne Feinstein: campaign newspaper clippings.
58 Friedrich Nietzsche, *Twilight of the Idols and Anti-Christ* (London: Penguin, 1990), p. 33.
59 Cronin, *Direct Democracy*, p. 145.
60 *Donahue* v. *Selectmen of Saugus*, 343 Mass. 93, at 96.
61 https://asia.nikkei.com/Opinion/Taiwan-mayor-recall-is-a-cautionary-tale-for-all-politicians (accessed 11 November 2020).
62 P.D. McClain, "Arizona 'high noon': The recall and impeachment of Evan Mecham", *PS: Political Science & Politics* 21(3) (1988), pp. 628–638.
63 www.sos.ca.gov/elections/elections_recall_faqs.htm#10 (accessed 11 November 2020).
64 *Stirtan* v. *Blethen* 79 Washington (1914) 10 at 14.
65 Benjamin Constant, "The liberty of the ancients compared to that of the moderns", in Marcel Gauchet (ed.), *Benjamin Constant: Écrits politique* (Paris: Gallimard, 1988), pp. 589–619 (p. 616).

Chapter 7

Citizen-initiated referendums: an empirical assessment

On 3 November 2020, a majority of the voters in Arizona voted to increase taxes by 3 per cent. Just over 51 per cent voted for Proposition 208, which would, according to the wording on the ballot, "distribute the revenue from the 3.50% income tax to teacher and classroom support staff salaries, teacher mentoring and retention programs, career and technical education programs, and the Arizona Teachers Academy". They also voted in the US presidential election, but that is another story. The policy was long overdue, and the voters took matters into their own hands. While the local business leaders opposed the measure, the voters nevertheless decided that it was time for the richest to carry a heavier (tax) burden.

But this example is rare. While referendums are widespread in Western democracies, citizens' initiatives (actual democracy "on demand") are relatively rare. While all but three of the countries in Europe (Belgium, Norway and Bosnia) have provisions for referendums in their constitutions, the initiative mentioned is in use in just six European countries.

After the Second World War, no countries in the Western world – with the exception of Switzerland – had the initiative. And even there, voters were (and are) only allowed to initiate constitutional changes, which require the signatures of at least 100,000 citizens[1]. (Though it should be said that this provision has been used to put into the constitution issues that would normally be regulated by ordinary legislation, such as the banning of new minarets supported by 57 per cent in a 2009 constitutional initiative.)

The paucity of provisions for the initiative changed after the fall of the Berlin Wall. Provisions for the initiatives were introduced in the Ukraine, Hungary, Latvia, Slovakia and Lithuania. Further, New Zealand and several German *Länder* were given the right to initiate legislation, a right that had been enjoyed (and, some would say, occasionally abused) in roughly half of the US states.

While citizens' initiatives in some of the Eastern and Central European countries have rarely succeeded due to harsh turnout requirements, there are some examples of high-profile legislation enacted as a result of a citizen-initiated process. For example, in 1996 citizens in Lithuania had the opportunity to vote on an initiative which stipulated that "at least half of the [national] budget [must be allocated] to citizens' social needs" (76 per cent supported the proposal). But this examples is rare.

However, it is in America that we have seen the most widespread use of the initiative, and it is, consequently, in this country that we find the best and the worst examples of its use. Twenty-four out of the 50 states have provisions for initiatives, though the provisions have been used with varying frequency (ostensibly due to different qualification requirements).

While the device has been used sparingly in other parts of the world, it has become an integral part of US political life, especially in the states on the Pacific coast such as Oregon, Washington and California. In these, major issues like immigration, taxation and more recently environmental issues have been put on the ballot[2]. This has generated considerable discussion about the pros and cons of this form of direct democracy.

Much has been written about the use of various types of referendums in the United States and Switzerland[3].

As we have seen, the system of direct democracy was based upon the ideas of the so-called American Populists – a rural movement that flourished in the United States from 1880 until 1910. Committed to radical reform and opposed to "big business", the Populists advocated state-ownership of the railways, anti-trust laws, and a number of other radical measures. However, it was their commitment to institutional reform in the form of direct election of senators, primaries, and the introduction of the initiative and the referendum that cemented their legacy in US political history.

While the Populists had initially contested elections as a third party, many of their policies were eventually adopted by the two major parties. Prominent Republicans and Democrats like Theodore Roosevelt and Woodrow Wilson – later US presidents – both supported the introduction of the citizens' initiative[4]. But while the device was gradually – and sometimes grudgingly – adopted by the major parties, it is worth stressing that it was "ordinary" men who secured the introduction of the device. One such was North Dakota farmer Lars A. Ueland, a lifelong Republican who abandoned party politics to campaign for the introduction of the initiative. As he is reported to have said:

> When I first became familiar with the principles of the initiative and the referendum, I was impressed with a sense of their value. The more I study these principles, the more I am convinced that they will furnish us the missing link – the means needed – to make popular self-government do its best. Programmes and reforms will then come as fast as these changes are safe – only when a majority of the people are behind them. I would rather have a complete Initiative and referendum adopted in state and nation than the most ideal political party that could be made[5].

Once elected to the North Dakota legislature (as an independent), Ueland was responsible for the introduction of the citizens' initiative. North Dakota was not, however, the first state to grant the people the right to initiate legislation. It had first been introduced in South Dakota in 1898.

Between 1898 and 1918 a total of 20 states adopted the citizens' initiative. California was one of them. In a succinct summary, Schwarzenegger summed up the early history of the institution thus:

> Among all the states, California is famed for its tradition of "direct democracy". Under the state constitution, legislators aren't the only ones who can create laws; the people can too, directly, by placing propositions on the ballot in state elections [if they can get signatures from 5 per cent of the voters in the previous Gubernatorial election]. The ballot-initiative system dates back to Hiram Johnson, California's legendary governor from 1911–1917. He used it to break the power of a corrupt legislature controlled by giant railroads[6].

Not everybody, however, was enthusiastic about this new institutional device. Some opponents challenged the use of citizens' initiatives in the courts, arguing that these provisions were unconstitutional.

The main argument was that this type of "democracy on demand" – being based on direct legislation – violated Article IV, Section 4 of the US constitution that states provide a "republican form of government".

However, the Supreme Court declared in 1912 that direct democracy did not violate the Federal constitution[7]. This ruling did not convince diehard opponents. Following the decision, the *Los Angeles Times* was vocal in its opposition to the citizens' initiative, which – in its view – would substitute "ignorance and caprice and irresponsibility" for the "learning and judgement of the legislature"[8]. Others, predictably, took a more positive view. Another newspaper, the *Arizona Star*, believed that the introduction of the initiative would lead to "the elimination of superstition, bigotry, intolerance and ignorance from American politics … an end to boss rule and … to grafting from the public crib; and an end to fraud, pomposities and political fakes"[9].

While this level of enthusiasm was unusual, the citizens' initiative was viewed favourably among constitutional reformers. Indeed, it was exported from the United States and included in the German Weimar Constitution in the wake of the First World War. According to this, one-tenth of the voters could demand that a vote was held. However, only two polls were held: in 1926 on confiscation of royal property (initiated by the left), and in 1929 on the repudiation of war reparations proposed by the far right. While both passed with overwhelming majorities, they were declared invalid due to low turnout[10]. This was to be a common fate for many initiatives in Europe when the mechanism was introduced in the 1990s.

The same has not been the case in the United States. At the time of writing a "total of 2,610 state-level initiatives have been on the ballot since the first ones went before the voters in Oregon in 1904, and 1,080 (41 per cent) have been approved", according to data compiled by the Initiative and Referendum Institute[11].

However, its use has varied widely. Between 1910 and 1919, a then record-setting 269 measures went to a vote, and 98 were approved. Use of direct legislation declined in the 1920s, rose again in the 1930s, fell precipitously in the 1940s and 1950s, and bottomed out in the 1960s. In the 1950s and 1960s, an average of fewer than eight citizens' initiatives passed per electoral cycle, down from an average of nearly 28 per election cycle in the 1920s. But these patterns reversed themselves in the 1970s. And since then the annual number of initiatives has stayed at the same (high) level.

The revival of the citizens' initiative was in large measure due to the impact of Proposition 13 in California in 1978, which sought to limit property taxes. This vote triggered a huge growth in the number of initiatives in all areas of government. In the 1990s, a total of 379 citizens' initiatives appeared on the ballots, with 167 being passed. In the last decade (2010–2019), a total of 301 citizens' initiatives have appeared on the ballot so far, with 127 being passed.

Most citizens' initiatives have been held in Oregon (341), with California a close second at 315. Other frequent users include Colorado (196), North Dakota (175) and Arizona (165)[12]. But the number of citizens' initiatives says nothing about the way in which this mechanism has been used. Has it led to an improved or decreased quality of decision-making and what are the kinds of policies approved or defeated?

Quality of legislation in a direct democracy

Charles de Montesquieu observed in *The Spirit of the Laws* that "the people are extremely well qualified for choosing whom they entrust with their authority". "But", he went on to ask, "are they capable of conducting an intricate affair, of seizing and improving the opportunity and critical moment of action?" His answer came promptly, "No; this surpasses their abilities"[13].

A more modern version of this sentiment was expressed by Lord Norton, who recently wrote, "Both Houses [of Parliament] vote on the principle of the measure, [and] they get to consider amendments. With a referendum, there is usually a single vote on a binary choice"[14].

This is a reasonable objection. Clearly, people need to delegate powers, we cannot all rule directly, but we need to control those who do. Delegation is necessary, yes, but this does not mean that we simply hand over power and accept the outcome whatever it is.

It is one of the advantages of representative democracy that parliamentarians deliberate carefully. But, the key problem with the model of delegative democracy is that it is based on an optimistic perspective of representative government. Woodrow Wilson (when he was governor of New Jersey), was closer to the mark when he wrote:

> It must be remembered by every candid man [and woman] who discusses these matters that we are contrasting the operation of the

> initiative and referendum, not with representative government which we possess in theory and which we have long persuaded ourselves that we possess in fact, but with the actual state of affairs, with legislative processes which are carried on in secret, responding to the impulse of subsidized machines and carried through by men whose unhappiness it is to realize that they are not their own masters, but puppets in the game[15].

Thus, the critics fail to appreciate that introducing the citizens' initiative does not mean that we are abolishing representative government. The device is perfectly compatible with representative government.

Hence, an idealistic – and perhaps unrealistic – assessment of the virtues of representative government should not be the main criterion in considering whether citizens' initiatives would benefit a nation. Mill, Burke and other illustrious figures who have discussed and defended representative government were writing in different times and were obviously unable to appreciate the modern pressures faced by parliaments today. Writing about the American experience, Shaun Bowler and Todd Donovan have noted, "notwithstanding the early claims made on behalf of the wisdom of legislators, recent studies of legislative behaviour suggest that legislators cannot be fully informed when they cast their ballots. They are expected to vote on bills they may not have read"[16].

While there are examples of seemingly ill-considered behaviour by voters in citizens' initiatives, the wisdom of legislators even under the American system can be questioned. There, lawmakers are allowed to deliberate without the ever-watchful eye of the government whips. It is conveniently forgotten that "the record of representative government is an imperfect one"[17].

As the historian Henry Steele Commager wrote in his assessment of the US system of representative government: "New York purged itself of socialists ... the Oregon legislature outlawed private schools and the Nebraska legislature forbade teaching in German ... the list could be extended indefinitely"[18]. In Britain, too, there are numerous examples of legislation – from the Dangerous Dogs Act to the Poll Tax – that have been forced through by government whips after insufficient thought, often with disastrous consequences.

Critics of direct democracy also often fail to consider how direct democracy might work in practice. The objection to citizens' initiatives, that they allow the voters to pass legislation without the deliberation and discussion of expert committees, is an important one. Yet, it must equally be accepted that the scrutiny by legislatures can be less than perfect. "Log rolling" (or vote trading) and "rent seeking" (the provision for a private good for a special group at the expense of the common good) are not unknown in both local and national assemblies across the world.

It would indeed be a problem that laws are not properly scrutinised by experts. The response to this criticism is provided by the indirect initiative. In nine US states (Maine, Massachusetts, Michigan, Nevada, Utah, Ohio, South Dakota, Washington and Wyoming), legislatures scrutinise the proposed measure prior to a vote.

While citizens' initiatives in these states are relatively rare, there is some evidence to suggest that this procedure meets the objections of the critics. It is worth noting that there are many different versions of the indirect initiative. Some of the states allow moderation or amendment; others require the measure to be approved or rejected exactly as it came to the legislature. If rejected or sharply amended, the sponsors may force the measure to a vote by the people. As it has been observed,

> While the indirect initiative is no panacea there are powerful arguments in its favour. Above all, that it involves the legislators in the legislative process. The indirect initiative strengthens rather than weakens representative democracy for forcing the legislators to come to grips with an idea they may have sought to avoid before. It brings into play forces of moderation, compromise and common sense often lacking in direct initiatives[19].

By allowing the legislature to debate – and, if necessary, amend – the proposition, an element of public deliberation is injected into the process. It is for this reason that some writers who are otherwise sceptical of the initiative have come out in favour of this application of the device. Thomas Cronin, in his much-cited study *Direct Democracy: The Politics of Initiative, Referendum and Recall*, concluded:

> The indirect initiative does indeed delay legislative change. But it also provides an opportunity for measures to get a formal hearing and to benefit from the experience of veteran legislators and their staffs. It is a sensible option for states not permitting the direct initiative[20].

Yet the indirect initiative may not always be necessary. There is increasing evidence that direct citizens' initiatives are *not* crudely drafted. Most initiatives are now sponsored or backed by powerful and professional campaign groups (who have access to professional and legal advice), which means that the technical quality of the proposed measures is relatively high. Dennis Polhill, in a study of the initiative process in Colorado, found that,

> Compared to bills that move through the Legislature, initiatives are no worse, and sometimes better. In Colorado, the Legislature drafts, considers, and disposes of about 600 bills per year in its 120-day session. Each legislator is allowed to sponsor five bills (although there are procedures that allow more). Initiatives are usually drafted by small groups of activists who are passionate and well-informed about their issues. It is not uncommon for development of a draft to take many months, even years. The procedure requires the same help that legislators get from the State Office of Legislative Legal Services (the bill drafting staff). The arduous task of getting on the ballot, the normal prospect of being substantially outspent in the campaign, the risk that any flaw is ammunition for the opposition, and the inevitability of court challenges upon passage provide important incentives for proponents to be both careful and reasonable in drafting their measure[21].

It is, therefore, difficult to conclude that initiatives are less likely to be the product of deliberation than laws passed by representatives without direct citizen involvement.

Policy implications of initiatives

It is often claimed that direct legislation by the people is likely to result in populist policies which may not necessarily be desirable, at least to the political classes: an example of this would be the reintroduction of the death penalty. There are, however, no examples of this happening outside the United States. In fact, referendums on the death penalty have resulted in its abolition, such as in Ireland in 2001. Though, it must be admitted, that there are examples of states in the United States where voters have opted for the restoration of capital punishment. For example, in California 67 per cent of the voters supported the reinstatement of capital punishment by voting for Proposition 17 of 1972, after the Supreme Court of California declared this form of punishment unconstitutional in *People* v. *Anderson*[22]. So, it has to be admitted, that the 25 US states with provisions for citizen-initiated referendums are also considerably more likely to have the death penalty than those who do not allow citizens to initiate and vote on legislation[23].

So, is the initiative to blame? It was in California. But it is difficult to draw too definite conclusions. Cultural factors probably play a more dominant role in this than does direct democracy; states with a large number of religious fundamentalists are significantly more likely to adopt capital punishment than are states with secular majorities. The initiative reflects the values of the societies in which it is used.

It is also often claimed that minorities suffer where direct democracy is in operation. While the initiative has occasionally been used to limit the rights of minority groups, such as in the case of the 1994 Proposition 187 in California (which sought to ban illegal immigrants from all but emergency treatment in hospitals), it is important to note that *all* such measures have been struck down by the courts[24].

Democracy, no matter how perfect, always requires the rule of law and minority protection. It is certainly the case that a number of initiatives have targeted minority groups, such as the constitutional measures aimed at preventing gay marriages in 2004 and 2006. Yet, while voters generally voted against marriage equality in initiatives that were held after the turn of the millennium, this has changed, largely as a result of different political attitudes.

"Interestingly, at least in national polls, the more people voted on gay marriage the better the idea fared", says Paul Jacob of the Citizens in Charge Foundation. So, the charge that direct democracy itself is inimical to LGBTQ rights is not well founded. Social attitudes, rather than the initiative, account for the results, very much like in a pure representative democracy. This view is supported by the 2012 citizens-initiated referendum in Washington, where 53 per cent on a whopping 81 per cent turnout, approved a measure that, according to the ballot question would, "would allow same-sex couples to marry"[25].

The same was true in other developed and long-established democracies. Thus, in Ireland and Australia voters adopted marriage equality measures by large majorities in, respectively, 2015 and 2017.

That there has been a tendency for voters to vote against marriage equality in referendums in more recently established democracies, does not, therefore, automatically suggest the citizens' initiative is to blame. True, there have been several votes on the subject that appear illiberal.

The citizens' initiative in Croatia in 2013, where 66 per cent of the voters voted affirmatively for the question, "Are you in favour of the constitution of the Republic of Croatia being amended with a provision stating that marriage is matrimony between a woman and a man?" being but one example[26]. However, this vote, like the initiatives on this subject in Slovenia in 2015, Slovakia in the same year, in Bermuda in 2016 and Taiwan in 2018, were either invalid due to low turnout (in the former three cases) or overturned by parliament (as in the case of the latter).

That authoritarian leaders occasionally use scapegoating of minority groups – such as LGBTQ people in plebiscites – is another story, one that reflects on the nature of dictatorships, not one that says anything about democracy. That a ban on gay marriage was a central part of Putin's proposed new constitution which was endorsed by a clear majority in a referendum in 2020 is not relevant for a serious discussion of the merits of citizens' initiatives. But it might be interesting, nevertheless, to note that the voters in Cuba (not assuredly a democracy) supported a new constitution in a referendum in 2019, which lifted the constitutional ban on gay marriage which had hitherto existed in the communist-governed island. The change came as a result of lobbying by Mariela Castro, the niece of former President Fidel Castro[27]. It is good to have friends and relatives in high places.

So, the results of referendums on this topic reflect social attitudes. Thus, in the case of Slovakia, the figures show that 81 per cent of the respondents to the Eurobarometer Survey were opposed to gay marriage[28]. Like in America, opinions might change, and once this has happened, so may legislation.

Some scholars have found that states in the United States that have provisions for citizen-initiated referendums score higher on performance indicators such as economic growth. Similar research in Switzerland has shown that cantons where voters have the right to initiate legislation are characterised by lower inequality and higher growth[29].

This research has been advanced by, in particular, John Matsusaka and Lars Feld, and will subsequently be referred to as the Matsusaka-Feld Hypothesis. For the purposes of this chapter, the hypothesis states that there is a positive correlation between macro-economic performance and provisions for direct democracy.

This is an important result, if it can be generalised. Given the largely critical debate about the consequences of direct democracy following the Brexit vote in the United Kingdom, this finding could challenge the largely negative assessment of the economic effects of initiatives, which have been advanced by political theorists and political scientists alike[30].

However, previous research has generally looked at differences within countries. (The exception is Simon Hug's study of the effects of direct democracy in former communist countries[31].) The aim of this part of the chapter is to test the proposition across countries. The fundamental assumption is the Matsusaka-Feld Hypothesis, i.e. that more opportunities for direct participation in citizen-initiated referendums is correlated with a number of welfare gains.

According to John Matsusaka, "the initiative provides the voters with a way to collect the dispersed information of ordinary citizens and bring it to bear on policy … the initiative allows nonpoliticians to compete against professional politicians in proposing new policies"[32].

As the quote indicates, contemporary political scientists and economists have found empirical evidence that cantons where the citizens have opportunities for initiating referendums and initiatives also have higher levels of growth and lower budget deficits[33].

Similar research at the state level in the United States has replicated this finding[34]. Why is this? The explanation is quite simple, politicians in pure representative democracies, so the argument runs, are likely to be more responsive to the party organisations that choose the candidates than to the less ideologically driven ordinary voters. The view was summed up in a recent study and is worth quoting:

> Representatives can be captured by special interest groups that engage in rent-seeking activities. Rent seeking involves redistributing income from those groups in society, which are not successfully lobbying the government to those which are … These considerations

> suggest that, from a societal point of view, income redistribution in representative democracies is inefficient as actual redistribution deviates from the preferred level and as those groups might benefit which are not the neediest ones[35].

Following the logic of this argument, politicians refrain from passing acts, which run counter to the voters' preferences if this legislation can be undone and nullified through citizen-initiated referendums and initiatives[36]. As voters are interested in increased welfare we would, *ceteris paribus*, expect politicians to enact legislation that leads to higher GDP growth. This is largely corroborated in Switzerland. The analyses of votes in this country have shown that their use is associated with higher pre- and post-tax income inequality. Overall, the statistical evidence suggests, that "stronger popular rights appear to decrease pretax and posttax income inequality"[37].

But lower taxes is not necessary a desired policy outcome. Indeed, it might be seen as a conservative preference. Might it be that initiatives simply help the richer and have adverse consequences for the less-well-to-do? In fact, the research on direct democracy and public policy in Switzerland (and earlier eras in the United States) found evidence to support a correlation between provisions for citizen-initiated referendums and higher income equality. In the words of one of the studies, the statistical evidence suggests that "stronger popular rights [to initiate referendums] appear to decrease pre-tax and post-tax income inequality"[38]. One is tempted to conclude that all good things go together.

Would initiatives lead to more democratic involvement?

While some see democracy as desirable on purely utilitarian grounds, others favour it for idealistic reasons. To them, institutions that encourage greater public engagement have an intrinsic democratic value. How does the citizens' initiative fare in this regard?

An often-noted consequence of this form of direct democracy is that turnout seems to be higher in states which employ the initiative rather than in those which do not allow the citizens to initiate legislation[39].

While the evidence is hotly debated, there are findings that corroborate this thesis. In a much-cited study, David Schmidt found that turnout in the American states which used initiatives was – on average – 5 per cent higher than in the states that did not. He also found that voter turnout was higher in states with initiatives on the ballot than elsewhere – 50 per cent compared to 42 per cent. The research showed that ballot initiatives tend to have a bigger impact in non-presidential-election years, where the difference in turnout is 45 per cent to 34 per cent, than in presidential elections, where the differential is only 57 per cent to 55 per cent[40].

A decade ago, it was found that each additional citizens' initiative on the ballot during a midterm election in America increases turnout by an average of 1.2 per cent. Researchers also found that citizens were more knowledgeable, interested and engaged in politics when there are propositions on the ballot[41]. An analysis of the 2006 midterm elections found higher turnout in states where voters had the opportunity to vote for citizen-initiated ballot propositions. Average turnout for the 18 states with initiatives was 45.1 per cent while the 32 states without initiatives averaged 39.6 per cent. Turnout across the United States was 40.4 per cent. Initiatives are clearly not the only factor in determining turnout, with some non-initiative states registering high turnout and some initiative states with low numbers voting. But citizens' initiative states tend to experience higher turnout; 13 of the 18 are in the top 50 per cent of states ranked by turnout, and only one is in the bottom 25 per cent[42].

Election officials in several states – but particularly in South Dakota in that year – attributed high turnouts to the presence of controversial citizens' initiatives on the ballot. In this state, where turnout was almost 58 per cent, there were eight initiatives, including proposals to increase tobacco tax to fund health and education services; stop state aircraft being used for non-official business; limit property tax increases; legalise marijuana for medical use; and abolish the video lottery (the state-run network of gambling machines). There was also a popular referendum (where citizens collected enough signatures to challenge a law passed by the legislature) on abortion. It should be noted that turnout in midterm elections tends to be 10 to 20 percentage points lower than that in presidential elections. As one observer noted: "The ballot issues are driving the vote. Very clearly, they bring great interest from all voters"[43].

Excursus: agenda initiatives: the tale of Uffe Elbæk and the Danish *Borgerforslag*

When Uffe Elbæk, a one-time Minister of Culture in Denmark, left the Social Liberal Party (Det Radikale Venstre) and established his party, Alternativet, in 2013, he had two concerns; democracy and the environment. He wanted more of both. He wanted a bill to address the climate disaster, and he wanted to involve the people. The latter would be a catalyst for the former, so he suggested that the voters were given the right to propose legislation, if they could gather a specified number of signatures. This would *not* lead to a popular vote but would force the Danish parliament to discuss a Bill. It was a modest proposal, yet one that many considered barmy. To have a provision for this – a so-called agenda initiative – is not revolutionary. As Table 7.1 shows, several countries already have these.

At the time eight other EU countries had the provision, and a similar institution had existed at the EU level since the ratification of the Lisbon Treaty and in some member states. The provisions have had different levels of success.

Some have done well. For example, in Poland, seven out of 24 measures submitted to the parliament led to the enactment of legislation[44]. And, in Finland (which adopted the provision in 2012) an agenda initiative for marriage equality was the first to be enacted by Eduskunta – the Finnish Parliament[45]. At the EU level, a handful of agenda initiatives have qualified but they have not been impressive[46]. According to Daniela Vancic, European Program Manager at Democracy International, "The only two successful European Citizens' Initiatives that have seen some political response have been Right2Water and Stop Glyphosate". And this was only indirectly. According to Vancic, "The EU Commission published a new EU directive on water inspired by the initiative (albeit 6 years after the submission of the successful initiative). With glyphosate, the Commission renewed the license for the pesticide for five years in the EU rather than the usual 10 years. So, there is definitely some scepticism by the campaigners in the Commission's response"[47]. When seen in context it is certainly not impressive. Every year, the EU passes on average 80 Directives and 700 Regulations. So, the two indirect "successes" constitute only 0.03 per cent of EU legislation.

As an entrepreneur in his previous career, Mr Elbæk's political start-up project was a surprising success. His party won nine seats in the 179-member Folketing in the election of 2015. And Uffe and his new colleagues got to work. To the surprise of many they were able to win support for the *Borgerforslagsloven*[48]. Most commentators were sceptical to say the least. Henrik Qvortrup, a well-known political commentator, was dismissive, "[the agenda initiative] creates the illusion that they [the people] have something to say"[49].

Table 7.1 Signatures required for initiatives and agenda initiatives in EU member states (national level)

Country	Population (millions)	Signatures required	Type of initiative
Austria	8.1	100,000	A
Finland	5.1	50.000	A
EU	446.0	1,000,000	A
France*	59.6	4,100,000	B
Denmark	5.8	50,000	A
Hungary	10.2	50,000	B
Italy	57.6	50,000	A
Latvia	2.3	230,000	B
Lithuania	3.5	50,000	A
Netherlands	16.3	40,000	A
Poland	38.6	100,000	A
Romania	22.3	250,000	A
Slovakia	5.3	350,000	B
Slovenia	1.9	5,000	B
Spain	39.4	500,000	A

Types of initiatives: A: agenda initiative; B: citizens' initiative with subsequent referendum. * According to Article 11 of the French constitution, a citizen-initiated referendum must be held if supported by *both* one-tenth of the voters *and* one-fifth of the members of the legislature. No such vote has been held to date.
Sources: National Constitutions and IRI Europe. At the EU level the requirement is one million signatures from at least a quarter of the member states (Art. 11, Para 4, *Treaty on European Union*).

Almost three years later, Mr Elbæk tweeted, "Tomorrow the first agenda initiative in Danish history will become law. And what a law? The *Climate Change Agenda Initiative*. Everybody ought to be happy. Both citizens and politicians. And, on a personal note, this is damn amazing"[50].

In the same year Mr Elbæk stepped down as leader of the Alternativet, and the party effectively folded. But he had achieved both his goals, more citizen involvement and a law on climate change that was proposed by the people. To paraphrase Friedrich Schiller, "Mr Elbæk has done his duty. Mr Elbæk can go"[51].

Overall, the agenda initiative has had some impact on legislation. To be sure, the results have not been overwhelming, but in its own limited way, the agenda initiative has impacted legislation. Bruno Kaufmann has described it as a "babystep"[52]. Perhaps, even this is an exaggeration. One could perhaps, with a similar metaphor, say that it is a kick in the womb. But it is a sign of life, and a promise of a life to come.

The initiative elsewhere in Europe

Outside the United States and Switzerland, the citizens' initiative is used sparingly and as an exception. For those wary of direct democracy, it is important to point out that there is an alternative to the frequent use of the initiative in California and the Swiss cantons.

There are a range of other countries that have experimented with the initiative, seemingly inspired by its use in the United States. Lithuania is the only European country that has made extensive use of the device, with six proposals being balloted from 1990 to 1996, but the Ukraine, Latvia, Hungary and Slovakia also have national provisions for citizens' initiatives.

In Lithuania, two of the initiatives have been successful. A vote on reducing the number of parliamentary deputies from 141 to 111 passed in 1996, as did a proposal (in the same year) that mandated the government to spend a specified amount of the national budget on social security. However, the other citizens' initiatives, which dealt with, among other things, matters regarding privatisation, were declared invalid as a result of low turnout. The 50 per cent turnout requirement seems to have been the main reason for the declining popularity of the initiative in the country.

High turnout requirements have also been a barrier to successful use of the citizens' initiative elsewhere.

Perhaps the most controversial initiative in the former communist countries took place in Hungary in 1989, when the Communist Party initiated a vote on whether the president should be directly elected. The party expected that the direct election of the executive would boost the Communists' chances of securing the election of one of the candidates. However, the plan failed to meet the 50 per cent turnout quorum as only 9 per cent of the voters cast a ballot[53]. Initiatives in Slovakia, on issues such as bringing forward the date of the next election, have also fallen due to low turnout.

Citizens in Latvia have a full range of initiative and referendum rights but "the restrictions and framework are rather complicated and not very citizen-friendly"[54]. The support of 10 per cent of the population is needed to trigger an initiative and turnout must be 50 per cent of the number who voted in the last parliamentary election. Constitutional amendments must be supported by half of the electorate.

In 1999, a citizens' initiative proposing one of three different pension systems for Latvia was defeated as none of the proposals won more than 50 per cent of the votes. However, in June 2000 the initiative process led to success for a popular measure without a vote taking place. Nearly 23 per cent of the population signed a petition for a draft law to prohibit the privatisation of the state-owned energy enterprise Latvenergo. The law was adopted by the government and so no referendum was needed.

It is clear that strict turnout and signature requirements have limited the use and success of the initiative across Eastern Europe. It could be argued that if, as stated above, citizens' initiatives encouraged political participation, then high turnout requirements should not be problematic. But this would fail to take into account the specific conditions in the region. The legacy of close to 50 years of communist rule and a limited democratic tradition cannot be ignored.

Initiatives in established Western representative democracies

But these newcomers to democracy and the American examples might not be well-suited to those who contemplate reform in established democracies. For this, New Zealand is a better example. Others are Germany at the state level and the Netherlands (see below)[55].

Given that New Zealand – a former British colony with a constitutional monarchy – operates a parliamentary system and lacks a written constitution it is interesting for Britain that it has recently adopted the initiative.

Proposals for the introduction of the citizens' initiative have a long history in New Zealand. As far back as 1918 a proposal for direct legislation had been introduced and in 1983 a similar measure was defeated in parliament.

The 1980s was a period of considerable constitutional and political reform in New Zealand. As part of a widespread reform of the country's democracy, the introduction of the initiative was discussed. Interestingly, the implementation of the initiative (known as the Citizens Initiated Referendum or CIR) went against the advice of the Royal Commission on the Electoral System 1986. The RCES stated that: "In general, initiatives and referenda are blunt and crude devices ... [that] would blur the lines of accountability and responsibility of Governments"[56]. Despite this, a proposal for initiatives was included in the centre-right National Party's election manifesto and the party passed the Citizens Initiated Referenda Act 1993.

Initiatives are often seen as alternatives to representative democracy. This was not the view taken by the majority who voted for the introduction of the initiative in New Zealand. As Chris Fletcher MP noted, "I see this Bill as being complementary to our current electoral system. I think that it is progressive legislation ... New Zealand will be the first Commonwealth country to introduce legislation of this kind to allow for citizens-initiated referenda"[57].

It is interesting that the political parties were so relaxed about a law that would give the people a considerably larger say. As one observer wrote:

> Neither the government nor the opposition seemed to have much enthusiasm for CIR, despite protestations from the Minister of Justice. The government had only been pushed into doing something thanks to internal party pressures before a major election. Having won the election, the government promoted CIR on the grounds that they would provide another channel for public opinion to be heard between elections; and they would increase public participation and "healthy debate" on "issues of national importance". The signature hurdle was set high to ensure that only "important" issues were brought forward[58].

Perhaps this had something to do with the fact that parliament was not bound by the result. As noted, there are a number of restrictions on the use of the initiative in New Zealand. The number of signatures required to trigger a ballot is very high – 10 per cent – thus severely limiting the number of issues ever likely to be decided by referendum (in California the signature requirement is only 5 per cent).

More importantly, however, the result is not binding[59]. David Lange, the then Labour prime minister, expressed reservations about this when the initiative was being considered in the 1980s: "[I]t is actually a fraud on the community for the Government to ask it for its opinion when the Government has said that it will not necessarily follow that opinion"[60]. The restrictions on its use have to a degree materialised. In fact, the government has been remarkably *unwilling* to listen, as we shall see shortly.

The promoters of any initiative must first get their proposed referendum question and petition form approved, and then collect the required signatures within 12 months. There is a $50,000 (£17,400) spending limit on promoting a petition, as well as a $50,000 spending limit on campaigning for any particular result if a referendum is called[61]. Such a cap on expenditure arguably acts as a deterrent to campaigners interested in using the initiative as a route to bring about political change. The idea behind this was to create a level playing field between promoters and detractors, so a particular result couldn't be "bought".

The first citizens' initiative under the new legislation was held in 1995. The question – "Should the number of professional firefighters employed full-time in the New Zealand Fire Service be reduced below the number employed in 1 January 1995?" – was unique in that it aimed to elicit a "no" response. Turnout was low and the measure passed easily. However, the government refused to take any notice of the result, citing the loaded question, the low "participation [27.7 per cent] and the general inappropriateness of dealing with a complex issue of industrial relations and budgeting priorities by such a blunt Yes/No question"[62].

Four years later, in the 1999 election, two initiatives were put on the ballot. One was to reduce the number of Members of Parliament from 120 to 99. Electors overwhelmingly voted in favour of the proposal, with 81.47 per cent voting for this proposal. However, there were no moves to amend the Electoral Act 1993 in line with this result. The question of the appropriate number of MPs was, to be sure, a term of reference for the MMP Review Committee, which was established in April 2000. Indeed, it referred to the CIR result, and the referendum proposer, Margaret Robertson, gave evidence before the Committee. But the Committee did not agree on this point, and so made no recommendation[63].

The other referendum held in that year asked, "Should there be a reform of our Justice system placing greater emphasis on the needs of victims, providing restitution and compensation for them and imposing minimum sentences and hard labour for all serious violent offences?"

The initiative was started by Norman Withers, who was appalled that a perpetrator of a violent assault on his mother (a shopkeeper) received (what he considered) a lenient sentence. In response to this perceived injustice he started an initiative. The measure passed by 91.7 per cent.

Although the referendum's provisions were not binding on parliament, some of the measures supported by the public have been subsequently introduced as changes to the Criminal Justice Act or Sentencing Act (2000) re parole. But it would be an exaggeration to say that the will of the people prevailed[64].

The fifth citizen-initiated referendum was held in December 2013, it was the sale or partial sale of state assets and companies, and in some ways echoed the one held in Uruguay, where there had been a not dissimilar referendum in 2003, which was approved by the voters. Yet, in New Zealand, the parliament is not bound by the result, and they rather unceremoniously disregarded the 67 per cent majority and went ahead with the privatisation notwithstanding[65].

While the initiative has had little direct impact on New Zealand's legislation, it is interesting that the introduction has had a discernible effect on the voters' perception of the MPs. According to a survey about direct democracy carried out by the New Zealand Election Study, in 1993, 63 per cent of the respondents agreed with the proposition "People like me have no say". Ten years on the percentage taking this view has fallen to 48 per cent[66]. To be sure this could be a result of other factors, such as the introduction of MMP[67]. It is difficult to determine this with mathematical accuracy. Yet, public perceptions of politics and politicians have grown markedly more positive since the mid-1990s. Except for an upsurge in 1998 – the year when Winston Peters, the then deputy prime minister from the New Zealand First Party, caused upset by describing the prime minister as "devious" and "untrustworthy" before he resigned – there was been an increase in the regard for the political process[68]. (Peters, later returned in a Labour-led government).

Unlike in many other Western democracies, in New Zealand "the level of trust in government was actually up on the last survey carried out as part of the global Edelman Trust Barometer. According to the survey, it increased by 5 per cent[69]. This cannot be ascribed to the Citizens' Initiative Referendum directly, but it is perhaps not entirely unreasonable to suggest that the provisions for voicing their opinion in a meaningful way has improved trust in political institutions among the Kiwis.

Smacking: a case study

In response to an amendment to the Crimes Act, Article 59 of which outlawed "the use of force for the purpose of correction", two petitions for CIR were launched in February 2007. The wording for the two referendums were: "Should a smack as part of good parental correction be a criminal offence in New Zealand?" "Should the Government give urgent priority to understanding and addressing the wider causes of family breakdown, family violence and child abuse in New Zealand?" In February 2008, with the Bill having been passed in the meantime, supporters of the referendums claimed that they had collected enough signatures. The petition was supported by Family First New Zealand, the ACT Party and the Kiwi Party. The first petition was presented to the Clerk of the House of Representatives on 29 February 2008, who vetted the signatures along with the Chief Electoral Officer. Of 280,275 signatures required to force a referendum, only 269,500 were confirmed – a shortfall of 10,775. As a result, Kiwi Party leader Larry Baldock started a new petition. This was successful. And two months later handed over 390,000 signatures. The referendum was held from 31 July to 21 August 2009. On 25 August 2009, the Chief Electoral Officer released the results of the Citizens Initiated Referendum. According to the results, 87.4

per cent of the voters supported the reintroduction of the right to "smack" children. Turnout was 56.09 per cent. Yet nothing happened. The law was not changed. Both Prime Minister John Key and Leader of the Opposition Phil Goff said the results of the referendum would not commit them to repealing the law[70].

While we should not throw caution to the proverbial winds, it is thus noteworthy that 77 per cent – according to the same survey – found that "citizen-initiated referendums enable citizens to get the politicians' attention".

It can thus be argued that the experience in New Zealand shows that, even if introduced in a very restrictive way, the initiative will engage the interest of voters and reduce mistrust of politicians. And while it is "one of the most under-utilized Acts on the statute book"[71], it is interesting that the provision for the initiative is compatible with a belief in representative democracy – as a complement rather than as an alternative.

So, whereas the evidence from America and Switzerland suggests that the initiative often results in a higher turnout, more political engagement as well as a number of policy factors (especially lower taxation), the evidence from New Zealand does not support this conclusion.

But the evidence is still relatively weak – and based on sparse examples. We cannot conclude on the basis of one example only. The problem is that we have to compare like with like. There are other countries that have introduced the initiative such as Hungary, Slovenia and other polities in the former communist countries. But given the historical differences between these countries and long-established Western democracies, it is questionable if we can compare these two categories of countries. To determine the effect of the use of initiatives and abrogative referendums, we need to look at established Western democracies. This leaves us with only two examples; local initiatives and referendums in Germany and the Netherlands.

Can we expect to find similar evidence in these countries? Do initiatives and referendums have the same effect in these countries as they seem to have had in the United States, Switzerland and, indeed, in New Zealand? One of the findings from survey evidence in the latter country was that voters became more trusting of politicians after the introduction of the *citizen-initiated referendum*. There are suggestions that this is also the case in Germany.

The initiative in Germany

"Germany is, without a doubt, primarily a representative democracy … and in the Basic Law, the people are given practically no direct democratic rights", according to Andreas Kost[72]. Yet, in practice, the citizens have recently had more opportunities to participate in politics, including the right to vote on a number of policy issues.

Direct democracy in the Federal Republic of Germany was long anathema to the constitution. Hitler's abuse of plebiscites (see Chapter 2) unfairly gave direct democracy a sordid reputation, which extended to the initiative. Any mention of direct democracy was controversial. This was a bit unfair. As noted above, there were two experiments with direct democracy during the Weimar era – on the confiscation of royal property (1926) and on the so-called Young Plan on war reparations (1929) – but both of these failed due to unforgiving turnout requirements[73]. The negative portrayal of the Weimar Republic's institution meant that the introduction of mechanisms of direct legislation by the people was out of the question when the Germans drafted a new democratic constitution after the Second World War[74].

Yet opposition to direct democracy elements was not total. Interestingly, the Founding Fathers of the *Grundgesetz* – the Basic Law of 1949 – had envisaged that referendums would be held in the event of a reunification of the two Germanies. However, no referendum was held at the time of the reunification in 1990.

Through a somewhat sneaky judicial manoeuvre the negotiators of the Unification Treaty defined the incorporation of the former East German States in a way that did not require a popular vote.

There was also a provision for referendums in the event of mergers of existing *Länder*, which even mentioned the use of the initiative (Article 29). This provision, as noted, was used when Baden and Württemberg merged into one *Land* after a referendum in 1951.

There was also a referendum on the future status of the Saarland in 1955, which was overwhelmingly endorsed by the voters. However, this was a treaty referendum and not one initiated by the people[75]. Apart from a handful of states (above all Bavaria), where the voters could demand referendums on acts passed by the Landtag (state legislature), the German Federal Republic was a barren land as regards direct legislation by the people.

This has changed since reunification. "Until the beginning of the 1990s only seven [of the 16] states offered direct democratic instruments at the state level … However, during the 1990s all German states changed their state constitutions to add a variety of direct democratic instruments at the state level as well as at the local level". Since 1996 there have been provisions for citizen-initiated referendums in all the German states[76].

Further, in Germany there is direct democracy at both the municipal level and at the state level. We will look at each in turn.

At the local level there is *Bürgerbegehren* and *Bürgerentscheiden*. These are, respectively, agenda initiatives and citizens' initiatives.

Nordrhein-Westfalen, Germany's most populous state, might serve as an example. Here citizens can "propose byelaws instead of those initiated by the elected council members"[77]. Until recently, the citizens had to provide a so-called *Kostenschätzung* (literally a statement of cost covering) which provides a breakdown of the fiscal implications of the proposal[78].

If the proposal is rejected, there will be a referendum on it (see Figure 7.1). In the popular vote the proposal will only be approved if a certain turnout requirement is reached (*Beteiligungsquorum*). This

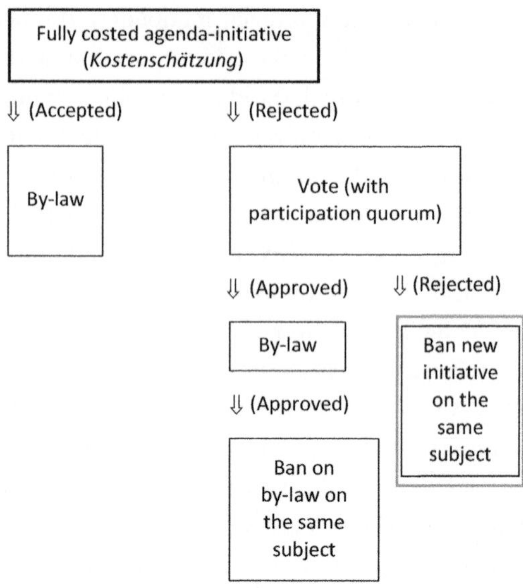

Figure 7.1 The process of direct democracy in German municipalities.

can vary between 10 and 30 per cent of the eligible voters[79]. If the by-law is approved, the Council is prohibited from passing any competing regulation. Conversely, if the proposal is rejected (or does not reach the quorum) the citizens are barred from proposing a similar regulation within a specified period, typically until the end of the term.

The effect of this is that "the elected Municipal councils have to compete with respectively, *Bürgerbegehren* and *Bürgerentscheiden*. Although there is no formal change [from representative to direct democracy], the councils are for all practical purposes forced to pursue a citizen-oriented set of policies, which does not ignore the opinion of the public"[80]. So, what have the effects of direct democracy provisions been? More generally, it has been found that authorities in areas with more direct democracy mechanisms "are more interested in communicating with their citizens due to the existing direct democracy options"[81].

While over 60 per cent of the 2,400 local referendums that have been held in the 12,000 municipalities across Germany have failed, the effect has been greater than the numbers suggest, and it has led to indirect changes. Furthermore, roughly half of the agenda initiatives have led to changes in by-laws[82].

The process is in many ways similar at the state (*Länder*) level. Though, here the two types are called, respectively, *Volksbegehren* (literally, people's demands) and *Volksentscheiden* (people's decisions). *Volkebeghren* – i.e. an agenda initiative – requires between 4 per cent in Brandenburg, in the former East Germany, to 20 per cent in Hessen and Saarland in the west. Often there is a limit on the time allowed to gather the signatures. This ranges from two weeks in Baden-Württemberg to six months in Niedersachsen.

At the *Land*-level, according to Andreas Kost,

> A [state-level] referendum [*Volksentscheid*] is only carried out if the relevant state parliament has not complied with an agenda initiative [*Volksbegehr*]. The goal of the referendum is to have a legislative decision by the citizens instead of the state parliament. The law can be implemented by adopting the draft with a majority of the votes specified; but only under the condition that this majority is between 15 percent (NRW) and 50 percent (Saarland) of those entitled to vote[83].

Yet, there have only been two dozen votes on policy issues at the state level. And again, many of these have failed because of high turnout requirements. Thus, a proposal to block a new train station in Stuttgart in 2011 failed because the 58 per cent of the voters who rejected the proposal did *not* constitute the minimum required 33.3 per cent of the eligible voters[84].

Bavaria still stands out as the most frequent user. And as other *Länder* have sought to catch up, the large southern state (the richest in Germany) has further deepened its provisions for direct democracy. Thus, in 1995, initiatives and referendums were introduced at the local level, largely at the instigation of the campaign group *Mehr Demokratie* (More Democracy)[85].

While the Bavarian Supreme Court introduced a turnout requirement in 1997, the voters have used the provisions extensively. In the first ten years there were over 835 local referendums and initiatives in Bavaria. In this state, the citizens have thus used the provision for citizens' initiatives to prevent the privatisation of drinking water, as well as to stop fracking.

According to Andrea Adamopoulos, of the pressure group *Omnibus*, Bavaria thus stands out as the *Land* where democracy on demand has been most successful[86]. As she says,

> A referendum on biodiversity took place in Bavaria last year [2019]. It was a huge success: within 14 days, over 1.8 million citizens went to their town halls and signed a petition on the topic of nature conservation and biodiversity. That has caused an enormous wave because since then there have been comparable initiatives or "round tables" in several German federal states, in which farmers' associations with citizens and representatives have agreed ecological points of view that things cannot go on as before. Some of the arch enemies were sitting together at a table and a lot has changed. Something has finally gotten into motion in agriculture: factory farming is being discussed more and more critically. This shows that not only the vote itself counts, but that a lot is set in motion by the voting process[87].

But Bavaria is no longer the only state where direct democracy has had a tangible effect on everyday politics. The voters in Berlin, for example, used the provisions for direct democracy to renationalise the public water supply. In 1999, a grand coalition in the State Senate approved the privatisation of drinking water. This was intended to lead to efficiency. Instead it led to a 35 per cent increase in the price of water. This led to a campaign for renationalisation. In 2010, the Senate rejected an agenda initiative. Following this, the activists gathered a record number of signatures, and after some attempts to kick the initiative into the long grass through various judicial delaying tactics, a popular vote was finally held in 2011. Over 90 per cent voted for renationalisation. Unlike previous referendums, the turnout quorum was met[88].

In addition to these examples, there was an initiative in Brandenburg on intensive animal farming or industrial livestock production. In the end there was no popular vote as the state legislature drafted legislation along the lines of the initiative. Sometimes the effect of direct democracy is a bit like the hound in the Sherlock Holmes detective story, the dog that didn't bark.

Referendums and initiatives in Germany are still institutions in their infancy but, so far, the effects have been positive, and perhaps it is time for these mechanisms to be introduced at the national or federal level.

Direct democracy in the Netherlands

Can this pattern be found in the Netherlands? Sadly, in this country, the brief experiment with citizen-initiated referendums was cut short. A bit of background is useful before we get to that.

The Netherlands is a bit of a paradox from the point of view of direct democracy. A model republic from the seventeenth century, many of the original ideas about tolerance, freedom and democracy were imported into democratic nations from the Low Countries. Yet, despite its democratic pedigree, the Netherlands was, until 2005, one of only a handful of democratic countries never to have held a nationwide referendum[89]. (At the moment the list of these countries includes only India, Israel, Japan and – perhaps surprisingly – the United States at the federal level).

Yet, the introduction of citizens' initiatives was a consistent feature of the centrist liberal party D66's electoral platform since its formation at the beginning of the 1980s. And just as consistently, the other main Dutch political parties (Partij van der Arbeid, PvdA (Labour), Christen Democratisch Appèl, CDA (Christian Democrats) and the Volkspartij van Vrijheid en Democratie, VVD

(Liberals)) opposed provisions for citizen-initiated referendums[90]. Indeed, a former leader of the VVD devoted a whole essay to attacking the referendum as an institution which would "sever the roots of democracy"[91].

In 1999, a constitutional amendment for a citizen-initiated referendum ("Het correctief referendum")[92] would have allowed voters to demand a vote on laws right after they were approved by parliament, if they secured a particular number of signatures. This, however, was, rejected by the Senate (Eerste Kamer) in 1999 when Hans Weigel, a former leader of the Liberal Party, cast his vote against the amendment, which consequently "failed to pass by one vote"[93].

Yet, at the local level, there were many experiments with direct democracy, as Arjen Nijboer, manager of Meer Democratie in the Netherlands, describes:

> Since the beginning of the 1990s many municipalities – by now about one third of all municipalities/cities – have introduced local regulations allowing for non-binding citizen-initiated referendums (mainly corrective/facultative, to challenge local council decisions. Like elsewhere in Europe, the interest in referendums grew considerably after the end of the Cold War, and after the Netherlands had seen a historically low turnout in the 1990 municipal elections. Local referendums were seen as a means of closing the "gap between citizens and politics", and their number increased quickly[94].

For this reason, the demand for the referendum continued. A few years later there was another push for a "corrective referendum". In 2015, the Dutch Tweedekamer (lower house of parliament) approved a law that introduced the institution. It had a short life.

The aim of the Dutch law was to hold politicians to account. But politicians didn't expect voters to actually challenge controversial legislation – but that's exactly what happened in 2016 when a referendum was called to block the European Union's Association Treaty with Ukraine.

As treaties with foreign countries must be unanimously approved by the EU states, the Dutch parliament could block the treaty. A concerted effort, sponsored by the Hungarian-American billionaire George Soros, and spearheaded by Prime Minister Mark Rutte, campaigned for ratification. Despite this, in April 2016, 61 per cent of the Dutch electors voted to block the European Union's Association Treaty with the Ukraine on a 32 per cent turnout. The outcome did not cause a revolution, nor did it fundamentally alter the relationship between the EU and the Ukraine. But it forced the Dutch government – and the EU as a whole – to find a compromise position, and to justify this to their voters.

But politicians do not like to be embarrassed. Now, rather than having to explain themselves to the voters, Dutch politicians abolished the right to demand referendums. Apart from Ireland, in 1928, no democratic country had taken away the right to demand referendums before. (The Fine Gael leader William Thomas Cosgrave abolished the provision for citizen-initiated referendums before the voters were asked.)

On 22 February 2018, the Tweedkamer voted to scrap the law, and repeal was supported by the Senate on 10 July of the same year. Before the law came into effect, the voters had the opportunity to vote one last time. In March of the same year a vote on surveillance powers became the country's last advisory referendum. By a 3 per cent majority, the voters opted to scrap the "Intelligence and Security Services Act" (*Wet op de veiligheids- en inlichtingendiensten*) – a provision that would have allowed the government sweeping surveillance powers. The result was valid as the turnout was over 20 per cent above the 30 per cent threshold. The citizen-initiated referendum had protected civil liberties. Alas for the voters, their politicians did not trust them to make decisions.

The referendum had provided a safety valve for letting out political steam. Those unhappy with specific policies could use the referendum to demand specific changes. In the absence of advisory referendums Dutch voters will no longer have a democratic safety valve.

The proponents of citizen-initiated referendums sought to counteract this move through the courts. The NGO Meer Democratie started three court cases during 2017–2018 against the abolishment of the referendum law. But they came to naught. In the words of Nijeboer,

> Sadly, we lost all 3 (as the position of the Dutch courts versus the parliament and the constitution is notoriously weak). The Dutch parliament has installed an advisory committee (the *Staatscommissie Parlementair Stelsel*) to advise on renewal of Dutch democracy. In December 2018, it came with a series of proposals including introduction of binding facultative referendums via a change of the Constitution. After this, the Socialist Party (SP) entered another proposal in parliament to do this. This is the 4th attempt in 30 years to add a binding facultative referendum to the Dutch constitution.

The referendum had provided a safety valve for letting out political steam. How did the parties get away with robbing the people of their right to veto legislation? Saskia Hollander, a country expert, believes that the abolition of the law was popular with those who voted for the established parties the Liberal VVD and the Christian Democrat (CD), "my hunch, but this is not scientifically validated, is that the parties who never wanted the Citizens Referendum Law in the first place knew that for their followers the referendum was not a not a very salient issue". The party D66 had originally sponsored the introduction of the initiative. However, personal ambition seems to have taken over from idealism. In the view of Hollander, "I think that for D66, a place in government was more important than the referendum", she says[95].

The political parties might live to regret this. Those unhappy with specific policies could use the referendum to demand specific changes. In the absence of advisory referendums disgruntled Dutch voters might resort to protest voting. That might not bode well for the established parties. And maybe, they belatedly realised this. As this book was about to go to press, there were indications of a change of heart in the Netherlands. A news website reported that Socialist Party Member of Parliament Ronald van Raak had proposed a Bill for the reintroduction of the corrective binding referendum. Though it will only really come about if the next, newly elected House of Representatives supports the referendum with a two-thirds majority after the elections in 2012. The Bill cleared the first hurdle, though it was opposed by the largest of the governing parties, the VVD. The rationale for the Bill was outlined by the proposer. Ronald van Raak said,

> In the elections in March, politicians demand the confidence of the voters, but do politicians also dare to give the people the opportunity to correct them? A large majority of the population wants a binding referendum. The idea that we can whistle back the politicians helps to increase confidence in politics[96].

That seems to be a succinct summary of the case for democracy on demand.

The effect of democracy on demand

Looking at case studies may reveal important insights, but they tell us nothing about the general trends and tendencies. So, can we discern anything about the overall policy effects of direct democracy institutions in countries where this mechanism is only used sparingly?

As we saw earlier in this chapter, a body of research point to welfare gains as a result of direct democracy provisions, though most of this research is based on US states and Swiss cantons. Feld, Fischer and Kirchgässner thus found that provisions for citizen-initiated referendums lead to more equality in Switzerland[97], and two of the same authors found that public debt was lower in municipalities in Switzerland when there were provisions for direct democracy institutions[98]. This research is generally part of the trend towards institutionalism that has characterised political science since the late 1980s.

Overall this research has suggested that democracies are better off than authoritarian regimes. For, example, in a much-cited article, Kenneth Schulz and Barry Weingast, found,

> A state's ability to raise money through public borrowing is enhanced when debtholders have mechanisms for sanctioning state leaders in the event of default. Institutions associated with liberal government provide such mechanisms. All other things being equal, states that possess these institutions enjoy superior access to credit and lower interest rates than do states in which the sovereign has more discretion to default unilaterally. Liberal states can not only raise more money from a given economic base but can also pursue tax-smoothing policies that minimize economic distortions[99].

Could something similar be found regarding the effect of citizen-initiated referendums? Are provisions for these likely to result in better policy outcomes? And, if so, how does the work-product of direct democracy compare with the effect of other political institutions, such as federalism, presidentialism, second chambers and electoral systems?

This can be assessed by comparing the work-product of the two types of political systems. For example, is there evidence that countries with provisions for citizen-initiated legislation have better public policies, for example are higher?

As the error bars in Figure 7.2 show, countries with provisions for citizen-initiated referendums tend to have higher GDP per capita, but there is an overlap and the tendency, and further the range, is wide so as to be statistically almost meaningless. So, generally speaking, the findings are not encouraging.

There is no statistical support for the proposition that provisions for citizen-initiated referendums make countries richer. Institutions matter but not provisions for initiatives. The more proportional the

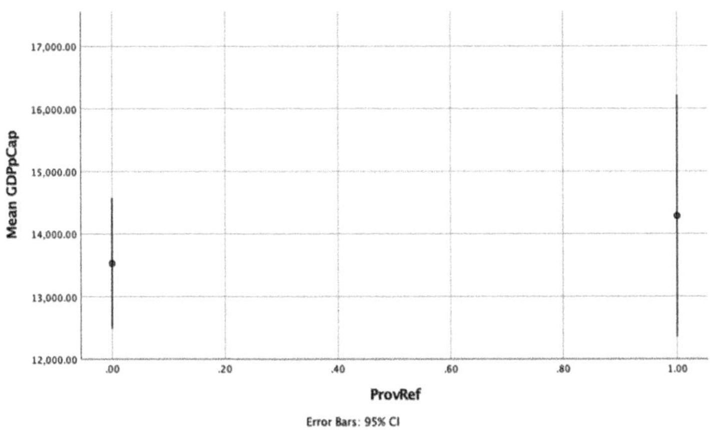

Figure 7.2 Simple error bar mean of Per Capita by Referendum Provisions.

electoral system the better, and federations are on average $8,600 richer.

But, maybe we should be driven by idealistic concerns rather than by utilitarian calculus, and introduce the initiative as this institution chimes with the ideal that all decisions in a democracy ought to be supported by the voters?

Perhaps Jeremy Bentham's words, here cited out of context, provide an answer:

> The utility of this remedial process would depend entirely upon the way in which it was administered; yet the rejection of a means so salutary can originate only in culpable indifference, anxious to save itself the trouble of discovering its expedients[100].

Notes

1 See A. Treschel and H. Kriesi, "The referendum as the centre-piece of democracy", in M. Gallagher and P.V. Uleri (eds), *The Referendum Experience in Europe* (London: Macmillan, 1996).

2 John M. Allswang, *The Initiative and Referendum in California, 1898–1998* (Palo Alto: Stanford University Press), p. 140.
3 See, for example, S. Bowler and T. Donovan, *Demanding Choices: Opinion, Voting and Direct Democracy* (Ann Arbor: University of Michigan Press, 1998); J F. Zimmerman, *The Initiative: Citizen Law-Making* (New York: Praeger, 1999); and T. Cronin, *Direct Democracy: The Politics of Initiative, Referendum and Recall* (Cambridge, MA: Harvard University Press, 1989).
4 Thomas Cronin, *Direct Democracy: The Politics of Initiative, Referendum and Recall* (Cambridge, MA: Harvard University Press, 1989).
5 Ibid.
6 Arnold Schwarzenegger, *Total Recall: My Unbelievable True Life Story* (New York: Simon & Schuster, 2021), p. 468.
7 *Pacific States Telephone and Telegraph Company* v. *Oregon*, 233 U.S. 118 (1912).
8 Quoted in Cronin, *Direct Democracy*, p. 52.
9 *Arizona Star*, 10 September 1910.
10 Hans Mommsen, *The Rise and Fall of Weimar Democracy* (Chapel Hill: University of North Carolina Press, 1996), p. 280.
11 www.iandrinstitute.org/docs/IRI-Initiative-Use-(2019-2).pdf (accessed 26 January 2020).
12 Initiative Use 1902–2006 and Ballotwatch, both at www.inadrinstitute.org.
13 Charles de Montesquieu, "De l'esprit des Loi", in *Oeuvres Complètes* (Paris: Pléiade, 1951), pp. 227–1216 (p. 241).
14 Philip Norton, *Governing Britain: Parliament, Ministers and Our Ambigious Constitution* (Manchester: Manchester University Press, 2020), p. 76. See A. Breuer, "The use of government-initiated referendums in Latin America: Towards a theory of referendum causes", *Revista de ciencia política (Santiago)* 29(1) (2009), pp. 23–55.
15 Woodrow Wilson, "The issues of reform", in W.B. Munro (ed.), *The Initiative, Referendum, and Recall* (New York: D. Appleton and Company, 1920), pp. 69–91 (p. 87).
16 Bowler and Donovan, *Demanding Choices.*
17 H.S. Commager, *Majority Rule and Minority Right* (Gloucester: Peter Smith, 1958).
18 Ibid., p. 28.
19 N. Peirce, "The indirect way for the Americans to take the initiative", *Sacramento Bee*, 12 February 1979.
20 Cronin, *Direct Democracy.*
21 D. Polhill, "Are Coloradans fit to make their own laws? A common-sense primer on the initiative process", The Independence Institute, 1996.
22 *People* v. *Anderson* 70 Cal. 2d 15, 447 P.2d 942 (1968).
23 Elizabeth Gerber, "Legislative response to the threat of popular initiatives", *American Journal of Political Science* 40(1) (1996), pp. 99–128.

24 Shaun Bowler, Stephen P. Nicholson and Gary M. Segura, "Earthquakes and aftershocks: Race, direct democracy, and partisan change", *American Journal of Political Science* 50(1) (2006), pp. 146–159.

25 On the same day, the voters supported the legalisation of marijuana by a 56–44 margin. See www.sos.wa.gov/office/news-releases.aspx#/news/1065 (accessed 29 July 2020).

26 R. Podolnjak, "Constitutional reforms of citizen-initiated referendum: Causes of different outcomes in Slovenia and Croatia", *Journal for Constitutional Theory and Philosophy of Law/Revija za ustavno teorijo in filozofijo prava* 26 (2015), pp. 129–149.

27 *La Razon*, "Hija de Castro impulsa el matrimonio gay en Cuba", 4 May 2018 (accessed 24 July 2020).

28 https://ec.europa.eu/commfrontoffice/publicopinion/archives/eb/eb66/eb66_highlights_en.pdf (accessed 29 July 2020).

29 John G. Matsusaka, *For the Many or the Few: The Initiative, Public Policy and American Democracy* (Chicago: University of Chicago Press, 2008); Lars P. Feld, Justina A.V. Fischer and Gebhardt Kirchgässner, "The effect of direct democracy on income distribution: Evidence of Switzerland", *Economic Inquiry* 48(4) (2010), pp. 817–840.

30 See for example, Andrew Glencross, *Why the UK Voted for Brexit: David Cameron's Great Miscalculation* (London: Palgrave, 2016); Harold D. Clarke, Matthew Goodwin and Paul Whiteley, *Brexit: Why Britain Voted to Leave the European Union* (Cambridge: Cambridge University Press, 2017).

31 S. Hug, "The political effects of referendums: An analysis of institutional innovations in Eastern and Central Europe", *Communist and Post-Communist Studies* 38(4) (2005), pp. 475–499.

32 Matsusaka, *For the Many or the Few*, p. 144.

33 L.P. Feld and M.R. Savioz, "Direct democracy matters for economic performance: An empirical investigation", *Kyklos* 50(4) (1997), pp. 507–538. For a more recent study see M. Qvortrup, "Mob rule or the wisdom of the crowds: Reflections on referendums and public policy", *The Brown Journal of World Affairs* 24(2) (2018), p. 57.

34 J.G. Matsusaka, "Fiscal effects of the voter initiative: Evidence from the last 30 years", *Journal of Political Economy* 103(3) (1995), pp. 587–623.

35 Feld et al., "The effect of direct democracy on income distribution".

36 E. R. Gerber and A. Lupia, "Campaign competition and policy responsiveness in direct legislation elections", *Political Behavior* 17 (1995), pp. 287–306.

37 Feld et al., "The effect of direct democracy on income distribution", p. 31.

38 Ibid.

39 B. Barber, *Strong Democracy: Participatory Politics for a New Age* (Berkeley: University of California Press, 1984).

40 D. Schmidt, *Citizen Lawmakers: The Ballot Initiative Revolution* (Berkeley: Temple University Press, 1989).
41 Dan Smith and Caroline Tolbert, *Educated by Initiative: The Effects of Direct Democracy on Citizens and Political Organisations* (Ann Arbor: Michigan University Press, 2004), p. 62.
42 Ibid.
43 Cited by S. Burrish, "Ballot measures spur high turnout", *Sioux Falls Argus*, 8 November 2006.
44 See Theo Schiller and Maija Setälä, "Comparative findings", in Maija Setälä and Theo Schiller (eds), *Citizens' Initiatives in Europe: Procedures and Consequences of Agenda-Setting by Citizens* (London: Palgrave Macmillan, 2012) pp. 243–259 (p. 254). See also Anna Rytel-Warzocha, "Popular initiatives in Poland: Citizens' empowerment or keeping up appearances?", in Maija Setälä and Theo Schiller (eds), *Citizens' Initiatives in Europe* (London: Palgrave Macmillan, 2012), pp. 212–227.
45 H.S. Christensen, M. Jäske, M. Setälä and E. Laitinen, "The Finnish citizens' initiative: Towards inclusive agenda-setting?", *Scandinavian Political Studies* 40(4) (2017), pp. 411–433.
46 Bruno Kaufmann, *European Democracy Passport* (Brussels: European Economic and Social Committee, 2020), p. 27.
47 Personal communication, Daniela Vancic, European Programme Manager, Democracy International, 24 July 2020.
48 Lov nr. 1672 af 26. December 2017.
49 Personal communication with the author, 17 July 2020.
50 https://twitter.com/uffeelbaek/status/1260688548363210758 (accessed 15 July 2020). Author's translation.
51 Friedrich Schiller, *Die Verschwörung des Fiesco zu Genua* (1783), Scene III, Act 4.
52 B. Kaufmann, "Transnational 'babystep': The European citizens' initiative", in Maija Setälä and Theo Schiller (eds), *Citizens' Initiatives in Europe* (London: Palgrave Macmillan, 2012), pp. 228–242.
53 Jon Elstr, Claus Offe, and Ulrich C. Preuss., *Institutional Design in Post-Communist Societies: Rebuilding a Ship at Sea* (Cambridge: Cambridge University Press, 1998).
54 B. Kaufman and M.D. Waters, *Direct Democracy in Europe: A Comprehensive Reference Guide to the Initiative and Referendum Process in Europe* (Durham, NC: Carolina Academic Press, 2004).
55 Susan Scarrow, "Direct democracy and institutional change", *Comparative Political Studies* 34(6) (2001), p. 663.
56 Quoted in Caroline Morris, "Improving our democracy or a fraud on the community? A closer look at New Zealand's citizens initiated Referenda Act 1993", *Statute Law Review* 25(2) (2004), p. 117.
57 Ibid., p. 116.

58 J. Parkinson, "Who knows best? The creation of the citizen initiated referendum in New Zealand", *Government and Opposition* (2001), pp. 403–421 (p. 414).
59 Helena Catt, "Citizen initiated referenda", in Raymond Miller (ed.), *New Zealand: Government and Politics* (South Melbourne, Victoria: Oxford University Press, 2001).
60 Morris, "Improving our democracy or a fraud on the community?", p. 117.
61 Catt, "Citizen initiated referenda", p. 387.
62 Richard Mulgan, *Politics in New Zealand*, 2nd Edition (Auckland: Auckland University Press, 1997), p. 284.
63 www.parliament.nz/NR/rdonlyres/067094C5-47A4-43AA-AE7F5D7C15B55D3E/36327/DBSCH_SCR_3542_3576.pdf (accessed 1 May 2007).
64 S.M. Pfander, "Evaluating New Zealand's restorative promise: The impact of legislative design on the practice of restorative justice", *Kōtuitui: New Zealand Journal of Social Sciences Online* 15(1) (2020), pp. 170–185.
65 www.nzherald.co.nz/nz/news/article.cfm?c_id=1&objectid=11172629 (accessed 11 November 2020).
66 www.parliament.nz/NR/rdonlyres/067094C5-47A4-43AA-AE7F-5D7C15B55D3E/36327/DBSCH_SCR_3542_3576.pdf (accessed 10 June 2007).
67 Jack Vowles, Peter Aimer, Susan Banducci, Jeffrey Karp and Raymond Miller (eds), *Voter's Veto: The 2002 Election in New Zealand and the Consolidation of Minority Government* (Auckland: Auckland University Press, 2004).
68 Arthur Banks (ed.), *The Political Handbook of the World* (Washington, DC: CQ-Press, 2006), p. 837.
69 www.nzherald.co.nz/nz/news/article.cfm?c_id=1&objectid=12018027 (accessed 24 July 2020).
70 Audrey Young, "PM: Smacking law review gives parents 'comfort'", *The New Zealand Herald (Auckland)*, 25 August 2009.
71 Morris, "Improving our democracy or a fraud on the community?", pp. 116–135.
72 Andreas Kost, *Direkte Demokratie*, 2nd Edition (Berlin: Springer, 2013), p. 67.
73 On the 1926 initiative, see Franklin C. West, *A Crisis of the Weimar Republic: A Study of the German Referendum of 20 June 1926*, Vol. 164 (Philadelphia: American Philosophical Society, 1985).

On the vote in 1929, see D. Nohlen and P. Stöver, *Elections in Europe* (Baden-Baden: Nomos Verlagsgesellschaft mbH & Co. KG, 2010), pp. 69–124.
74 See Ottar Jung, "Direkte Demokratie Erfahrungen und Perspektiven" (2016). https://silo.tips/download/direkte-demokratie-erfahrungen-und-perspektiven-otmar-jung (accessed 11 November 2020).

75 E. Wiskemann, "The Saar moves toward Germany", *Foreign Affairs* 34(2) (1955), p. 287.
76 B. Geissel, "Direct democracy and its (perceived) consequences: The German case", in Saskia P. Ruth, Yanina Welp and Laurence Whitehead (eds), *Let the People Rule? Direct Democracy in the Twenty-First Century* (Colchester: ECPR Press, 2017), pp. 155–167 (p. 156).
77 See e.g. § 26 Abs.1 *Gemeindeordnung*, NRW.
78 Personal communication, Professor Andreas Kost, 28 September 2020.
79 This section is based primarily on Kost, *Direkte Demokratie*, pp. 43–44.
80 Ibid., p. 45.
81 Geissel, 'Direct democracy and its (perceived) consequences', p. 163.
82 Kost, Direkte Demokratie, p. 46.
83 Ibid., p. 61. It should be noted that there is no majority requirement for ordinary laws in the states of Bavaria, Hessen and Sachsen.
84 www.lpb-bw.de/volksabstimmung-stuttgart21 (accessed 14 September 2020).
85 On the campaign, see Michael Seipel and Thomas Mayer, *Triumph der Bürger. Mehr Demokratie in Bayern – und wie es weitergeht* (Munich: Mehr Demokratie, 1997).
86 On Bavaria see B.M. Weixner, "Direkte Demokratie in Bayern", in Andreas Kost (ed.), *Direkte Demokratie in den deutschen Ländern: eine Einführung* (Berlin: Springer-Verlag, 2016), pp. 29–59.
87 Personal communication, Andrea Adamopoulos, 29 July 2020.
88 Jung Ottar, "Ein Neuer Modus", *MD Magazin* 88(1) (2011), pp. 4–8.
89 Piet Gilhuis, *Het Referendum: Ein rechtvergelijkende studie* (Hague: Alpen aan den Rijn, 1981). On Dutch local democracy, see also W.J.M. Voermans and G. Waling, *Gemeente in de genen: Tradities en toekomst van de lokale democratie in Nederland* (Amsterdam: Prometheus, 2018).
90 Joop J.M. Van Holsteyn, "'To refer or not to refer, that's the question': On the first national referendum in the Netherlands", paper presented at the ECPR general conference, 8–10 September 2005, Budapest.
91 W. J. Geertsema, *Het Referéndum: Bijl aan de Wortels van de Democratie* (De Haan: Houlten, 1987).
92 Paul Lucardie and Gerrit Voerman, "The Netherlands", *European Journal of Political Research* 43(4) (2004), pp. 1084–1092.
93 R.B. Andeweg and G.A. Irwin, *Governance and Politics in the Netherlands*, 2nd Edition (Basingstoke: Palgrave, 2005), p. 87.
94 Personal communication with the author, 29 July 2020. See also Arjen Nijeboer, "People's vengeances: The Dutch referendum" (2006), www.arjennijeboer.nl/wp-content/uploads/elcr-peoples-vengeances-the-dutch-referendum.pdf (accessed 29 July 2020).
95 Personal communication, Saskia Hollander, 31 July 2020.

96 Ronald van Raak quoted in "Kamer steunt initiatief SP voor correctief bindend referendum", *Reformatorisch Dagblad*, 22 September 2020.

97 L.P. Feld and G. Kirchgässner, "Does direct democracy reduce public debt evidence from Swiss municipalities", *Public Choice* 109(3–4) (2001), pp. 347–370.

98 Feld et al., "The effect of direct democracy on income distribution".

99 K.A. Schultz and B.R. Weingast, "The democratic advantage: Institutional foundations of financial power in international competition", *International Organization* 57(1) (2003), pp. 3–42 (p. 3).

100 Jeremy Bentham, *The Theory of Legislation* (London: Kegan Paul, 1931), p. 107.

Conclusion: bringing it all back home

> A people having sovereign power should do for itself all it can do well, and what it cannot do well, it must do through its representatives.
>
> Montesquieu, *De L'Esprit des Lois*[1]

Referendums and ballot propositions can be good for you. More referendums lead to longer life expectancy and they make you richer. For every additional nationwide referendum, the average citizen adds $884 to their bank balance.

In recent years we have seen how voters have become more sophisticated. For example, in 2020, a large majority of the voters in California opted for Democratic Presidential Candidate Joe Biden, but they voted against liberal policies on affirmative action and workers' rights. At its best, that is how the system of democracy on demand works.

But politicians have tried to abuse the system. Some have abused big-data and targeted voters in ways that undermine democracy. At other times they have waged one-sided campaigns. Luckily, there are ways to address this, as we have seen above.

This might not convince everyone, of course. "Readers may rightly ask", a scholar wrote, "how we can justify the existence of mechanisms of direct democracy at all given the apparently regressive, xenophobic, and illiberal policies and attitudes that have been crystalized by these votes?"[2]. At first sight, and superficially, the justification for direct democratic mechanisms is not strong. But – and this is the point – the findings in this book do *not* support this dire view of direct democracy.

The word "apparently" in the first sentence is indicative. The experiences with initiatives and referendums show that voters can have relatively nuanced views. In Switzerland, where the populist *Schweizerische Volkspartei* have sponsored many referendums, these have, more often than not, been lost[3]. It has turned out that the Swiss were not, in most cases, opposed to immigration[4]. It is hard to show that the Swiss consistently have voted for conservative causes when they have, recently, voted to retain anti-discrimination legislation to protect minority groups (2020), and when they have voted for tighter gun control the year before[5].

One of the conclusions of this book is that referendums, while they are slightly more common in countries dominated by centre-right parties, have not helped populists like the ones mentioned above. It is true that "when courts or governors in several American states attempted to expand social rights (such as same-sex marriage, and euthanasia), they were derailed directly by citizens through referendums)"[6]. But this reflects social attitudes rather than provisions for referendums. States that have conservative outlooks are likely to have less liberal legislation, and this is as likely to have been enacted by legislatures as much as by referendums. Direct democracy cannot be directly blamed for social attitudes. Yes, a divisive campaign might have a negative impact on minority groups but so too can an election. As recent referendums in Ireland have shown, when combined with citizens' assemblies, referendums can yield progressive results even in conservative societies.

But should we have referendums at all? Couldn't we just have periodical general parliamentary and presidential elections and elections to local bodies? The answer is emphatically in the negative. If history, as the philosopher G.W.F. Hegel mused, is the "unfolding of freedom", then restricting the use of referendums would be a step backwards[7].

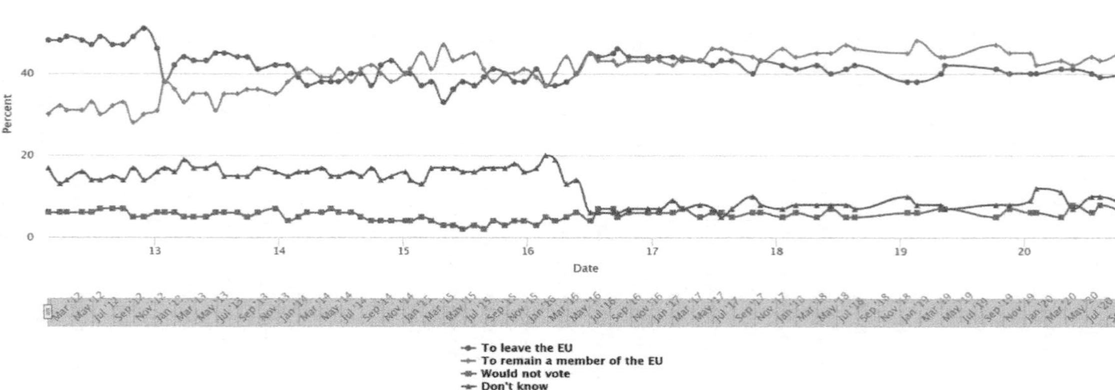

Figure 8.1 Support for Brexit 2012–2020.

There is another reason at a lower philosophical level which also justifies the use of direct democracy. In 2019, the Conservative British politician Sir Oliver Letwin made the observation that "elections are divided on the basis of all sorts of concerns that people have about whom they want to have govern them. The Brexit issue is a different kind of issue"[8]. As Figure 8.1 shows, in the United Kingdom in 2019, a majority were in favour of reversing the decision to withdraw from the European Union. In the general election in December of that year, the parties in favour of a second referendum on Brexit won a majority of the votes, but not a majority of the seats.

The pure representative system meant (and means) that the will of the majority can be ignored. This is a policy failure that necessitates referendums, especially of the variety initiated by the people themselves. This is not a new or revolutionary insight. As far back as 1910, Arthur Balfour, then the leader of the Conservative Party, noted the same, "the referendum … is a decision of the people on a particular thing, but a general election, be it a good thing or a bad thing, is not the decision of the people on a particular measure"[9].

A citizen-initiated referendum (and the citizens' initiative) provides a way of allowing voters to stray away from "their" parties and vote in accordance with their convictions on issues that do not follow party-lines. And sometimes, the same is true for constitutional referendums. In Scotland over 30 per cent of those who vote for the Scottish National Party do not support Scottish independence. A vote for the SNP is not automatically a vote for secession from the UK. Likewise, it is possible to vote for the Liberal Democrats and be opposed to marriage equality and abortion. Referendums are there to provide voters with an option to "agree to disagree". It is a device that extends – not limits – democratic choice.

In an ideal world, the referendum should be a complement to representative government rather than an alternative to it. Hence the institutions of direct democracy should "serve as intermittent safety valves against the perverse or unresponsive behaviour of representative institutions and politicians"[10].

However, there is no guarantee that voters are given this opportunity to let out political steam, when they are unable to ask for it themselves, as they are in Malta and Switzerland. In places like Ireland and Australia, the courts have intervened in cases where the elected politicians have usurped unconstitutional powers. In Ireland, since *Crotty* v. *An Taoiseach* (1987), the Irish Supreme Court has held that all amendments to the constitution must be approved by the voters. But this is only true for constitutional issues, and it does not provide an outlet for citizens who are concerned about other radical and potentially irreversible changes. The people cannot rely on well-meaning but unrepresentative judges.

There is an answer to this problem. It lies in allowing voters to either directly initiate legislation (as in, for example, California, Uruguay and Lithuania) or in allowing voters to veto legislation, if they can gather the required number of signatures to trigger a referendum (as in the Netherlands until 2019 and in Italy).

This book has made an argument that these institutionalised citizen veto-players serve to empower voters; they force the political elites to pay heed to the views of the voters and lead to more consensual results. By developing mechanisms for letting out political steam in the form of referendums, the political systems seem to have become more legitimate. And, it appears that countries with more referendums have suffered lower levels of political distrust in the political elites; "giving people more voice is widely considered a promising remedy against the current crisis of democracy"[11]. And while we cannot see a direct statistical effect of initiatives, these have not had a detrimental effect on prosperity and policy outcomes.

Traditionally the referendum was used but in exceptional circumstances[12]. It was a mechanism reserved for momentous constitutional change; a bulwark against radical and irreversible constitutional change. But in more recent years, the referendum has become more than a constitutional safeguard[13].

The traditional system of "party-democracy" is at odds with an electorate which is more interested in single issues, causes and campaigns. It is "likely … that a shift in political attitudes has taken place, the effect of which has been to make the citizens either more confident in their ability to make key policy decisions or less confident in the ability of their elected representatives to do so"[14].

It is in this context we should see the debate about direct democracy. The referendum – and even more so the citizens' initiative – at least on paper, provides the "political consumer" or "customer" with the opportunity of selecting their personal choices, and thus provides another avenue – another *input* – into the political system.

But this does not mean that the old system is entirely obsolete. Direct democracy is *not* a substitute for representative government. It is not a system that should be used on a daily basis, but as a last resort; a democratic safety valve to be used on rare occasions. By allowing people to vote for individual issues in referendums, this mechanism of direct democracy provides a means for upgrading politics.

But the question, of course, is if the voters are competent enough to make informed choices. It is often claimed that direct legislation by the people is likely to result in populist policies which may not necessarily be desirable, at least to the political classes. The introduction of mechanisms of direct democracy – so the argument runs – would allow voters to vote for higher spending and lower taxes, and the system would collapse.

The problem with this line of argument is that it is not sustained by the empirical studies reported in this book, let alone in the literature surveyed as part of research for this volume[15]. True, the infamous Proposition 13 in California did result in lower taxes, and the result was poorer public services. Yet, opponents of democracy on demand have conveniently overlooked that "California's *Propositions*

99 (1988) and *108* (1990) increased taxes and public spending"[16]. Basically, the voters in the Golden State learned their lesson.

The political system has changed. People are no longer content with the package deal provided by the political parties. Like individualised consumers who want to choose bespoke products that fit their own needs, the citizens increasingly want to cherry-pick policies. It is in the light of this overall societal change we should see the recent growth in the number of referendums and initiatives as a positive development.

Often, the results have been cosmetic, but referendums have overall provided a corrective to the prevailing – and still unchallenged – system of representative government. Referendums do not always work. There are examples of populist measures to lower taxes and increase spending, but these have not taken place in recent times. In more recent years, there have been a fair number of cases of referendums in which the voters have voted for higher taxes, and other so-called "progressive" measures such as legalisation of marijuana and gay marriages. The referendum – and its close relative the citizens' initiative – has not resulted in the introduction of a deluge of populist measures. It might be argued that the voters –when given the choice – have acted responsibly.

Critics have argued that direct democracy is both time-consuming and costly, and that it would lead to democratic fatigue. In extreme cases they are right. People do not want politics all the time. Yet in manageable doses, direct democracy works and provides an effective complement to the representative system of government.

Of course, we have no proof that voters are always competent and enlightened, though there is some (limited) evidence that voters in countries with more referendums have a greater knowledge of the issues (in this case matters pertaining to European integration). There are, to be fair, a good number of examples of referendums which have been less than edifying (the referendum on Brexit is, some argue, a case in point). Further, referendums, even those held in countries where the voters often go to the polls (such as Ireland), suggest that there are limits to the levels of enlightened participation. Class voting and domestic politics often override and supersede the issues on the ballot[17]. Referendums are not always about the issues on the ballot paper. But, then again, nor are general elections!

These shortcomings have led to demands for greater regulation. In America, especially in California, there have been many examples of the courts striking down direct legislation on the grounds that citizens did not know what they were voting for. Similarly, in 2019, a Swiss court "overturned the result of a 2016 referendum which sought to give tax breaks to married couples", on the grounds that the "voters had not been in the full possession of the facts when they took part in the ballot, and should therefore be allowed a re-run [of the referendum]"[18]. A case could perhaps be made for the view that the abuse of social media in other referendums in the same year could necessitate a rerun of these referendums.

Of course, direct legislation must comply with the rule of law and be subject to the same constitutional limitations as legislation enacted by legislatures. Like all other laws, those enacted by the people – in whichever form – need to be regulated and comply with ideals of fairness and the *Rechtsstaat.*

As we saw in Chapter 4, mechanisms of regulation, such as limits on campaign spending, bans on advertising, etc. may be necessary – though more often than not politicians use these justified concerns as an excuse to impose draconian regulations, which limit the rights of the voters and strengthen the powers of the elected representatives. Regulation often seems to be a result of partisan considerations and not a consequence of an impartial assessment of the need to ensure fairness. As Paul Jacob once put it, "even a cursory look at the actions of legislatures forecloses the possibility that increased regulation comes from a genuine attempt to improve the process"[19].

So, is direct democracy a panacea or the opposite? The answer lies somewhere in between, but closer to the former than to the latter. Countries that have referendums etc. are not markedly better than countries that only allow their citizens to vote in general and other candidate elections – though there is evidence to suggest that they are marginally more successful economically – and, above all, they trust the people, the ultimate masters, to make decisions. "A nation does not have to be judged fit for democracy; it becomes it *through* democracy", the Nobel Prize winning economist Amartya Sen said once[20].

This book has found evidence in support of the proposition that the people who live in countries that have more referendums and more direct democracy, *all other things being equal*, are better governed, slightly richer and have fewer social ills.

Introducing *more* democracy on demand will improve societies, make them richer, make politicians more accountable and make the citizens more responsible. It is for this reason that we can, once again, paraphrase Marx and Engels: "Democrats in all countries unite – You have nothing to lose but your chains!"

Notes

1 Charles de Montesquieu, "De l'esprit des Loi", in E. Desfossés-Néogravure (ed.), *Oeuvres Complètes II* (Paris: Gallimard, 1951), p. 240.

2 David Altman, *Citizenship and Contemporary Direct Democracy* (Cambridge: Cambridge University Press, 2019), p. 11.

3 D. Skenderovic, "Immigration and the radical right in Switzerland: Ideology, discourse and opportunities", *Patterns of Prejudice* 41(2) (2007), pp. 155–176.

4 Though it needs to be added that they have, on occasion voted against multicultural measures such as in the infamous minaret ban in 2009. M. Antonsich and P.I. Jones, "Mapping the Swiss referendum on the minaret ban", *Political Geography* 29(2) (2010), pp. 57–62.

5 www.swissinfo.ch/eng/in-depth/vote-may-19-2019/44927148 (accessed 6 May 2020).

6 Altman, *Citizenship and Contemporary Direct Democracy*, p. 89.

7 Georg Wilhelm Friedrich Hegel, *Lectures on the Philosophy of History* (translated from the German edition of Johannes Hoffmeister from Hegel papers assembled by H. B. Nisbet) (New York: Cambridge University Press, 1975), p. 43.

8 Sir Oliver Letwin quoted in the *London Evening Standard*, 12 September 2019.

9 Arthur Balfour quoted in C. Emden, *The People and the Constitution* (Oxford: The Clarendon Press, 1933), p. 295.

10 Ibid., p. 13.

11 Laurent Bernard, *Campaign Strategy in Direct Democracy* (Basingstoke: Palgrave, 2012), p. 199.

12 Stephen Tierney, *Constitutional Referendums: The Theory and Practice of Republican Deliberation* (Oxford: Oxford University Press, 2012), p. 29.

13 Maija Setälä and Theo Schiller, *Citizens' Initiatives in Europe: Procedures and Consequences of Agenda-Setting by Citizens* (Basingstoke: Palgrave, 2012), p. 12.

14 Tierney, *Constitutional Referendums*, p. 9.

15 For a balanced view see Russell J. Dalton, "Direct democracy and good governance: Does it matter?", in S. Bowler and A. Glazer (eds), *Direct Democracy's Impact on American Political Institutions* (New York: Palgrave Macmillan, 2008), pp. 149–167.

16 David Altman, *Direct Democracy Worldwide* (Cambridge: Cambridge University Press, 2011), p. 167.

17 On this see J. Foley and P. Ramand, "In fear of populism: Referendums and neoliberal democracy", *Socialist Register* 54(54) (2017).

18 www.euronews.com/2019/04/12/swiss-court-overturns-result-of-2016-marriage-tax-referendum-over-misleading-claims (accessed 6 May 2020).

19 Paul Jacob, "Silence isn't golden: The legislative assault on citizens' initiatives", in M. Dane Waters (ed.), *The Battle over Citizen Law Making* (Durham, NC: Carolina Academic Press, 2001), pp. 97–108 (p. 98).

20 www.wmd.org/assemblies/first-assembly/keynote (accessed 11 November 2020).

Index

Index

Index